The
Branded
Mind

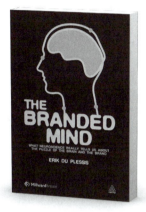

The Branded Mind

What neuroscience really tells us about the puzzle of the brain and the brand

Erik du Plessis

KoganPage

LONDON PHILADELPHIA NEW DELHI

Elements of this book are taken from an article published in *Admap magazine*: 'Account planners need to care more about share of voice', Peter Field (*Admap*, September 2009 © see email Warc), which can be viewed at www.warc.com/admap

Extracts from the following title have been used with permission of Broadway Books, a division of Random House, Inc: *The Male Brain: A breakthrough understanding of how men and boys think* by Louann Brizendine, M D; copyright © 2010 Louann Brizendine, M. D.

First published in Great Britain and the United States in 2011 by Kogan Page Limited

120 Pentonville Road	1518 Walnut Street, Suite 1100	4737/23 Ansari Road
London N1 9JN	Philadelphia PA 19102	Daryaganj
United Kingdom	USA	New Delhi 110002
www.koganpage.com		India

© Erik du Plessis, 2011

The right of Erik du Plessis to be identified as the author of this work has been asserted by him in accordance with the Copyright, Designs and Patents Act 1988.

ISBN   978 0 7494 6125 6
E-ISBN   978 0 7494 6298 7

British Library Cataloguing-in-Publication Data

A CIP record for this book is available from the British Library.

Library of Congress Cataloging-in-Publication Data

Du Plessis, Erik.
    The branded mind : what neuroscience really tells us about the puzzle of the brain and the brand / Erik du Plessis.
        p. cm.
    Includes bibliographical references.
    ISBN 978-0-7494-6125-6 – ISBN 978-0-7494-6298-7   1. Neuromarketing.   2. Advertising–Psychological aspects.   3. Marketing–Psychological aspects.   4. Branding (Marketing)   I. Title.
    HF5415.12615.D8 2011
    658.8'342–dc22   2010037756

Typeset by Graphicraft Limited, Hong Kong
Production managed by Jellyfish

CONTENTS

PART FOUR Towards insights 161

PART FIVE Some marketing implications 171

PART SIX My conclusions 235

FOREWORD

Ah, to know what is going on in someone else's head. At some point we have all wished we could. Is she attracted to me? Does he really mean that? There is a powerful allure to knowing what someone is thinking.

But without the ability to mind read, we are condemned to communicate using crude surrogates: words, facial expressions and body language. Humans have been using spoken language for at least fifty thousand years and physical expression for far longer, but both remain open to potential misinterpretation and misdirection. So pity us, the marketer researchers, doomed to use these crude tools to understand the motivations behind people's behaviour and provide information to guide important business and social decisions. But lo! Help is at hand. Science promises us the Holy Grail. We *can* read minds. We just need to attach some electrodes and we will know what is going on in your head. Whether you prefer Coca-Cola to Pepsi. Whether cigarette warning labels make you want to smoke. Whether we have pushed your 'buy button'.

But are claims like these really true? Does the application of neuroscience mean that established research techniques are outdated? Or could neuroscience actually learn from established methodologies? These are questions that Erik Du Plessis sets out to answer in this book. In the process, he introduces us to the labyrinthine complexity of the human brain, a curious creature called the rat-brain robot, and the role that emotions, moods and culture play in our lives.

The Branded Mind builds on Erik's previous book, *The Advertised Mind*. Going beyond the role of transient emotions in directing attention, *The Branded Mind* explores the impact of longer-lasting feelings on decision making. Emotions direct our attention quickly and effectively and, as a result, they can call our attention to advertising and ensure continued engagement. But emotions are also transitory, lasting only for a few seconds; our relationship with brands lasts far longer than that. What, then, determines our brand allegiance?

Erik argues that this is the domain not of emotion but of feelings and, in the even longer term, personality and culture. What determines which brand you buy? Erik proposes that this is the domain of the 'reward circuit,' which relies on the release of dopamine and other neurotransmitters. It is the anticipation of how much pleasure we will get from consuming one brand versus another that determines which one we buy. Importantly, the anticipated pleasure derives not just from functional rewards but from emotional and social benefits as well. We are motivated by anything that makes us feel balanced and happy. It might be the pleasure of quelling our hunger with a Big Mac or the satisfaction of announcing our status by driving a Mercedes.

Successful brands, therefore, create lasting emotional tags in people's minds that help ensure that the brand will flourish in the long term.

After detailing his understanding of how the brain works, Erik goes on to explore some implications for practitioners of marketing and neuroscience: why the dichotomy between rational and emotional is unwarranted, what neuroscience can learn from market research, and why a one-size-fits-all approach to market segmentation is wrong.

It is not for nothing that this book's sub-title is *What neuroscience really tells us about the puzzle of the brain and the brand*. Our understanding of how the brain works is informed by a multitude of disciplines and tools. The new techniques of neuroscience are rapidly expanding that understanding. We have many new pieces of the puzzle, but not everyone agrees on what the new learning means or how it fits with the old. However, even though we cannot yet literally read minds, the application of neuroscience to market research holds a lot of promise. Knowing precisely when and how someone reacts to something is of significant importance, particularly in understanding how people respond to dynamic stimuli such as video advertising.

As one of the leading advertising pretesting companies in the world, Millward Brown has a strong interest in applying scientific techniques to expand on what people can readily tell us. In 2010, after six years of experimentation, the company established a neuroscience division under the direction of Graham Page with the goal of supplementing its existing advertising research offer with techniques that uncover the inner workings of the human mind. To date, the application of electroencephalography (EEG) brainwave measurement, eye tracking, and implicit association tests has not overthrown our existing learning and methodologies, but it has added new insights. Only time will tell just how far reaching the impact of that new learning will be.

In this book, Erik is not trying to sell you on a specific neuroscience technique. He is simply trying to lay out what is known about how the brain works today and offer his interpretation of how it all fits together. In the process, he challenges some of the currently accepted wisdom about how we make decisions and the value of neuroscience and market research. And he does so with his customary intelligence, no-nonsense style and good humour. Even if your interest is intellectual rather than practical, *The Branded Mind* is well worth reading.

Nigel Hollis, Chief Global Analyst, Millward Brown

ABOUT THE AUTHOR AND CONTRIBUTORS

Erik du Plessis

Chairman, Millward Brown South Africa

Erik is Chairman of Millward Brown (South Africa) and the author of *The Advertised Mind* published by Kogan Page in 2005 and since translated into nine languages. He was Visiting Professor at the Copenhagen Business School teaching neuromarketing from 2007–09.

Erik worked as a market analyst, researcher and brand manager at a wine company before joining BBDO advertising as media director and research director. He then went on to start his own company, Impact Information, which built the largest database in the world of tracked television commercials (now more than 60,500). This company became Millward Brown South Africa in 2001.

During his career, Erik has consulted with nearly every major company in South Africa (FMCG, services, financial, public service, automotive) on brand management, research, advertising strategy and media planning.

Erik is one of the most published non-American, non-academic authors in the *Journal of Advertising Research* with contributions spanning Recall vs Recognition, Ad-liking, and the effect of DVRs (this was published in the recent special issue on advertising laws based on the conference at the Wharton Business School and also in the *Harvard Business Review*). He has also contributed several papers to *ADMAP* on the same topics.

In 1998 he was the joint winner of the TELMAR (New York) Emerging Author Award with John Philip Jones and Erwin Ephron. His book *The Advertised Mind* (2005) won the coveted WPP's Atticus 'Grand Prix' Award 2005 for original published thought, chosen from 450 entries.

Erik is in constant demand at industry conferences around the world. More details can be found on his website: **www.erikdup.com/**

Nigel Hollis

Executive Vice President and Chief Global Analyst, Millward Brown.

Nigel Hollis is Chief Global Analyst at Millward Brown where he provides thought leadership to the company while consulting with clients on their key marketing and business issues. He has extensive experience on branding, successful marketing communications, interactive research, applying research to pre-testing, tracking and optimization in these areas.

Nigel has worked with a wide range of global marketers including Nestlé, SABMiller, HP, Unilever, Microsoft and Pepsi-Cola. He is also a four-time recipient of the WPP's distinguished Atticus Award for original thinking.

Before joining the Millward Brown team, Nigel worked as senior research manager for Cadbury Typhoo in Birmingham, UK. He holds a BA (Hons) in economics from Lancaster University in the United Kingdom.

Nigel is a frequent speaker on major industry platforms around the globe and a keen contributor to leading industry journals and trade publications. He is a member of the Editorial Advisory Board of the International Journal of Market Research. Recently Nigel was awarded the David K Hardin award by the American Marketing Association Foundation.

In 2008, Nigel authored *The Global Brand,* a book that explains how marketers can create and develop lasting brand value in the world market. He continues to share his thoughts on marketing research, and global branding on his blog *Straight Talk with Nigel Hollis* (**www.mb-blog.com**).

Graham Page
Executive Vice President, Millward Brown Consumer Neuroscience Practice

Graham Page leads Millward Brown's Neuroscience Practice which is responsible for integrating cutting-edge neuroscience techniques with existing Millward Brown research solutions.

He has worked for Millward Brown since 1992 providing brand owners in many different industries with answers to their marketing questions. Before moving into his current role, Graham spent a decade working on research innovations, including six years as the Head of Global Innovations. Prior to that, Graham spent three years working on major client projects in the United States.

Over the last six years Graham has led a pioneering research team looking into how neuroscience techniques might be used to better understand consumers' responses to brands and marketing. This involved working with leading academics in the field, including Professor Jane Raymond of Bangor University, running a multitude of client projects with Fortune 100 marketers, and pure experimentation. The culmination of this work was the establishment of The Neuroscience Practice in 2010, which has overseen neuroscience-derived research projects all over the world.

Graham holds a BA in experimental psychology from Oxford University. He is an award-winning writer and speaker about brand issues on a wide range of topics including neuroscience, the effects of emotion in marketing, the drivers of brand success, viral marketing, consumer segmentation, brand elasticity and corporate reputation.

ACKNOWLEDGEMENTS

The first one I should thank is my wife who suffered my frustrations and moods with me and was forgiving throughout.

This book is not a product of my brain alone, although the errors are.

Most of all I need to thank Nigel Hollis for hours of debating, for days of reviewing the text and questioning my conclusions, and for contributing to the way that things are said. Nigel has been a true friend and supporter in this process spanning three years during which I often felt that it might not be worthwhile writing a book like this because it has to deal with contentious issues.

John Philip Jones previewed some very early manuscripts while touring Anglo-Boer war sites with us. He even rewrote some sections for me. If it had not been for his encouragement – despite disagreeing with some of my thoughts – this book would probably not exist.

My writing career was started by Prof. Giep Franzen who asked whether they could publish *The Advertised Mind* as a first monogram in Dutch for the University of Amsterdam.

This would have been the end of my writing career had it not been for Bob Meyers, CEO of Millward Brown, who suggested that I write an updated English version. Three years after this appeared Eileen Campbell, then CEO of Millward Brown asked me at a conference in Mexico when the next book is due. She explained: the one about brands rather than just advertising. Dominic Twose probably knows what Damasio proposes better than anyone, and Graham Page drives the bio-measurement technology of Millward Brown.

In neither of the books did Millward Brown insist on text being changed to fit in with the Millward Brown philosophies as to how research should be conducted. In both books there are issues I raise that Millward Brown might not want to see in print, but they allowed me to go my, erroneous, way.

Prof. Flemming Hansen died in 2010, and deserves a special mention not only because of his contribution to consumer behaviour theories but also for starting the first neuromarketing course at a business school, for his efforts to start conferences and a journal on the topic. From a personal perspective he was a unique friend and by inviting me to teach neuromarketing I learned a lot more about what this discipline will be than I otherwise would have.

Prof. Yoram Wind and Prof. Byron Sharpe deserve mention for their invitation for me to talk at their Wharton Business School conference about the effect of 30 second ads that are fast forwarded – even though I could not attend they allowed a video to be showed. This gave me a new perspective on the contributions that neuroscience can give to popular marketing issues.

Thomas Ramsoy, now teaching Neuro-Decision Making at Copenhagen Business School taught me about neuroscience and the views that neuro-psychologists have of what they can contribute to neuromarketing.

Charles Foster (CEO Millward Brown – Africa), Travyn Rhall and local MB staff like Christine Malone and Hendrik van Vuuren (both now in the United States) all indulged in my passion for this book and made it possible.

PART ONE
What it is all about

Introduction

Brain science has undergone a revolution. It has made the front page of *Time* magazine, and it is regularly reported in the popular newspapers that brain scientists have proved something or other. Brain science books like Malcolm Gladwell's *Blink* (2005), Antonio Damasio's *Descartes' Error* (1995), Read Montague's *Your Brain Is (Almost) Perfect* (2007) and Martin Lindstrom's *Buy-ology* (2008) are to be found on the popular bookshelves rather than the specialist sections of bookstores.

The term 'neuromarketing' is now freely used in the marketing media and is one of the hottest topics at conferences. It was only coined in 2002.

At the last estimate there were some 100 organizations offering neuro-marketing measurements. Similarly the claims about marketing companies that are investing in these technologies appear to be overwhelming. Some business schools now have courses called 'neuromarketing' or something similar.* Creative directors are now stating confidently at conferences that 'Neuroscience has proved...'. They are especially prone to point out that research respondents lie, or cannot tell the truth, because they just don't know why they buy brands, and neuroscience has proven this. The popular media have articles that claim the 'buy button' has been found. Organizations like Commercial Alert are pressing the US government to stop funding research at Baylor College because it is using brain scanning equipment for commercial purposes – to find the buy button.

To most marketers it appears as if there is some revolution out there that they are not part of, and need to become part of as soon as possible. In this milieu it is not surprising that snake oil salesmen will abound.

Having written *The Advertised Mind*, which is now available in nine languages, I am often asked questions about neuromarketing by journalists. As a visiting professor at the Copenhagen Business School, where I co-lecture with a neuro-psychologist, I had to get my material sorted into bite-sized chunks for lectures. As the Chairman of Millward Brown (South Africa), I am exposed to the evaluation of these neuromarketing technologies in

---

* I started a discussion on LinkedIn entitled 'Is Neuromarketing taught at Management Schools/Universities?' in the group Professors in Management Schools as well as in the group 'Neuromarketing'. See these for responses about where neuro-marketing is taught.

terms of their viability and what they actually measure, in a situation where there is an abundance of actual empirical consumer research.

I really sympathize with the average marketer's problem of trying to make sense of what neuromarketing is about and even whether it leads to new marketing thinking.

The meta- and the micro-problem

The real problem for a marketer is that neuromarketing has achieved very little, and at the same time very much.

At a meta-level, neuroscience made a great breakthrough in 1995 when the neurologist Antonio Damasio published the book *Descartes' Error*, which changed the paradigm about the role of emotions. Since Descartes, 300 years ago, said 'I think, therefore I am', which we have philosophically equated with 'I am rational, therefore I am', we have seen emotions as something that interfere with rationality. Damasio changed the whole paradigm by positing 'I have emotions, therefore I am rational.' This could be the biggest philosophical thought that we have seen in 300 years. In itself this changes some of the thinking by philosophers and psychologists and of disciplines like economics, evolutionism, sociology and consumer behaviour. It is probably on a par with Darwin's insights on evolution. It should be noted that when Darwin published *The Expression of the Emotions in Man and Animals* in 1872 he recognized the importance of emotions.

Damasio's statement has been latched on to by people talking at marketing conferences and writing marketing books, some interpreting it as saying that we are not rational, but we are emotional. This is not what Damasio proposes, and in his subsequent book (1999) he laments the fact that some people present his thinking this way.

At a micro-level, we are now able to measure some things about the biology of the brain. We can insert people into fMRI machines and plot the topography of their brains or even see which parts are active when the person performs a thinking task. These machines weigh 4 tons and generate a magnetic field that is 600,000 times that of the earth. We are very limited in the type of experiments we can use them for. We can also place electrodes on people's heads and read the electronic waves in their brain.

Over-claiming

There are really two 'experiments' that most marketers are aware of: 1) Read Montague (a neuro-computational psychologist) repeated the Pepsi Challenge while his respondents were in fMRI machines and reported this in *Your Brain Is (Almost) Perfect*; 2) Martin Lindstrom scanned 2,081 people (mostly by electroencephalography – EEG) on a variety of tasks and published the results in *Buy-ology* (2008). Martin Lindstrom's subtitle for his book is *How Everything We Believe about Why We Buy Is Wrong*. Read Montague's conclusion is that, while neuroscience is delivering on its promise to view the brain, it still has more to learn from psychology than psychology has to learn from neuroscience.

I believe, like Montague, that neuroscientists still have more to learn from disciplines like marketing and the social sciences that have studied consumer decision making and have mountains of empirical data.

Emotions and feelings

Nearly all the work that has been done in this area considers the role of emotions, and most talks about this area include the role that the neuroscientists and psychologists have proposed for emotions. Briefly, this role is that emotions are the result of things in our environment and they ready us for action, ie they happen very fast and seldom last longer than a few seconds. This works very well when we try to explain the attention being given to an advertisement.

However, it does not work when we try to explain the feelings component about brands, which is really the soma that Damasio's theorem is based on. (We will discuss soma in subsequent chapters.) This has been overlooked by most people in the hype of the new definition of what emotions are all about.

Where does this leave us?

I won't be going along with the hype about neuromarketing and making unreasonable suggestions about how to market a brand. However, after reading this book the reader will have a good idea about what we know about how the brain works – and also what we don't know yet. The reader should understand enough to be able to ask sensible questions when presented with an argument that states 'Neuroscience has proved that...' or at least be very sceptical.

On a much more pragmatic level, I have also written about some marketing practices that are supported by our knowledge from neuroscience as being good practice.

The puzzle

This book is about how people think and how people think about brands. What people do involves making decisions, which is simply making choices between available options. A very large portion of what people do involves decisions about brands. These are not only the brands they eat and drink, but the brands they work for to get money, the brands they use to save this money at, the brand of store they buy things from, the brands they drive to, the brands they work for, the brand of area that they want to live in (even the country), the brand of house style they live in, the brand of neighbourhood they want to be in, the brand of political party they vote for, the brand of books they buy, the brand of newspaper they buy, the brand of television they watch, the brand of movie they go to, the brand of husband or wife they desire, the brand of child they want to raise, the brand of school or church this brand of child will go to, the brand...

All of these brands are decisions people take, ie behaviour. Like a jigsaw puzzle, the brain consists of many pieces, each unique in appearance and function. All these work interdependently, and in harmony, to produce the big picture. The big picture is termed 'behaviour'. If only one piece of the brain is faulty then the big picture is often faulty.

To complete a jigsaw puzzle you need to know the picture on the cover of the box, and you need to study the individual pieces when trying to assemble the puzzle. If you do not know what the final picture looks like and merely proceed by trying to assemble the pieces you will waste your time. Similarly, just looking at the picture on the cover tells you very little about the way the puzzle is assembled.

Something similar is true of the brain. The biological sciences study the pieces of the brain. The social sciences study the total picture, ie the output from the brain. Naturalists study the brain in action in animal behaviour. Sociologists study the brain and its interaction with other brains. Engineers contribute by designing machines that measure the brain or even simulate the brain. Even artists study the brain and the way it gains pleasure from music and art.

It can truly be said that everybody in the world has a view about the output of the brain (the picture on the cover of the box). We all need to know how other people and animals will react to actions we take. Without such a view of the brains of other people and animals, people will be unable to function in society. Without such a view they will not be able to bring up their children.

Until recently it has been impossible to study the pieces of a living human brain. It was really only possible to observe abnormal behaviour in people and, upon their death, to inspect their brains for abnormalities. We are then left to make the assumption that these abnormalities were the cause for the abnormal behaviour. With the highly interactive nature of the pieces of the brain, this was truly unsatisfactory.

On occasions brain surgery removed parts of a brain, and then we could observe changes in behaviour. Again the highly interactive nature of the pieces of the brain limited such studies. We could do experiments on animals, but we could not ask them questions after the operation to determine what had changed. We could really draw only very broad generalized conclusions from such experiments.

Technology has now enabled us to measure (or scan) the parts of living human brains in action. Until recently this has been accessible only to neurologists and neuro-psychologists, but this has changed. It is now possible to selectively 'knock out' specific brain areas for a while and then to observe changes in behaviour. From this has come an integration of the scientists who study the puzzle of the human brain.

In a jigsaw of a nature scene all pieces contribute to the big picture, but even within this big picture they contribute to elements of the picture: some are parts of a tree, some are parts of the mountains, some are parts of the lake, and most are parts of more than one element of the big picture. This is why one needs to understand the big picture as well as the pieces. The big picture teaches us what we should expect from the smaller pictures: we know there should be some with one straight edge, some with two straight edges, some brown pieces – and we know that brown pieces are more likely to be part of the tree in the big picture.

The big picture in this book is not just the human brain. This is only one of the elements discussed. Included in the picture are elements of culture, personality and so on, all of which affect the brain. Included in the book are also elements of brands and marketing.

When you assemble a jigsaw puzzle you often change the way that you view specific pieces. You will group them in different types (tree pieces, lake pieces, edges, etc); you will turn them around to provide different perspectives; you will sometimes decide that a piece has been put in the wrong place. This is happening in our view of the brain today.

The insights that we now have as a result of brain scanning techniques and a greater interest by the different sciences about how these insights affect thinking about the brain can be compared to the process of reconsidering the pieces of a jigsaw puzzle. This book considers what the views of the pieces, systems and elements are and how this might change.

Be warned that what is happening in the sciences of the brain – and in marketing – is not a zero-based exercise. Everything we know about the brain has not changed since we've been able to scan it – much of what we knew, or suspected we knew, is being verified.

This is also true for what we knew about brands and marketing. Nearly everything that we believed was best practice remains best practice. In some cases we now understand some things better than before, and in some cases we will work out better ways of doing what we did before.

This book is about the consumer's brain

Neuromarketing is a very recent discipline – the word was only coined in 2002. It really is about the border between neuroscience and marketing. It forces marketers to review what they believe about the consumer's brain, and how this might affect their marketing activities. That is what this book is about, and in this chapter I give a preview.

Why I wrote this book

This is the second book I have written. The first book, *The Advertised Mind* (2005), is about how the human mind works and the implications that this has for advertising. I wrote *The Advertised Mind* over a period of nearly 10 years. It started because I had an interest in the difference between recall and recognition measures of advertising memories – a hotly disputed debate even to this day among research companies and advertising agencies. Both these measures are ways that advertising memories are measured; therefore it appeared reasonable to understand what memories are if we wanted to understand what the measures are measuring. This led me to reading what the cognitive psychologists are working on – learning and memory – and talking to some of the big names in this area about the implications for advertising.

At the time my company had a system that tracked every new television commercial in South Africa. By pure serendipity we asked respondents to rate all the advertisements in terms of their likeability. We soon discovered that the more people liked an advertisement the more likely they were to recall the advertisement. This should not have been a surprise to anyone. The link was obvious: people give attention to things they like, and attention creates memories. This then gave rise to two considerations: how do you create advertisements that people like, and how do you treat these in your media strategy to benefit the most from what you created?

At that time a new paradigm about the reason why we have emotions – to give attention and to influence our decisions – raised by Antonio Damasio and Joseph LeDoux, both neurologists, became popular and the topic of many marketing conferences. The use of brain scanners for non-medical reasons became more common, giving rise to the terms 'neuro-economics' and 'neuromarketing'. This helped to make *The Advertised Mind* quite popular – and brought me several invitations to speak at conferences. It also gave me the opportunity to be a visiting professor at the Copenhagen Business School.

The question I have been asked is: why spend three years writing another book? It is a question I have asked myself several times over the last two years. There are several reasons for writing this book:

- *The Advertised Mind* dealt with the implications that modern insights about the way the brain works have for advertising. It does not really address the issue as far as the brand itself is concerned. It became obvious to me soon after the book appeared that this is a major weakness.

- The main function of emotions for human survival is attentioning. Brands are seldom bought for reasons relating to attention. They are bought to affect bodily states like hunger, thirst and being cold, to create moods of well-being, or to comply with cultures and social groupings. They are bought because people have different personalities that react differently to different brands, or for status or to project personalities. All of these things can be broadly classified as feelings. When, therefore, we want to consider the implications of modern brain research then we cannot avoid embarking on the understanding of a much greater concept than mere emotions; we must begin to understand feelings.

- A number of articles in journals, talks at conferences and books appeared after *The Advertised Mind* based on the work of Antonio Damasio and brain scanning studies that are a bad interpretation either of what he said or of the results of brain scanning studies. Damasio denounced this in his subsequent book (1999), but few of the speakers or authors seem to have read this. I felt frustrated by this, and a major reason for writing this book is to enable marketers and advertisers to better judge what is being said at conferences – and in their companies when suppliers make claims based on 'Neuromarketing shows that...'.

Why do we make decisions?

This might sound like a very trite question. However, if you want to understand 'brand decisions' then you need to understand 'decision making'; and then you need to know what 'decision making' is trying to achieve.

The objective of decision making is to motivate us to do something. This 'something' is to make us either feel less bad or feel good. We buy food brands so that we feel less hungry or we buy music brands so that we will feel good. This hedonistic view of why people do what they do has spurred a lot of debate. Yet, when one understands how the brain works, it becomes obvious that this is what we do.

The objective for marketers becomes one of making sure that the brand they market will make their consumers feel good.

How do people differ from animals on this view?

A lot of the arguments against such a simple hedonistic (selfish) view of people are based on the objection that it reduces people to mere animals at the whims of our feelings. Well, we are animals; that much is beyond dispute. However, we are different from other animals in that we have proportionately the largest frontal lobes of all animals. As the insights and understanding of the brain grows, so it is becoming clearer that we are less at the whim of our feelings because we have big frontal lobes that moderate the effect of our feelings. The frontal lobes allow us to plan for the future by considering options, and actually a wide range of options beyond those that we are physically confronted with at a point in time.

We are considerably better than other animals in the making of plans. Plans involve a view of the future outcomes of what we do, ie how will we feel sometime in the future if we choose a specific alternative now? Most animals have limited planning ability. Some might migrate to where there is better grazing. Some might even store food for the future. Zoologists are amazed when they find evidence of animals using tools. This is about where it stops. Humans plan much further. We will plant so that we can eat months into the future. We will get jobs so we can get money, which we save in financial institutions, so that we can buy food from a store, to which we drive in a vehicle. All of this we do so that we will feel good at some future point in time. All of this involves brands.

How does this happen in the brain?

This book explains the modern view of how this works inside the brain. A very brief overview will have to serve now.

Perceptions about the state of the environment (threats, delights), the state of the body (hungry, tired) and the state of the mind (relaxed, anxious) are all channelled to the frontal lobes. Neuronal recruitment is based on our experiences (memories). This channelling is actually just a process of interpretation (ie what is it?) based on our previous experiences (ie memory or knowledge).

The channelling goes through the limbic system, which is the oldest part of the brain in evolutionary terms. Part of the interpretation of what we are experiencing now is also how we feel about it. This feeling part of the interpretation is added to the developing interpretation mostly in the limbic system, so that when the interpretation reaches the frontal lobes it knows not only what it is that we perceive but also how we feel about it.

The frontal lobes can consider alternative actions. This happens again by way of neuronal recruitment. There is also the (absolutely automatic) ability for these processes to be sent back via the limbic system, so that included in the thought of alternative actions there is also a 'How will I feel?' component. The frontal lobes can now start certain reactions: walk away, run toward, pick up and take to the till and so on. They can also decide to do nothing if that might be what would make us feel best.

This is a vast oversimplification of the process, but is essentially what this book will explain in terms of the biology of the brain.

How do we buy a brand?

The difference between us and the other animals on the planet is that we live in a world that we have changed over many millennia to suit our needs. We did this by our ability to plan for the future and to create. We learned that to herd cattle means we do not need to hunt, and by cultivating food we do not need to forage. We learned to trade, and we learned to specialize. We learned to make tools with which to hunt, herd or cultivate food. We learned to build shelter. We even learned that some people produce better-quality food than others and we preferred to buy their produce (ie branding).

We know that at some stage in the future we will be hungry. So we know that we will have to go to the shop to buy some food. We know that to buy food we need money, so we get a job. We know we need a way to keep the money we earn safe and to pay for the food, so we get a bank and a credit card. We know that the store is a long way to walk, so we get a car – and so on.

In reality what is happening is that we are planning our future based on our knowledge that we will at some stage feel hungry. We are pre-empting our feeling of hunger by planning. We also know that at some stage we will feel bored, and so we plan for this by buying a computer game – which presupposes we have bought a computer. We know that we will, at some stage, feel a need to relax, so we buy a CD. We know we will need company, so we try to keep friends.

How do we know that these things will happen to us? Mainly we know this because they have happened to us in the past or we expect them to happen to us in the future – for example, we may 'expect' to get married, have children and so on. We have a memory of these situations and we have a memory of what we did to turn the situation from feeling bad to one where we feel better.

This process, described very simplistically here, underlies a lot of marketing and advertising theories. The Percy–Rossiter grid is based on this. The problem–solution advertising style is based on this. But, more than just these two examples, all of marketing is based on this.

Yes, there are philosophical viewpoints that argue against the above description of behaviour as not explaining all behaviours. The questions raised involve issues like deferred gratification, sympathy, and some obvious questionable behaviours like setting yourself alight with petrol in protest at some government action. The issue about sympathy is being solved by neuroscientists having found what appears to be the 'sympathy neuron'. It is a great benefit for the survival of a society (or tribe) if evolution has blessed the members with a 'sympathy neuron'. In all cases the decision to do what we might consider to be deviant, abnormal behaviour is explained simply by the person who indulges in it having a greater expectation of feeling good by these behaviours.

From a marketing perspective the analogy would be saving money and insurance products. It is the expectations that create a better feeling of good than the immediate consumption of the money.

Marketing practice

People plan to satisfy their future needs by buying things now, or sometimes they buy things 'on impulse' for immediate consumption. Even for an impulse purchase that we consume immediately, the act of consumption is after the act of purchasing, ie in the future. Ultimately they buy brands because they believe the brands will make them feel better now or in the future. Interestingly, as I will show, even if they just expect that the brands will make them feel better in the future, buying them now makes people feel better now.

The brand choice decision that they make now is based on the interpretations that reach their frontal lobes. These interpretations are not only the interpretation of their current environment but also the interpretation of their thoughts (ie there seems to be an 'as if' circuit that allows the brain to evaluate how they would feel if they did something). This might sound confusing now, but read the rest of the book and you will see the circuitry.

This interpretation of the brand that includes how one feels about the brand I call the 'brand soma', based on Antonio Damasio's term 'soma', which describes the feeling component of the interpretation of things that we see, hear or smell. A marketer's objective is to influence this brand soma. The brand soma is based on memories (or knowledge or experience) and neurologically simply the chemical state of the synapses between neurons.

The task of the marketer is to ensure that the brand soma is positive, at least more positive than that of the competing brands. This summarizes best what lesson this book has to teach marketers.

So what is this book about?

Much of what I have touched upon in this chapter explains how understanding brands involves not just the brands themselves, but human decision making and even the limens between neurons in human brains and how this came about through evolution.

There is a lot being said and claimed under the term 'neuromarketing'. This book looks constructively and (I hope) unsensationally at this area of endeavour by scientists and marketers.

The two really important lessons for marketers have come from Joseph LeDoux and Antonio Damasio. LeDoux explained how emotion influences attention. This has given a good biological explanation of how ad liking works. It has placed the ARF Copy Validation Project in a new light and has led to a better understanding of emotional measures of advertising. Damasio's brand soma theories have explained better how measures of feelings influence the decisions we make (including brand decisions).

This does not suggest that the brain scanning experiments that marketers are doing are wasted. At this stage there is a lot to be learned about the brain, and each experiment contributes to this knowledge – whether the outcome is positive or negative. It will be in everybody's interest for these experiments to be published, so that the results from different studies can be compared and be the foundation of a solid science.

At this stage I think that the insights gained about how the brain operates, biologically, are especially useful in giving us insights into the bases of marketing theories that already exist, thereby allowing us to have confidence in what we are doing and also to decide which marketing theories are less solid. I also think that marketing theories, and especially empirical databases, have more to contribute to neuroscience than the other way around. We have databases of decisions people have taken as a result of some marketing activities or as a result of certain mindsets. These should be used to guide neuroscience experiments.

Good examples of this include the following:

- Baars and Ramsoy (2007) illustrate the interaction between taxi drivers' skills and the development of the hippocampus (see Chapter 17). This is about how changed brain structures lead to skills and possibly activities leading to changed brain structures. A very good question is whether this could happen to brand preferences.

- Read Montague's Pepsi experiment (discussed in Chapter 22) is a brilliant example of marketing theories leading to a neuromarketing experiment, and how the marketing theories provide a basis for interpreting the results of the neuromarketing experiment.

- I discuss market segmentation in Part 5, especially to point out that one might expect different market segments to yield different reactions in the brain for the same stimuli (brands). Simply averaging the brain scan measures over a random sample of people could lead to useless results. Here marketing science and segmentation results should lead brain scan experiments.

- Further to the above point, segmentation studies often result in demographic differences between segments. Baars and Ramsoy's taxi driver experiment raises the question about the effect of age on the brain structures. Could the interaction between demographics as a segmentation variable be a result of this age effect on the brain? Segmentation studies often have personality variables as differentiators. It certainly sounds reasonable that personality differences might be a result of brain structural differences. Could marketers provide good empirical segmentation evidence to brain scientists, on which the scientists could base their experiments?

- In all markets there is a price-sensitive segment. Is this a neurological condition? Similarly there are brand-loyal segments. Are these due to differences in the way the brain operates? If this is so, what are the things a marketer can do to increase loyalty to the brand? I would be sceptical if the outcome of experiments about this is not simply: do good marketing. But at least there will be good neuroscientific reasons for doing so.

The new paradigm

In 1995 the neurologist Antonio Damasio introduced a new paradigm about how we should view emotions as being a fundamental component of rationality, thus replacing the 300-year-old paradigm of Descartes. This major paradigm shift has brain scientists (from neurologists to psychologists) excited, and they are reviewing what their disciplines believe. This modern view about the role of emotions has found its way into papers presented at most marketing conferences, sometimes misinterpreted. Most of this book is about the Damasian paradigm shift. Therefore the new paradigm is presented very early in the book.

From Descartes to Damasio

As I wrote the book I often found myself asking: so what is new? Isn't this stuff we knew and used all along? This is what happens when there is a paradigm shift. Many people say 'But we knew this all along', and many others say 'This is overrated rubbish, because it doesn't fit with what we knew all along.'

I have been interviewed by magazines, technical journals, radio programmes and blogs since the appearance of *The Advertised Mind* (2005). In most cases it is obvious that the journalist has heard of new insights into the human brain due to scanning techniques, and believes that this is what I have written about. In some cases journalists believe there is some new 'magic' whereby marketers will peer into the human brain and make people misguidedly buy brands that are bad for them. Nothing can be further from the truth of what is happening.

However, what is happening is much more spectacular. There is a new paradigm that affects the way we view the role of emotions or feelings in human life.

The momentous moments in science and history are when there is a paradigm shift:

> Paradigm shifts tend to be most dramatic in sciences that appear to be stable and mature, as in physics at the end of the 19th century. At that time, physics seemed to be a discipline filling in the last few details of a largely worked-out system. In 1900, Lord Kelvin famously stated, 'There is nothing new to be discovered in physics now. All that remains is more and more precise measurement.' Five years later, Albert Einstein published his paper on special relativity, which challenged the very simple set of rules laid down by Newtonian mechanics, which had been used to describe force and motion for over two hundred years. In this case, the new paradigm reduces the old to a special case in the sense that Newtonian mechanics is still a good model for approximation for speeds that are slow compared to the speed of light.
>
> (Wikipedia, 'Paradigm')

Who is Damasio?

Much of this book is about the work of Damasio, who is mostly responsible for the paradigm shift. So let us introduce the reader to him as early as possible:

> António Rosa Damásio (born 1944) is a Portuguese behavioral neurologist and neuroscientist working in the United States. He is David Dornsife Professor of Neuroscience at the University of Southern California, where he heads USC's Brain and Creativity Institute. Prior to taking up his post at USC, in 2005, Damásio was M.W. Van Allen Professor and Head of Neurology at the University of Iowa Hospitals and Clinics. His career at Iowa lasted from 1976–2005. Besides being a well-known researcher in several areas of neurology, he is a best-selling author of books which describe his scientific thinking.
>   ... Damásio's books deal with the relationship between emotions and feelings, and what their bases are in the brain. His 1994 book, *Descartes' Error: Emotion, Reason and the Human Brain*, was nominated for the Los Angeles Times Book Award and is translated in over 30 languages. His second book, *The Feeling of What Happens: Body and Emotion in the Making of Consciousness*, was named as one of the ten best books of 2001 by New York Times Book Review, a Publishers Weekly Best Book of the Year, a Library Journal Best Book of the Year, and has thirty foreign editions. Damásio's most recent book, *Looking for Spinoza: Joy, Sorrow, and the Feeling Brain*, was published in 2003. In it, Damásio explores philosophy and its relations to neurobiology, suggesting that it might provide guidelines for human ethics.
>
> (Wikipedia, 'António Damásio')

None of his books are written with marketers in mind. He deals with things on a philosophical level. However, the paradigm that he proposes has some really important implications for marketers – which is why I wrote this book.

The book that has had the most influence on what we consider in this book is *Descartes' Error*.

Who was Descartes?

With Damasio's book being *Descartes' Error*, it makes sense to first know who Descartes was:

> René Descartes (31 March 1596–11 February 1650), was a French philosopher, mathematician, scientist, and writer who spent most of his adult life in the Dutch Republic. He has been dubbed the 'Father of Modern Philosophy', and much of subsequent Western philosophy is a response to his writings, which continue to be studied closely to this day. In particular, his *Meditations on First Philosophy* continues to be a standard text at most university philosophy departments.
>
> ... Descartes frequently sets his views apart from those of his predecessors. In the opening section of the *Passions of the Soul*, a treatise on the Early Modern version of what are now commonly called emotions, he goes so far as to assert that he will write on his topic 'as if no one had written on these matters before'.
>
> ... His most famous statement is 'Cogito ergo sum' (English: I think, therefore I am; or I am thinking, therefore I exist).
>
> (Wikipedia, 'René Descartes')

Damasio criticized Descartes's views over 300 years after Descartes died. Descartes basically stated 'I am rational therefore I am', and by doing this he separated the emotional life from the rational. For 260 years most philosophy was based on emotionality being the opposite of rationality. People like Sigmund Freud (himself a neurologist by training) built a whole system that today is called psychology. Much of Freud's thinking is based on emotions interfering with rationality. A phobia is just an irrational emotion.

Sometimes people who have not yet begun to appreciate that Damasio has posited that one should not think 'emotion versus rational' but that emotions are part of rationality will mistakenly present at conferences that Damasio has said that people's decisions are emotional, not rational. Much of this book is to explain to marketers that this is wrong. Damasio did not say that we are driven by our emotions to the exclusion of rationality. What he said is that the two are inextricably interlinked – and this is because of the way our brains are built.

In The *Feeling of What Happens*, Damasio sounds irritated by the way he is often misrepresented:

> These findings suggest that selective reduction of emotion is at least as prejudicial for rationality as excessive emotion. It certainly does not seem true that reason stands to gain from operating without the leverage of emotion. On the contrary, emotion probably assists reasoning, especially when it comes to personal and social matters involving risk and conflict. I suggested that certain levels of emotion processing probably point us to the sector of the decision-making space where our reason can operate most effectively.
>
> I did not suggest, however, that emotions are a substitute for reason or that emotions decide for us.
>
> (Damasio, 1999)

What is the paradigm shift that we are looking at?

Here is the quote from the back cover of *Descartes' Error* (1995): 'Damasio's experiences [are] with modern-day neurological patients affected by brain damage. Far from interfering with rationality, the absence of emotion and feelings can break down rationality, and make wise decision making almost impossible.' This quote itself explains the new paradigm: 'Emotions cause rationality'. (In terms of the definitions I use later in this book 'Feelings cause rationality').

If you do not know how you feel about something you might behave inappropriately toward it – to the extent that people observing your behaviour would find it irrational:

- Not being scared of a snake is irrational.
- Not eating when you are hungry is irrational.
- Not avoiding speeding motor cars on the street is irrational.
- Not being kind to someone you love is irrational.

Of course:

- You might decide that you like snakes, and then explain to people that you like snakes and have learned how to handle them, which then makes your behaviour 'rational'.
- You might decide not to eat because you are on a diet. This would be rational if you say that you feel good about your decision because you want to feel slim and desirable.
- I cannot think of any reason why it would feel good to walk into a speeding car.
- If you are unkind to someone whom you love, people will really question your motives.

The new paradigm is that emotions are not in conflict with rational behaviour but cause rational behaviour. Descartes is credited with establishing the 'old paradigm', which is why Damasio titled his book *Descartes' Error*.

Damasio's somatic marker theorem

I believe that this is the most important chapter in this book, and I urge the reader to read it slowly and think about it.

On somatic markers, Damasio said:

Consider again the scenarios I outlined. The key components unfold in our minds instantly, sketchily, and virtually simultaneously, too fast for the details to be clearly defined. But now, imagine that before you apply any kind of cost/benefit analysis to the premises, and before you reason toward the solution of the problem, something quite important happens: When the bad outcome connected with a given response option comes into mind, however fleetingly, you experience an unpleasant gut feeling. Because the feeling is about the body, I gave the phenomenon the technical term somatic state ('soma' is Greek for body); and because it 'marks' an image, I called it a marker. Note again that I use somatic in the most general sense (that which pertains to the body) and I include both visceral and non-visceral sensation when I refer to somatic markers.

What does the somatic marker achieve? It forces attention on the negative outcome to which a given action may lead, and functions as an automated alarm signal which says: Beware of danger ahead if you choose the option which leads to this outcome. The signal may lead you to reject, immediately, the negative course of action and thus make you choose among other alternatives. The automated signal protects you against future losses, without further ado, and then allows you to choose from among fewer alternatives. There is still room for using a cost/benefit analysis and proper deductive competence, but only after the automated step drastically reduces the number of options.

Somatic markers may not be sufficient for normal human decision-making since a subsequent process of reasoning and final selection will still take place in many though not all instances.

Somatic markers probably increase the accuracy and efficiency of the decision process. Their absence reduces them. This distinction is important and can easily be missed. The hypothesis does not concern the reasoning steps which follow the action of the somatic marker.

In short, somatic markers are a special instance of feelings generated from secondary emotions. Those emotions and feelings have been connected, by learning, to predicted future outcomes of certain scenarios.

When a negative somatic marker is juxtaposed to a particular future outcome the combination functions as an alarm bell. When a positive somatic marker is juxtaposed instead, it becomes a beacon of incentive.

(Damasio, 1999)

Damasio uses the term 'somatic' as referring to 'how the body feels'. When we have experiences we lay down memories not only of the event, but also how we felt when we experienced the event. So, when we interpret events, we recall not only memories of the event but also how we felt about it. This is Damasio's 'somatic marker'. This feeling component becomes part of the input to the cognitive process so that we can decide how to respond to the event: it will make us feel bad and we should avoid it, or it will make us feel good and we should be motivated toward it.

04 The brain – the coming together of disciplines

In The *Advertised Mind* (2005) I had a chapter similar to this based on the description that Stan Franklin (*Artificial Minds*, 1997) used. I briefly repeat it in this book for the following reasons:

- Many believe one should be qualified to operate a brain scanning tool to be involved in neuromarketing. This is not true.

- One need not be a neurologist to be interested in how people think. Few neurologists are especially interested in how people think. They are more interested in fixing problems of the brain via chemicals or surgery.

- There are many other sciences (engineering, statistics, psychology, operations control, HR, market research, etc) that are concerned with how people think, and have valid empirical data to contribute to the developing science of the brain.

- There are many people selling neuromarketing techniques to unsuspecting marketers. Very important-sounding words are used as part of the sales technique. I hope to forewarn users of these techniques before the whole industry gets a reputation for charlatanism.

- In some instances the advances are made more in the areas of non-brain scanning (or neurological brain scanning) – areas like artificial neuronal networks, chemistry, psychology, sociology and engineering. To appreciate what happens in the brain one should not discard these insights.

- Ultimately we are studying the brain from the outside in – even if we have a lot of knowledge from the inside out. We want to understand behaviour, and behaviour is represented in massive databases in companies that have done market research. These databases can contribute a lot to the study of the human brain (behaving normally).

Since before the days of Plato and Socrates people have been interested in what constitutes 'mind' or 'How do we think?' Over the centuries mind was assumed first to be in the stomach and later the heart. There has also been a big debate about whether your mind is part of your body or something outside the body, with the church preferring the latter idea.

Marketers spend a lot of money trying to determine what consumers want, and how to best give this to the consumer. Economists work hard at trying to work out what the population wants, and how governments can best give this to the population. Cognitive psychologists devote their attention to how we learn and how we can best teach students. Clinical psychologists study mind abnormalities and how these can be treated. Psychiatrists do the same, but are looking at chemical interventions. Anthropologists study how the human mind changed and adapted in societies. Artificial intelligence scientists try to work out how to build an artificial mind that will be indistinguishable from a human brain.

In his book *Artificial Minds*, Stan Franklin uses the schema in Figure 4.1 to explain how the different disciplines that study the brain approach the brain. The vertical axis (Outside in–Inside out) denotes whether the person is looking at pieces of the brain and then trying to put them together and 'create' a whole brain, ie working from the inside of the brain to the outside, or whether the person is looking at the whole brain and trying to deduce what parts should be inside. The horizontal axis (Analytic–Synthetic) denotes whether the person is working with a real human brain or something artificial.

FIGURE 4.1 The 'brain sciences'

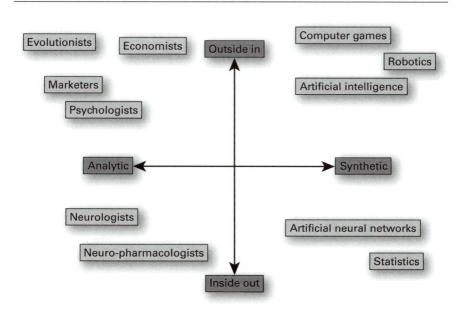

PART TWO
The decision-making puzzle

The most important chapter in Part 1 is the one dealing with Damasio's concept of the soma. This is, of course, a high-level view of how one's feelings are part of the interpretation of things and thoughts to form a basis for decision making, which leads into the question of how this is really executed in the brain.

The soma is part of the interpretation of objects (and concepts or ideas). This interpretation of something is based on our experiences, which are really our own memories. Memories are stored in the brain by a biological process very different from that of computer memories. Too often we think about the brain in terms of what we know about computers, but this confuses. We need to understand the biology of memories to make any sense of what the brain is about. We also need to understand how these memories are used to interpret things.

Since Damasio's soma is really the 'how I feel' about things, we need to understand what feelings are. Unfortunately, feelings are ill defined in the literature, so we need to set up some definitions based on the functions of feelings. Once we have set up the functions of feelings and hence are able to classify feelings into types of feelings, we can review the biology of feelings. This gives us the biology of the soma.

Against this background we can evaluate brain scanning methods to see what they measure in terms of what we need to be measured.

Interpretation, memory, experience, learning

05

The human brain is all about survival. To do this efficiently the brain has to learn from experiences so that when it encounters something in the environment it has memories with which to interpret the object. It is this process of interpreting things in the environment, including whether they are threats or pleasures, that allows for survival. The details of this very fundamental process in the brain are explained in this chapter. Out of necessity the chapter repeats some things that were mentioned in *The Advertised Mind* (2005). Without understanding how things are interpreted and how this activates brain regions, the neuromarketer will misinterpret brain scan data (and examples of this are given). Following the Hinton diagrams can be a bit tedious, but I strongly recommend working through the example.

Why the memory system is important

Your brain is basically just one big memory system. In the 1960s, neurologists were amazed that they could not find a single area that is the 'memory storage'. At that stage they were thinking about the brain as if it was like a computer and therefore were looking for components that had to do with memory (long-term and short-term). Eventually they had to conclude that memories are stored all over the brain.

The neurons of the brain just conduct electronic impulses, and the chemical status of the synapses between the neurons determines whether the next neuron will fire. The structures of the brain are made up out of neurons and synapses. Everyone's brain is made up of the same structures, and each of these structures, when activated, will lead to something similar happening in each brain. In this sense our brains are biologically (evolutionarily) hard wired and are the same. However, the synapses and even the connections between neurons will differ for each of us based on our experiences (memories). In this sense we are soft wired. By 'soft wired' I mean that memories are laid down for individuals based on their experiences.

Feeling good, culture, personality and memories

This book is about feelings, and the brain systems that induce feelings, and our reaction to feelings. It certainly would appear that the feelings in our brains are started by specific, hard-wired brain systems. If a specific system fires, the person will feel hungry or scared or frightened, depending on the system.

However, what actually starts the process will differ significantly between individuals. My stomach does not like curry, and my 'feeling' reaction at a conference where only curries are served is very different from that of the typical British or Indian person. I love to lecture and teach at conferences. My feeling when invited is very different from that of most people not used to public speaking. I love biltong, because I am South African. Biltong is fresh meat hung outside to age. Few British people visiting South Africa will eat it. Most South Africans overseas will drive miles to buy it.

Obviously different centres in the mind of different people become activated by the same stimulus. The difference is the soft wiring of the brain, which leads to similar hard-wired responses by parts of the brain.

Just studying the activations of certain brain structures is useless unless you understand the way that neurons (memories) work. Memories are there so that we can interpret anything that our senses experience, as well as anything we might be thinking about. Memories also tell us how we will feel as a result of what we experience. Unless we understand memories we will not understand the brain.

The brain

It is big

The brain mainly consists of neurons (which are just specialized body cells). A person has 10^{10} neurons (10,000,000,000 or 10 billion). It is very difficult to make comparisons that adequately describe how many this is, because whatever one compares this to is something that is an equally inconceivably big number. Consider that the total population of the earth is 6.6 billion.

If each person were represented as a neuron then all of them together still represent only 60 per cent of the neurons in your head!

As you will see, the neurons themselves do not do that much in the brain. What really matters is the synapses (connecting points between the neurons). This is where memories are stored. Each neuron is connected to up to 10,000 other neurons. The estimates for an adult human brain is that it has 10 quadrillion synapses! If we continue the analogy then this would equate to us waiting until the number of people on earth had nearly doubled, and then each of them being in touch with up to 10,000 other people on Facebook.

A neuron has no intelligence of its own (and does not even remember anything – this is in the synapse). All a neuron does is to 'ping' all the neurons that it is connected to.

Let's continue our world population analogy of 10 billion people each in contact with 10,000 others via Facebook. Suppose somebody writes a virus that accesses a computer's address book and sends a copy of the virus to all the contacts. Then the first computer will infect 10,000 others, this will infect 10,000 × 10,000 others = 100,000,000. This will infect 10,000,000,000,000,000 others. Amazingly it will take only three cycles (if there is no duplication between the address books of people) to have the computers of all 10 billion people on earth infected.

This massive interconnectivity is the real power of the human brain. In Part 1, using the jigsaw puzzle as an analogy, it was stressed that no single element of the brain should be viewed as operating in isolation. This interconnectivity of the brain makes it impossible for any element to operate individually.

Neurons

Neurons are electrically excitable cells in the nervous system that process and transmit information. Neurons are the core components of the brain, the spinal cord in vertebrates and the ventral nerve cord in invertebrates, and the peripheral nerves.

A neuron has an axon along which electrical impulses are transmitted and up to 10,000 dendrites that receive impulses from the axons of other neurons. All neurons in resting state have an electronic impulse of –40 millivolts. When a neuron is stimulated it sends an electronic impulse of +70 millivolts through its axon to other neurons. This impulse travels at about 100 miles per second, which is fast given the short distance it has to travel, but is nowhere near as fast as an electronic impulse travelling across the ocean on a telephone line. (An electromagnetic wave in a coaxial cable travels at about 66 per cent of the speed of light.)

When a neuron has been stimulated it returns to its resting state of –40 millivolts. In other words, there is no trace of the experience – or no memory.

A neuron can fire up to 1,000 times a second. This is actually very slow, even when compared to first generation computers. However, when we take into account the above interconnectivity of the neurons in the brain and that it takes about three or so cycles of recruitment then, in the hypothetical case of every neuron being connected uniquely to 10,000 other neurons, every neuron in the brain could have been recruited.

We will tell how people can differentiate between pictures of cats and dogs in less than one tenth of a second and they will also form a memory of these pictures in that time. They can, inside this one tenth of a second, recognize whether they have seen a picture before.

In Chapter 24 we will tell how Sands Research shows that people decide inside the first 800 millisecond (1000th of a second) whether they have seen an advertisement before. We will also discuss how this is why an exposure to a fast forwarded advertisement on a DVR (Digital Video Recorder) is as good as, or even better than, an exposure at normal speed.

This becomes very important when we discuss the measurements of the brain's activities in Chapter 17. With the event we are trying to measure happening so fast we need equipment that measures very frequently – up to 2,000 times per second.

Synapses

The synapse is where an axon from one neuron meets the dendrites of another neuron. There is a small gap between the axons and the neurons, which contains chemicals. The state of the chemicals inside the synapse determines a threshold (called the limen, which is where the term 'subliminal' comes from). If the incoming impulses are above this threshold the receiving neuron will fire. Every time two neurons fire simultaneously the state of the chemicals will change in such a way that the threshold decreases, thus increasing the likelihood that the receiving neuron will fire when there is a future impulse.

Think of it this way: the teacher repeatedly shows the class the letter 'a' and they have to say 'a'. Each time this happens the synapses between the eyes seeing the letter 'a' and the mouth saying 'a' are stimulated simultaneously. This simultaneous stimulation leads eventually to the children sounding 'a' in their mind (or verbally) every time they see the letter 'a'.

When a neuron causes another neuron to fire this is called 'recruiting'. We will be using this term often in the rest of the book. If neuron A fires and the threshold of the synapse with neuron B is low enough then neuron B will be recruited (fires). Neuron B will then recruit other neurons based on the chemical state of its synapses with them. Each time this happens the thresholds of the synapses that are involved will decrease. This makes it more likely that next time neuron A stimulates neuron B it will fire.

It is important to recognize that there are two processes that happen concurrently: 1) the neurons being recruited (interpretation of the incoming sensory experience) are determined by the state of the synapses (ie memories); 2) this process causes the state of the synapses to be changed (ie memories are formed or reaffirmed).

Figure 5.1 describes the electronic process in a neuron. For our purposes it is important that the whole process of firing takes about 2 milliseconds

FIGURE 5.1   Action potential of neurons

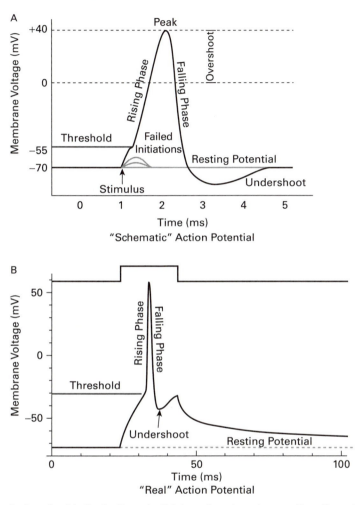

A. view of an idealized action potential shows its various phases as the action potential passes a point on a cell membrane.

B. Recordings of action potentials are often distorted compared to the schematic view because of variations in electrophysiological techniques used to make the recording.

SOURCE: Wikipedia: Neurons

(2/100,000 seconds) when viewed from a static point on the cell membrane. The electric potentials generated by single neurons are far too small to be picked up by EEG (Electroencephalography). EEG activity therefore always reflects the summation of the synchronous activity of thousands or millions of neurons that have similar spatial orientation. Because voltage fields fall off with the square of the distance, activity from deep sources is more difficult to detect than currents near the skull.

Most of the bio-measures that are supplied under the term neuromarketing are obtained by EEG, which measures electronic activity via electrodes on the respondents scalp. Given the speed of electronic activity demonstrated above one can appreciate why the EEG machine typically needs to take up to 2,000 readings a second. Fortunately EEG measures a fairly gross area of the brain – ie activity in many neurons.

Because EEG is the most common used bio-measure for neuromarketing we will devote Part 5 of this book to exactly what is being measured: interpretation, memory formation, attention, etc.

Artificial neural networks

Now that we know about the physical properties of neurons and synapses we can look at how they operate. What has been described above is a system of neurons in the brain. Since the features of neural networks in the brain have become known, scientists have become interested in finding out what such systems can do.

Once again I stress that there are many disciplines that contribute to our understanding of the puzzle of the brain. Neurology, with brain scanning methodologies, is just one, and not all that powerful in isolation. With current technology it is impossible to watch all the individual neurons in a system at work. There are too many, and things happen too fast. This is where the scientists who work with artificial neural networks come into play.

In this chapter we move on from biologists' field of study to that of artificial neural network scientists. It is very important to understand this aspect of study, because it explains memory formation and interpretation: how we learn and how we know what we see, hear and so on.

What neural networks do

In Figure 5.2 you will see we have four neurons with their dendrites and synapses.

To see how such a system works, let's make neuron A fire (Figure 5.3).

Having fired, neuron A will return to its resting state, but owing to the synaptic sensitivities neurons B and C will fire (are recruited) (Figure 5.4).

Having fired, B and C will return to their resting state, but D is now recruited (Figure 5.5).

This system will settle into a state of reverberation: ie neurons C and D will fire alternately.

Readers can now set up any such system and follow what happens. In all cases the system will settle into a state of reverberation within a few cycles of recruitment. This is one of the beauties of such systems: it is impossible to set up a state of synaptic sensitivity that does not lead to a state of reverberation. Remember that a neuron can fire 1,000 times per second, so this all happens very fast. Obviously, four neurons is a simplistic example.

DE Rumelhart extended this to a much bigger system in an experiment with his students. He created a list of 40 items commonly found in a room. His students then had to indicate how often they saw one of these items when they saw another. For example, you will often see a stove and a fridge in the same room, but less often a computer and stove. He then set the synaptic sensitivities for the resulting Hinton diagram based on the number of students indicating that they experienced these items at the same time. Effectively this creates a situation simulating what happens in the brain: every time one sees a stove and a fridge the synapses between these neurons will become more sensitive (lowered threshold). Because one seldom sees a computer and a stove, the synapses between the neurons will not become sensitized. He then 'fired' the node 'oven' and 'ceiling' and observed what other neurons were recruited, and how the system settles into a state of reverberation. The output of the system (final reverberation) is things that describe a kitchen (Table 5.1). He then fired the nodes 'desk' and 'ceiling'. This time the reverberation that the system settled into describes a study (Table 5.2).

FIGURE 5.2   A neural network of four neurons

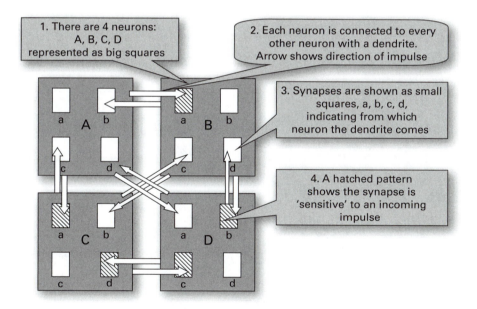

1. There are 4 neurons: A, B, C, D represented as big squares

2. Each neuron is connected to every other neuron with a dendrite. Arrow shows direction of impulse

3. Synapses are shown as small squares, a, b, c, d, indicating from which neuron the dendrite comes

4. A hatched pattern shows the synapse is 'sensitive' to an incoming impulse

FIGURE 5.3 Step 1: neuron A fires, sending impulses down its dendrites

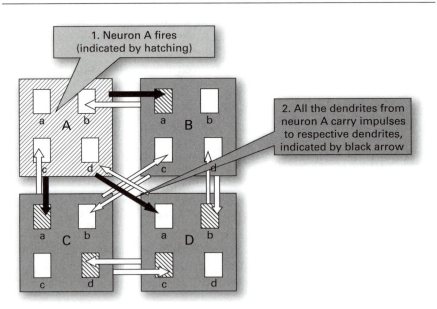

FIGURE 5.4 Step 2: neurons with sensitive synapses are recruited (fire)

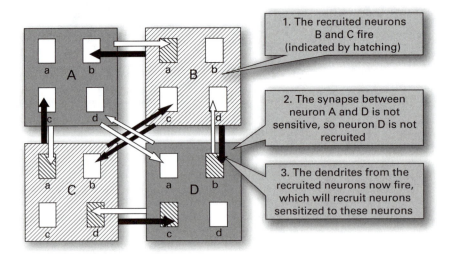

FIGURE 5.5   Step 3: neurons with sensitive synapses are recruited (fire)

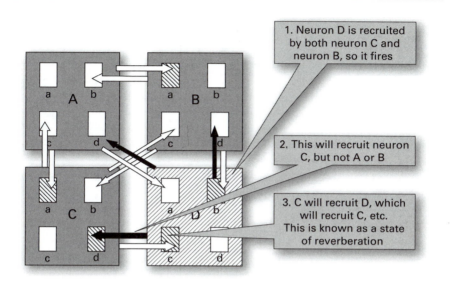

1. Neuron D is recruited by both neuron C and neuron B, so it fires

2. This will recruit neuron C, but not A or B

3. C will recruit D, which will recruit C, etc. This is known as a state of reverberation

Gestalts

This phenomenon that the output of the neuronal system is more than the input is termed a gestalt. A good example of the above is the use of icons in text messages, ☺ or ☹. Another good example is that you read letters but a whole word comes to mind as well as what the word means. This is what your brain does all the time, and you have no control over it. You are not even aware that this is what you are doing. You have no control over your senses (other than that you can close your eyes, but when they are open you cannot stop them from seeing). Nature does not trust you with doing a good enough job in this regard.

There is a continuous flow of stimuli from your senses to the brain. These all start a process of recruitment. This process of recruitment is based on the state of the synapses (thresholds), which again is based on your experiences (memories).

People are surprisingly unaware of how this happens to them. When I do talks at conferences I put the audience through the following exercises, and invariably get them to chuckle at themselves. I ask them to close their eyes and *not* see an elephant. I keep repeating the words '*Do not* see an elephant!' I then say 'Particularly do not see a pink elephant with big ears. Do not see him flying. Do not see the cap on his head. Don't read his name.' This is impossible to do, because my words are stimulating neurons that recruit

TABLE 5.1 A gestalt of a kitchen

Cycle	1	2	3	4	5	6	7	8	9	10	11	12
Oven	▓	▓	▓	▓	▓	▓	▓	▓	▓	▓	▓	▓
Computer												
Coat hanger												
Scale												
Toilet												
Bath												
Television												
Dresser												
Coffee pot			▓	▓	▓	▓	▓	▓	▓	▓	▓	▓
Cupboard						▓	▓	▓	▓	▓	▓	▓
Toaster												
Fridge		▓	▓	▓	▓	▓	▓	▓	▓	▓	▓	▓
Sink		▓	▓	▓	▓	▓	▓	▓	▓	▓	▓	▓
Stove		▓	▓	▓	▓	▓	▓	▓	▓			
Curtain			▓	▓	▓	▓	▓	▓	▓	▓	▓	▓
Fireplace												
Ashtray												
Coffee cup			▓	▓	▓	▓	▓	▓	▓	▓	▓	▓
Easy chair												
Sofa												
Reading lamp												
Painting												
Clock						▓	▓	▓	▓	▓	▓	▓
Desk-chair												
Books												
Carpet												
Bookcase												
Typewriter												
Bed												
Telephone							▓	▓	▓	▓	▓	▓
Desk												
Very small												
Small							▓	▓	▓	▓	▓	
Medium sized												
Large												
Very large												
Frame					▓	▓	▓	▓	▓	▓	▓	
Door												
Wall		▓	▓	▓	▓	▓	▓	▓	▓	▓	▓	▓
Ceiling	▓	▓	▓	▓	▓	▓	▓	▓	▓	▓	▓	▓

SOURCE: DE Rumelhart, in Cohen, Kiss and Le Voi (1993).

TABLE 5.2   A gestalt of a study

Cycle	1	2	3	4	5	6	7	8	9	10	11	12
Oven												
Computer			■	■	■	■	■	■	■	■	■	■
Coat hanger		■	■	■	■	■	■	■	■	■	■	■
Scale												
Toilet												
Bath												
Television												
Dresser												
Coffee pot												
Cupboard												
Toaster												
Fridge												
Sink												
Stove												
Curtain												
Fireplace												
Ashtray				■	■	■	■	■	■	■	■	■
Coffee cup			■	■	■	■	■	■	■	■	■	■
Easy chair												
Sofa												
Reading lamp												
Painting				■	■	■	■	■	■	■	■	■
Clock												
Desk-chair				■	■	■	■	■	■	■	■	■
Books		■	■	■	■	■	■	■	■	■	■	■
Carpet						■	■	■	■	■	■	■
Bookcase		■	■	■	■	■	■	■	■	■	■	■
Typewriter		■	■	■	■	■	■	■	■	■	■	■
Bed												
Telephone			■	■	■	■	■	■	■	■	■	■
Desk	■	■	■	■	■	■	■	■	■	■	■	■
Very small												
Small												
Medium sized												
Large					■	■	■	■	■	■	■	■
Very large												
Frame												
Door		■	■	■	■	■	■	■	■	■	■	■
Wall		■	■	■	■	■	■	■	■	■	■	■
Ceiling	■	■	■	■	■	■	■	■	■	■	■	■

SOURCE: DE Rumelhart, in Cohen, Kiss and Le Voi (1993).

neurons based on experience to interpret what I am saying (ie creating a gestalt). I then ask them to see a dog, specifically a dog they know. This immediately removes the picture of the elephant from their minds. I then tell them to keep thinking about the dog and *not* think of an elephant. I keep telling them to *not* see an elephant. Obviously they cannot, because just by me repeating the word 'elephant' they see the elephant again. I stop talking and ask them whether they noticed the drone of the air conditioner, and they agree that until I mentioned it they did not hear it. Of course, they did hear it, but they were not listening to it (ie it was forming gestalts, but they were giving attention to the gestalts my words were forming).

Even when you sleep your brain is getting impulses from your senses. They do not 'switch off'. You will be awakened by a loud noise, the lights suddenly going on or somebody touching you. Your senses remain working all the time, and everything comes to the brain and starts a process of recruitment.

This is not only true for what happens outside your body. Consider how you will wake up because your bladder is full, or you are thirsty, or you are cold, or hot, or not breathing comfortably, or not lying comfortably.

Your brain is a pool of developing gestalts

A useful way of thinking about your brain is that it is like a pool in which a handful of pebbles are dropped. Each pebble starts a wave, so you have waves continuously developing in your brain. In fact, since your brain is three-dimensional, you might even want to think of this as like a fireworks show.

The very real question that brain scientists were faced with was: so how do you decide which of these waves you give attention to (or which becomes a 'consciousness', in their terminology)? Even more important, from the perspective of the marketer, how does the consumer switch attention from one gestalt to another?

This is where emotions, feelings, moods and so on come into play. These interact so that you can survive rather than just be overwhelmed by sensory input from the environment. This is what the next section of the brain and brand puzzle is about.

What do artificial neural networks do very well?

Studying neural networks is one of the branches of artificial intelligence and statistics. Their approach can be seen as: 'Well, we know what a neuron does. Let's put a lot of these together in a machine and see what the machine does.' What they found not only is very interesting, but explains a lot about how we think, and has some serious implications for marketers. What they found was that such an artificial neural network system is particularly good at: 1) classifying objects (in statistics this is called cluster analysis); and 2) predicting things (in statistics this would be done by regression analysis). As a result artificial neural networks are now a fully developed branch of statistics, and are included in software packages like SPSS (Statistical Package for the Social Sciences).

Classifying

The natural sciences are very concerned with classifying things when new specimens are found: rocks, insects, plants, etc. They use statistical and computerized neural network programs. These programs are presented with specimens and then told what group the specimens are; this is called the training phase. After the system has dealt with a lot of known examples, it will be presented with new examples and will tell what they are, based on what the neural network has learned.

When I give talks at conferences I show people 80 slides of cats and dogs, asking them to shout whether it is a cat or a dog or neither. I start off by showing these at the rate of one per second, and end up flashing the slides at a tenth of a second. (The whole exercise takes less than two minutes.) It never happens that anyone is not able to get all the pictures right!

I also have a few tricks to demonstrate the issues I need to explain about the brain and its neural network. Before I start the slide show I tell them that, since the slides are going to come at them very fast, we need to clarify what the decision rule will be. What is the difference between a picture of a cat and a picture of a dog? There is no rule that applies to all cats and dogs. I then ask them how, if they cannot explain the difference between dogs and cats to me, they are going to know whether a slide depicts a dog or a cat. Yet the audience assure me they can do the task. The correct answer seems to be: 'I know that I know what is a cat or a dog.' This is how neural networks in computers work. They do not come up with a decision rule as a statistical cluster analysis program or a pre-programmed computer program would; they just come up with an answer. I have a slide of a bear in the middle of the exercise. Remember, the instruction was to shout 'Cat', 'Dog' or 'Neither'. The whole audience, to the last person, will shout 'Bear, I mean neither.' This is because the process of interpretation (classification) is what the neurons in the brain do fastest. So when the audience see a bear they know it is a bear, and shout that it is a bear before they think that this is not what they are supposed to say.

I then change the task (when I have a bilingual audience), marking some slides with a smiley and asking the audience to shout cat or dog in these cases in their home language. It is very seldom that an audience can do this inside the allotted one second. One would have thought that introducing their home language into the task would have made them faster. It does not. The reason is that they need to make a decision. They need to decide between languages. The reader might ask: 'Is it not a decision to decide between cat and dog?' Interestingly it is not. It is just knowledge. You know. By the time the picture is interpreted it is classified.

I then ask the audience whether they memorized the pictures I have shown them (many for only a tenth of a second). The answer is obviously 'No'. I then show them a series of pictures, some of which they have just seen; they have to shout whether the picture was among those they have seen. Again I do this at the rate of one per second, with some pictures being on the screen for only a tenth of a second. The audience have no problem with this task, thereby demonstrating how fast a memory is formed.

An interesting feature of the brain is that when you are asked a question you will often answer 'I don't know' as fast as you would give the correct answer. Sometimes you might even answer 'I know the answer, but I just cannot think of it right now.' The brain knows what it knows as fast as producing the knowledge itself. This is amply demonstrated by the last task mentioned above. People do not compare the pictures against a 'file' in their memory. They simply know – in a fraction of a second – whether they have seen the picture before. The brain does not scan its memory as a computer does when you click the search button. This is all as a result of the huge interconnectivity of the brain.

Predicting

Stock market analysts use artificial neural network systems to predict what is going to happen in the stock exchange. The network is presented with (trained on) a lot of historical time series, and then asked to predict what will happen as new data become available. We all experience this predictive action of our brain so continuously that we seldom think about it:

- We need only to hear a few notes of a tune to start whistling the rest. Even as we whistle the rest we do not think about the whole tune; the next notes just 'come to mind'.

- When people talk to us we think about what they are going to say, and often interrupt them when they are slow in getting to the point, we predict what they will say.

- Humour is often seen as 'a story with a surprising twist' – in other words we are predicting where the story is heading only to find that we suddenly have to rethink what we thought.

- When we cross the road we are predicting where oncoming cars will be. We are predicting where we will be.

- When we sit down for a Sunday roast we already know what the roast will taste like. (Later in the book I will show that often the actual taste of the roast is not as good as the expected taste.)

These are all examples of our biological neural networks behaving as artificial neural networks do – being predictive based on experience.

Marketing implications of classifying and predicting

Readers might validly wonder what all of this has to do with them and with marketing.

When the consumer sees your brand it is classified as something. It is not classified as 'a pretty carton with stuff inside it'; it is classified as milk. It is probably classified as fresh milk or long-life milk or some other variant. But the classification might be wrong. Consumers are going to react to your brand based on their classification and what they think that class of products does, even if they are wrong. If marketers know their brand is fresh milk and consumers think it is long-life, the consumers might not buy it – or be very disappointed when they use it on their camping trip. They will blame the marketers.

As brand manager it is your job to manage your brand in terms of what people will classify it as, which also means you need to know what classification scheme people use. This means that you need to do a brand cluster analysis at some stage for your markets, and not define them from a manufacturer's perspective. In South Africa the wine industry classifies its wines in terms of the amount of excise duty paid on the product. This is totally irrelevant for the consumer.

It is quite popular among new brand managers to propose packaging changes as their first 'marketing activity'. Obviously brands need packaging changes – to keep them looking modern, to make people think something has changed in the brand, and so on. Unfortunately I have witnessed a few brands in South Africa where packaging changes led to disasters. In the United States, Tropicana changed its pack and sales dropped by 20 per cent – presumably because people did not recognize it as 'my brand' anymore. For new brands this is even more important, especially when you think you are creating a new product category. The consumer will always try to classify you in terms of existing product categories. Remember, the consumer is not wrong.

When a consumer sees a brand the neural network is already predicting things about it – predicting whether it will solve a need that might arise, when it might be used, how it will be used, who in the family will be glad it was bought, or disappointed, how the consumer will feel when it is being used, and so on.

Once again the neural network might be wrong. Remember, it is only trained on past experiences of the brand (including promotions, word of mouth, etc). It is the brand manager's job to know what these predictions are based on, and to find ways to improve the predictions the consumer's mind makes about the brand.

I believe that the jingle has become a lost art, and that marketers are much poorer for this. There are many jingles from my youth that I remember, and start to sing (in my mind) when I buy the brand. These contain the brand promise, and I am reminding myself why I should buy the brand. It is easy in today's supermarket environment for marketers to use jingles in front of the shelf. Get the consumer to mentally rehearse the brand position as they are buying.

When designing new brands the question should not be: 'How much do you like the pack design?' The questions are: 'If you see this pack, what do you think it is?' and 'What will it do when you use it?' From here you can explore how it will make people feel when they use it.

This auto-classification becomes especially important as far as advertising is concerned. People automatically classify what they see or hear. They mostly know whether they are looking at an advertisement or programme. They mostly know whether they are looking at an advertisement for a bank or a motor car. They mostly know which brand's advertisement they are looking at. More importantly, they might be wrong, but they do not know this. Based on this 'knowledge' they might give attention to the advertisement or not, and this lays down memories (involuntarily). If they are assuming they are looking at the advertisement for the wrong brand or wrong product type, these memories are laid down in such a way that they do not support the brand.

It is the brand manager's job to make sure that what people think they know happens 'in the name of the brand'. One of the banks in South Africa ran a campaign, which Millward Brown tracked, showing a high-jumper clearing the bar. Despite good media pressure, when we asked people whether they had seen a commercial for this bank the answer remained 'No'. We then realized that there was a very similar advertisement on the air for Gatorade also showing a high-jumper. We started to track this and found Gatorade's recall increased each time the bank advertised.

This problem becomes even more vexing for a trade association doing generic promotions. The consumer is used to brands, and appears to find it difficult to interpret messages about a category. Because there are no brands on these ads the consumer seems to inject a brand – mostly the brand leader. It might be thought that this means that the brand leader will gain most from a generic campaign, and it does. But the corollary is also true: when a product category gets bad publicity, it mostly sticks to the brand leader. (This presents some very interesting strategy problems.)

Later in the book I will show an experiment where the Millward Brown team showed people fast-forwarded advertisements and achieved very high recall of these. In fact what we were measuring was that people recognized the ads at fast-forward speed, ie ads that people have seen before their neural networks 'classify' them spontaneously as 'an ad for...'.

Interpretation, memory recall, 'comes to mind'

Here we are really looking at the jigsaw piece concerned with what comes out of memory – the gestalt. Marketing researchers have had a field day playing with the two pieces of the marketing puzzle called 'recall' and 'recognition' – there are many pages of the *Journal of Advertising Research* given over to this.

Evolution has given us, and all animals, a memory for only one reason: to interpret what is happening inside and outside our bodies. All animals need to interpret the environment and the body. The only way this can be done is by reference to experiences – memories. Every animal needs to know 'When I see that, or hear that, or smell that, or feel like this, then there is a good chance that I soon will feel good/bad.' The lay-language expression for this is 'comes to mind'. When something appears in my environment then the issue for survival is 'What comes to mind?' Whatever comes to mind will be determined by my experiences (memories). This is also true if I think of something that is not in my environment but just a mental concept. The same process occurs, the new thought will be interpreted in the same way and what 'comes to mind' will be based on my experiences (memories).

We have shown that different inputs into our neural system will produce different gestalts. Artificial neural networks work on a feedback system where what is output for the system gets fed back into the system as further prompts, and this will produce a more specific or even a different output gestalt. The longer we think about something, the more specific or the more detailed or even the more different the resultant gestalt.

A good analogy is that of a well-stocked cupboard. When the door is opened (you give attention), things fall out. This cascade of things falling out will continue until the door is closed (you give attention to something else). What makes this analogy truly amazing is that the opening of the cupboard takes place inside a tenth of a second! Things do not pour out in a nice sequential way, as they do from a computer, but like a torrent of memories (interpretations), and these include your feelings.

Introducing the rat brain robot

06

In the preceding chapter I explained what neurons and synapses do. Basically the chemical composition in synapses changes when something is experienced. This change is a memory of what happened, and allows the brain to interpret any stimuli it is presented with in its environment. Neurons and synapses do not do much more than this. In this chapter I introduce a robot that is guided by 300,000 living rat neurons. In terms of the continuity of the book we will now understand how these living brain cells guide the robot. In subsequent chapters I will explain how the survival of the robot rat is not dependent on the number of brain cells it has, but on its feelings. In this chapter we introduce the rat brain robot because we will be using this model to answer the question 'What is needed in the brain of the consumer to make decisions?'

One of the most interesting experiments in modern times was done in 2008 when Ben Whalley at the University of Reading managed to combine a real rat brain with a robot in such a way that the neurons in the brain controlled the machine. This event did not receive the popular publicity I believe it should have. Here is the news item as it appears on the BBC site:

A robot controlled by a blob of rat brain cells could provide insights into diseases such as Alzheimer's, University of Reading scientists say.

The project marries 300,000 rat neurons to a robot that navigates via sonar.

The neurons are now being taught to steer the robot around obstacles and avoid the walls of the small pen in which it is kept. By studying what happens to the neurons as they learn, its creators hope to reveal how memories are laid down.

Hybrid machines: The blob of nerves forming the brain of the robot was taken from the neural cortex in a rat foetus and then treated to dissolve the connections between individual neurons.

Sensory input from the sonar on the robot is piped to the blob of cells to help them form new connections that will aid the machine as it navigates around its pen.

As the cells are living tissue, they are kept separate from the robot in a temperature-controlled cabinet in a container pitted with electrodes. Signals are passed to and from the robot via Bluetooth short-range radio. The brain cells have been taught how to control the robot's movements so it can steer round obstacles and the next step, say its creators, is to get it to recognize its surroundings.

Once the robot can do this the researchers plan to disrupt the memories in a bid to recreate the gradual loss of mental faculties seen in diseases such as Alzheimer's and Parkinson's.

Studies of how neural tissue is degraded or copes with the disruption could give insights into these conditions.

'One of the fundamental questions that neuroscientists are facing today is how we link the activity of individual neurons to the complex behaviours that we see in whole organisms and whole animals,' said Dr Ben Whalley, a neuroscientist at Reading. 'This project gives us a really useful and unique opportunity to look at something that may exhibit whole behaviours but still remains closely tied to the activity of individual neurons.'

The Reading team is not the first to harness living tissue to control robots.

In 2003, Dr Steve Potter at the Georgia Institute of Technology pioneered work on what he dubbed 'hybrots' that marry neural tissue and robots.

In earlier work, scientists at Northwestern University Medical Center in the US wired a wheeled robot up to a lamprey in a bid to explore novel ways of controlling prosthetics.

(http://news.bbc.co.uk/1/hi/technology/7559150.stm)

Of course, there are robotic machines that can do what this robot rat does much more efficiently and are less cumbersome to maintain. But these machines are controlled by computers, which run on hardware and software. The rat brain is wet-ware, and this is what our brains are.

The robot rat is guided by the memories that have been laid down in the synapses of the living neurons. In *The Advertised Mind* (2005) I describe a computer program called Darwin III that simulates neuronal networks and learns, like a baby, simple behaviours without being told to learn them.

The robot rat not only shows how neurons learn, but allows us to compare it with other living species that show much more motivated behaviours. Motivated behaviour does not depend on the size of the brain, but rather on the fact that we (and other species) have feelings, and it is the presence of feelings in the brain that causes us to have motivated behaviour.

Let's look at this robot rat

I have uploaded a 58-second video of this robot rat on my website. Visit: **www.erikdup.com/neuro-videos_pages_sites.php**. Essentially what the scientists did was to take 300,000 neurons from a rat, untangle them, place them in a dish with a solution that fed them, and allowed the neurons to grow new connections with each other and with electrodes. They built a little robot, basically a little machine on tractor wheels, which can change direction. The electrical output from the electrodes that the rat brain had grown on to was then transmitted to the robot, and input from the robot's camcorder was transmitted to the rat brain. The robot body moved around the maze, and the brain learned to avoid obstacles!

The obvious question is 'What is needed to make the robot rat do things that real rats do?' In other words, real rats need to do much more than merely avoid static objects. The naive answer would be that maybe the scientists just need to give it many more neurons.

Table 6.1 shows the number of neurons that different animals have. Whilst the robot rat has many fewer neurons than a normal rat would have, it still has more than a fruit fly. A fruit fly, with only a third of the neurons that the robot rat has, will avoid static objects, avoid moving objects, know when it is hungry, find food to eat, and even decide between brands of fruit, eating the one it prefers, and so on.

TABLE 6.1   Number of neurons in animals' brains

Animal	Neurons in the brain/whole nervous system
Sponge	0
Ant	10,000
Pond snail	11,000
Fruit fly	100,000
Honeybee	850,000
Cockroach	1,000,000
Rat	15,000,000
Frog	16,000,000
Dog*	160,000,000
Cat*	300,000,000
Chimpanzee	6,200,000,000
Human*	10,000,000,000
Elephant	20,000,000,000

* Only neurons in cerebral cortex counted.

SOURCE: Wikipedia, 'List of animals by number of neurons'.

What brain systems does the robot rat need to be more like a human (or just more like a fruit fly)?

One of the obvious questions that comes to mind, now that living brain cells can 'manage' a robot, is: so what else is needed to create those cute (or fearsome) cyborgs that they have in sci-fi movies? Do they merely have to move from 300,000 neurons to 10,000,000,000 neurons? Whilst this seems like an answer, it is not. After all, the fruit fly needs only 100,000 neurons to do most of the things needed to be like a human.

For the robot rat to become more like a fruit fly it will need to delegate some very basic functions like breathing and heartbeat to a part of the brain that does not need to learn or think. In fact, the brain should not have responsibility for these functions. In all animals these functions have been located in the brain stem, which handles these functions mostly autonomously. Evolution did not trust us to have control over these things. If we had to 'think' about keeping our heart beating we just might forget.

The robot rat will need to monitor the robot body's well-being. It needs to know when the body is running out of energy so that it can be replaced, when it is overheating so it can rest, and so on. There has to be a feedback system from the rat body to the rat brain, which is constantly monitoring the body. This is called the homeostasis system. (Many of these functions are handled by hormones controlling the state of the body.)

Not only does the rat brain have to monitor the state of the body, but it has to monitor the state of the brain. (In humans this is done mostly via moods and arousal – the things we call 'state of mind'. There is no reason to suspect that the fruit fly does not sometimes feel at peace or feel agitated.)

The rat brain will also need to monitor the environment. It is not enough to have eyes and ears, but it needs to know when to react to changes in the environment that could spell danger. When a fruit fly sees anything that could be danger it will experience a fright and fly away. In humans this is called emotions.

With all these monitoring devices in place the robot brain will need something that allows it to plan. Planning simply means that the fruit fly decides in which direction it wants to fly or walk, and then sets this in action, ie the parts of the brain that control its wings will do what is needed to fly in the desired direction. The doing part, ie the connections from the brain to the muscles and limbs, is in the cortex, the outer layers of the brain. The planning function is in the frontal lobes – the area of the brain that in evolutionary terms developed proportionately more in humans than animals.

When it makes a decision on which direction to fly the fruit fly will have many options. It needs to consider some of these and decide on one. The best guideline is to decide which direction would make it feel the best. Generally that would mean towards something that it recognizes as food, or as sex, or it might simply be a sunny spot if its monitors tell it that it is cold. This is done by way of the amines in the brain, the most important of these being dopamine.

Even with these systems in its brain the robot rat will still not survive. It needs a memory system. Only once it can remember 'When I did this I felt better, or worse' as well as 'When something like that was in my environment I felt worse, or better' will the robot rat be able to use these systems to survive. Without the ability to learn from experience these systems are largely useless. Fortunately this is what neurons do, and the robot rat already has 300,000 and is using them to avoid obstacles.

You might think that this is a very complex system to build. However, remember that I have merely described what a fruit fly has and what it does with its allotted 100,000 neurons.

Besides the systems described, there appear to be two more systems that are important to humans, and to rats. These systems help survival by creating groups of people (or robot rats) that can work together to survive better.

If robot rats are to work together as a society, it will be less efficient if the robot rats are all the same, rather than slightly different from each other. The group will be better off if some robot rats are leaders, some are followers, some are thinkers, some are warriors, and so on. When we talk about humans, these traits are often grouped under the term 'personality'. On my website I have uploaded a video of the experiment at the University of Reading (**www.erikdup.com/neuro-videos_pages_sites.php**). In this they changed the adventurousness of a rat by altering its genetic structure, which implies that some of what we call personality is caused by genetic variation (presumably the rest is determined by experience, ie learning, and some by brain chemicals, ie mood disorders).

I would also include in this discussion an acculturation system. This system is needed so that the robot rats in one group do not confuse themselves with robot rats that belong to other groups. Since the members of the group work together to increase their own well-being (survival) they are competing with other groups for resources.

The system that is really fascinating when we compare ourselves to animals (or robot rats) is our ability to plan. Sometimes we arrogantly assume that we are the only species that plan. This is patently not so. Even for an insect to move from one leaf to another involves a plan of some sort. For a snake to set out to find food involves a plan of some sort. Humans just have a much more evolved ability to come up with more advanced plans than other species. Most of this happens in our frontal lobes, which are proportionately much bigger than those of any other species. This planning ability is very dependent on the systems described above: our plans are often strongly influenced by our personality, our culture, our memories and our 'feel good' system.

Once we have these systems in place in the robot rat's brain it will behave like a fruit fly with 100,000 neurons, and it will behave like a real rat with

15 million neurons, and it will behave very similarly to a human with 10^{10} neurons.

I do not suggest that these are the only systems in the brain. There are many other systems: systems for sight, systems for motion, systems for hearing, systems for speaking, and so on. I chose the above systems because they relate to feelings and behaviour, which is what this book is about.

'Movere' is Latin for 'to move', 'to be motivated'

The difference between animals and plants is the survival strategy they evolved. Plants survive by procreating profusely in the hope that the seeds land on more fertile soil or in better climatic conditions. The individual plant cannot flee from danger or move to a more attractive location.

Animals do not procreate profusely, but survive by moving about. Animals can flee from danger in the environment, and move toward things that are good for survival: food, water, pleasant climate, sex and so on.

A sea squirt (ascidiacea) is an animal that looks like a tadpole, born from an egg. When it is born, it has a brain with neurons. It uses this to move around until it finds a rock on which to anchor itself. Once it has anchored itself and has no need to move anywhere, its brain is consumed (along with the tail and fins). It is known as the creature that eats its own brain!

The robot rat can avoid walls, but was not really interested in doing anything else. In fact it merely formed memories of what happened, but did not really have a great use for these memories. However, things changed when I postulated what it should do to be a normal rat: *take care of its own body and brain.*

Move! But where to?

It is all fine and well to have a brain that tells us what to do to move, ie move limbs or wings or fins. But mostly it would be beneficial if we could know in which direction to move.

For most creatures it seems that at first they simply move. There are random impulses coming from the cortex that make the limbs move. Babies move their limbs without any purpose, and it is assumed that they don't even 'know' that the limbs are theirs.

However, neurons involuntarily lay down memories all the time. Over time the baby learns that certain movements (neural activities in its cortex) have certain outcomes that are favourable. Soon the baby learns that if it desires a specific outcome it has to execute certain moves. I discuss in

The Advertised Mind (2005) the experiment with Darwin III where artificial neural network scientists (or artificial intelligence scientists) conducted an experiment teaching a computer how to 'learn' like a baby by simulating the behaviour of neurons.

A good example of this at its primeval best is some simple cell amoebas that exist in a pond of primeval slime in Australia that had developed a simple neuronal system and a muscle. When the sun comes up they overheat, and the neuron makes the muscle twitch, which moves them around in the pond. When they reach the shaded area the neuron stops firing. As it becomes cold in the evening the neuron sets the muscle twitching again, and this might move them towards an area that has some warmth. These amoebas 'learn' to twitch in a certain direction when they are uncomfortable due to heat and in another direction when they are cold. A good equivalent would be Mexican jumping beans, where the pupa inside jumps when it senses heat.

This is the basic reason why we have brains: to move. The second reason is that we will move towards what will make us feel better. Combined, these lead us to the word most used in marketing: *motivation*.

Feelings

07

So far we know how the laying down of memories happens in the brain, as part of an involuntary process, and how this is the way we interpret stimuli in our environment. In other words, we understand what the 300,000 neurons in the robot rat's brain are doing. We also understand how, even if 300,000 neurons sounds like a lot, this does not allow the robot rat even to begin having life-saving functions such as the fruit fly has – and it needs only 100,000 neurons. We now turn to understanding that the difference is 'feelings'. Unfortunately 'feelings' are under-researched and still poorly understood as motivators. At modern marketing conferences many presenters talk about emotions, but only in so far as these influence advertising theories, and specifically how attention is given to advertising. Probably the major contribution of this book to the future of neuroscience and neuromarketing is extending the word 'feelings' to include more than mere short-term emotional reactions.

Why we need to understand feelings

The modern 'insight' that is exciting brain scientists is the role of feelings in our decision-making processes. Since brand choices are decisions, marketers are now more interested in understanding feelings.

The robot rat's brain consists of 300,000 neurons. Neurons store memories by way of the state of the synapses, and interpret things based on the state of the synapses. This allows the robot rat to form memories of its experiences of its environment. Whilst forming memories of the environment is vital, it is not enough to enable the robot rat to live. The robot rat also needs feelings.

For the robot rat to live independently it at least needs to:

- react to the state of the body (we call this homeostatic feelings);
- react to the state of the environment (we call this feeling emotions);
- react to the state of the brain (we call this feeling moods); and

- socialize:
  - by being specialized in a different way from others in the tribe (we call this feeling personality);
  - by having behaviours that are similar to those of the tribe (we call this feeling culture).

Currently there is a lot of excitement about the new insights deriving from brain scanning techniques. At this stage these techniques cannot measure the formation or laying down of memories in consumers' brains. These actions happen too fast and are too dispersed throughout the brain for the techniques really to measure much. In other words there is not a specific location in the brain that contains the memories of Coca-Cola, or any specific brand, that we can scan.

It is not possible to read on a brain scan whether memories of a brand exist, or where they are, or whether they have been activated by some stimuli, or whether they have been refreshed, or how strong the memories are or even what other memories they are associated with!

Here is a brief overview of the structure of this chapter:

- An important way that feelings work is by being a background to your emotions and thereby determining what you will give attention to or, in neuro-speak, which of the developing gestalts becomes a consciousness. (For example, I feel hungry, I see food, and the perception gets more attention than it would have if I had not been hungry.)

- Feelings probably also should be seen not only as helping to select what attention should be given to, but also as motivating behaviours directly. (For example, I am hungry and decide to go somewhere where there is food to eat.)

- The word 'feelings' is ill defined in the literature – there is especially a lot of confusion with the word 'emotions'. I devote some space to this so that I can use my own definition.

- Feelings appear to originate in the deep brain area called the limbic system. I describe this.

This leads to a discussion in Chapter 8 of each of the types of feelings mentioned above.

From many gestalts to one: attention and touchpoints

The most important task of any marketer is to get people to give attention. The modern view of marketing includes the word 'touchpoints' to indicate ways in which the brand tries to 'touch the consumer' and points to where the consumer comes into contact with the brand. The whole basis of touch-points is that they are designed to get attention for the brand.

When consumers are in front of a shelf the marketer hopes they will give attention to the brand, and to achieve this the marketer uses packaging design and shelf promotions, or even buys better positions on the shelf or buys gondola ends.

When marketers run an advertisement (on its own, or as part of a campaign, in any medium) they hope that it will get attention for the brand. When marketers sponsor an event the idea is to get attention for the brand. The idea behind a viral ad on the internet is that people will send it to others (increase reach) and that the recipients will give it attention – hopefully attention for the brand.

It is, unfortunately for marketers, true that most marketing activities get very little attention. Even worse, where the activity gets attention it does not necessarily get attention for the brand.

It might very well be that, because it is so difficult to get attention for the brand by nearly any means, some marketers and marketing theorists argue that attention is not necessary. Such arguments do mean that marketing activities become non-accountable, and this might suit the agencies responsible for creating attention for the brand.

Besides the argument that attention is irrelevant to brand-building activities it is often argued by advertising agencies that they can easily get attention for the advertisement. All they have to do is show a couple copulating, or shout loudest, or be vulgar, etc. The fact is that they are right: this will get attention. And they are right when they argue that it will be the wrong type of attention.

We cannot ignore this argument when we discuss attention. This argument has to do with the 'volume' of the input signals that are forming gestalts that then forces them to become consciousnesses. We will discuss how emotions and feelings contribute to making a gestalt a consciousness. There are many ways to make a gestalt a consciousness, and marketers who understand that they need to have their touchpoints receive attention need to understand the alternatives.

Attention

Our inspection of parts of the puzzle of the brain started with us looking at the features of neurons and their synapses. We then showed how artificial intelligence scientists managed to show how such neuronal systems work on a very small scale. Where we left off was that the senses are feeding a continuous stream of information to neurons in the brain, and these start a process of recruitment of more neurons, based on experiences (memories, the state of the synapses).

This was known well before the modern paradigm about the role of feelings. What scientists could not really figure out was: if your brain consists of all these developing gestalts, how does it happen that you give only one gestalt attention at a time? And how do you know when to switch your attention from the gestalt to which you are giving attention to one that could be more important?

Cognitive psychologists studied this phenomenon especially during the Second World War. The problem then was radar operators not giving attention to a new blip on their screen. You can imagine how boring it must be to sit in front of a screen for hours and how difficult it is to give attention – even if the lack of attention could cost many people their lives.

Even in the 1980s the cognitive psychologists' solution was that you have a supervisory attentioning system in your brain. This attentioning system somehow correlates all the incoming sensory information and decides what should be a priority. Other than stating that there should be such a system, little was known about the way such a system would work, or even where it would be inside the brain.

Now we know that it is in the limbic system (mostly), that the developing gestalts are given an importance based on our feelings about the gestalt, and that this plays a major role in determining which gestalts receive attention.

Susan Greenfield, a professor of synaptic pharmacology at Oxford University, tackled the issue of consciousness in her book *Journey to the Centers of the Mind: Toward a science of consciousness* (1995). She describes how interpretation of stimuli consists of concentric waves of neural recruitment forming gestalts, much like the effect of pebbles thrown in a pond. So we can easily use her analogies.

In the first place there are gestalts that will naturally not grow big, and others that will. She suggests that this has to do with the strength and nature of the epicentre of the gestalt. Is the thing that initiated the gestalt strong? In other words, was it a big rock or a pebble in the pond? In marketing terms one would talk about the advertisement being big or loud. By strong she means 'not only in correspondence to an external stimulus that was conspicuous in physical terms (loud, bright, big, moving, and so on) but strong in cognitive terms (having associations with reward or pain, or being made special or significant by a past individual history)'. Are the numbers of neurons that can be recruited many and well connected? In other words, do we have a lot of well-connected memories that will easily lead to the recruitment of many neurons and therefore a big gestalt? We all have a lot of memories about ourselves, and devote a lot of synapses to this. If the thing that evokes the gestalt (starts the process of recruitment) is relevant to a large bundle of memories it will raise a bigger gestalt. This explains why people react to anyone mentioning their name near them – even if they were not paying any attention to the speaker.

We know that these obvious enhancers of gestalt formation are active in our own minds. We also know that we are continuously forming gestalts as we go through our day, and very few of them are the result of loud noises, life-threatening situations or even things that directly relate to ourselves. We are simply conscious of things around us, and more so of some than others.

So how does it happen that some gestalt formations become more prominent than others? Greenfield explains that this is especially as a result of the chemicals of the brain. These come from the brainstem, which produces amines. She calls these the fountains of the brain. There are at least five major amines (chemicals) released by these fountains: serotonin, acetylcholine, dopamine, neropinephrine and histamine. It appears that many more are being discovered.

The neurons involved with this are unlike those that we have described. They do not make short connections to neighbouring neurons but very long connections to the centre of the brain and the cortex. They also connect to areas where they can influence many neurons. In reality they are connections between the very oldest parts of the brain and the newest. It is also suggested that their communications are not specific, but very general. These neurons are seen to bias the receiving neurons in a process called neuromodulation. This is a process of biasing the response of a neuron for relatively short periods of time ranging from seconds to hours. Owing to the structures of these systems in the brain they tend to affect classes of events rather than just specific events. 'For a while after eating a big meal, we might refuse a slice of cake which at other times we would have eaten with gusto… Neuromodulation gives a neuron a recent history, a working past; without it all neurons in a certain area would respond in an invariant and predictable way' (Greenfield, 1995). In this way some groups of neurons become more excitable (dopamine) or less excitable (serotonin). Not only do the amines control the overall level of arousal of the brain, but they also manage specific areas in the brain. Thus the gestalts that are forming might become bigger or smaller depending on the amines in the areas that the gestalt is developing through.

On the question of how some gestalts become bigger than others, Greenfield comments on the situation where the input stimuli are of a low 'noise' aspect, which will be referred to when we discuss the fact that advertising is mostly processed at a low level of attention. One is never not conscious of anything – except when you have been knocked unconscious or possibly sometimes when you are asleep. In other words, you are conscious of the most dominant gestalt, even if it in itself is really very small. The more relaxed you are the more likely it is that this is also due to you attending to fairly minor (unexciting) gestalts. And, in answer to those who argue that advertising works in a non-conscious way with little attention, this might be the issue: you are mostly watching television as a relaxation.

Greenfield suggests:

> We are frequently highly conscious of minimal stimuli, such as a whisper or a light touch on the skin. The concentric theory could account for these observations in two ways, both of which endow the stimulus with more significance than might be imagined from the actual weak intensity. First, the weakness of the stimulus, in physical terms, should not be assessed on its own but, rather, in the signal-to-noise ratio. If someone whispers in a library we are immediately aware of it…

> The other way in which a physically weak stimulus could be powerful is if it triggers a large gestalt either because it has strong cognitive associations and/or because arousal is high. At a party, the whisper or small gesture of a lover may have immediate significance (trigger many associations) even in a crowd of people.
>
> (Greenfield, 1995: 171)

What she is suggesting is that one should be very careful to generalize situations to 'all advertising in all viewing situations'.

Everybody knows what feelings, emotions and moods are – do the scientists?

It is only during the last decade that a real understanding of feelings, emotions and moods and their roles in decision making has begun to be achieved, specifically after Damasio's book *Descartes' Error* (1995) and LeDoux's book *The Emotional Brain: The mysterious underpinnings of emotional life* (1996).

While these two books by neurologists are the books that get most credited for the changing paradigm about emotions, there are others that appeared at about the same time:

- Ronald de Sousa, *The Rationality of Emotion* (1990). He is a professor of philosophy at the University of Toronto.
- Oatley and Jenkins, *Understanding Emotions* (1996). They are professors in psychology at the University of Toronto.
- Paul E Griffiths, *What Emotions Really Are* (1997). He is a professor of history and philosophy of science at the University of Pittsburgh.

Previously emotions were seen as the causes of disorders (mood disorder, emotional disorder, etc) and mostly as things that interfere with rational decision processes. These bodily functions were largely studied as things that should be cured (or avoided). As the pieces of the puzzle in this book unfold, it will be seen that this view has taken a 180-degree change. Now these bodily functions are seen to be essential to survival, an important feature of evolution and necessary to be studied for their positive effects on rational decision making.

Unfortunately, as these new insights are evolving there is not yet a common definition. Different authors use the terms ('feelings', 'emotions', 'mood' and also 'traits') in different ways, and often do not define their specific interpretation. This contributes to confusion. In subsequent chapters we will be explaining how these bodily functions work, but here we first need to clarify our definition. Consider the statement: 'EVERYBODY KNOWS WHAT FEELINGS ARE, UNTIL ASKED TO EXPLAIN WHAT THEY

ARE.' I put this in capitals in the hope that you will stop for a moment and consider a personal definition, or description, of what a feeling is.

Most people would now feel confused. So you are experiencing a feeling: confusion. You can probably describe what causes you to feel confused, as well as what the result of feeling confused is. But you will find it difficult to actually describe the feeling, especially in a general sense, rather than just being confused by this sentence. And, if it is difficult to find words to describe the feeling, then it is even more difficult to describe the collective noun 'feelings'.

Now try the same exercise with 'emotions'. Some people would say that the emotion they are feeling is confusion. But haven't we just now said that confusion is a feeling? Once again, try to describe what an emotion is.

Now try your hand at the word 'mood'. Again you can probably name the mood you are in at the moment, at least saying that you are in a good or a bad mood. You might even say that you are sad, or happy, etc. But try to describe what a mood is, without using a lot of examples, and without using the word 'feeling'.

Then try as an exercise, even if only in your mind, to list a lot of 'feeling' words and decide whether they are emotions or moods. You might even find that many of the words you list are personality traits rather than feelings. Think about 'optimistic', 'extroverted', etc.

Before I give the definitions that I will be using in this book, let's look at Wikipedia to see whether the experts do better than what you just did at describing feelings, emotions and moods:

> Feeling in psychology is usually reserved for the conscious subjective experience of emotion. As such, it is inherently beyond the reach of scientific method. Phenomenology and heterophenomenology are philosophical approaches that provide some basis for knowledge of feelings. Many schools of psychotherapy depend on the therapist achieving some kind of understanding of the client's feelings, for which methodologies exist. Some theories of interpersonal relationships also have a role for shared feelings or understanding of another person's feelings.
>
> (Wikipedia, 'Feeling')

I do not find this very helpful, especially for a simple word like 'feelings', which is a word everyone uses regularly. Let's now have a look at how nearly incomprehensible the definition in Wikipedia is for the simple term everybody uses very often: 'emotions'.

Just for fun, imagine that on some faraway planet some intelligent beings developed a robot rat using human neurons. To their disappointment this rat now does less than a fruit fly. They read in Damasio's book that what this rat needs is emotions. So they send a rat to earth, and your job is to describe to the rat what an emotion is. If you use Wikipedia then this is what you will be telling the rat. (Let me make it clear up front that I think these definitions may in some contexts be unnecessarily complex and even

misleading. They certainly do not reflect the way ordinary people understand the words, and ordinary people do understand these terms, because
they use them in normal conversations without others becoming confused.)
So you say to the robot rat from outer space:

> Emotion is very complex, and the term has no single, universally accepted
> definition. The study of emotions is part of psychology, sociology, neuroscience,
> ethics, and metaphysics.
>
> According to Sloman, emotions are cognitive processes. Some authors
> emphasize the difference between human emotions and the affective behaviour
> of animals.
>
> We often talk about brains as information-processing systems, but any
> account of the brain that lacks an account of emotions, motivations, fears, and
> hopes is incomplete.
>
> Emotions are measurable physical responses to salient stimuli: the
> increased heartbeat and perspiration that accompany fear, the freezing
> response of a rat in the presence of a cat, or the extra muscle tension that
> accompanies anger.
>
> Feelings, on the other hand, are the subjective experiences that sometimes
> accompany these processes: the sensations of happiness, envy, sadness, and
> so on.
>
> Emotions seem to employ largely unconscious machinery – for example,
> brain areas involved in emotion will respond to angry faces that are briefly
> presented and then rapidly masked, even when subjects are unaware of having
> seen the face.
>
> Across cultures the expression of basic emotions is remarkably similar, and
> as Darwin observed, it is also similar across all mammals. There are even strong
> similarities in physiological responses among humans, reptiles, and birds when
> showing fear, anger, or parental love.
>
> Modern views propose that emotions are brain states that quickly assign
> value or valence to outcomes and provide a simple plan of action. Thus,
> emotion can be viewed as a type of computation, a rapid, automatic summary
> that initiates appropriate actions. When a bear is galloping toward you, the
> rising fear directs your brain to do the right things (determining an escape
> route) instead of all the other things it could be doing (rounding out your
> grocery list). When it comes to perception, you can spot an object more quickly
> if it is, say, a spider rather than a roll of tape. In the realm of memory, emotional
> events are laid down differently by a parallel memory system involving a brain
> area called the amygdala.
>
> One goal of emotional neuroscience is to understand the nature of the many
> disorders of emotion, depression being the most common and costly. Impulsive
> aggression and violence are also thought to be consequences of faulty emotion
> regulation.
>
> (Wikipedia, 'Emotion')

Wikipedia has a list of emotions, divided into basic emotions and other
emotions. I reproduce this list below. It might be useful for you to consider
these words and decide whether you feel they are emotions, moods, feelings,
personality traits, etc.

Basic: Anger, Fear, Sadness, Happiness, Disgust
Others: Acceptance, Affection, Aggression, Ambivalence, Apathy, Anxiety,
Compassion, Confusion, Contempt, Depression, Doubt, Ecstasy, Empathy,
Envy, Embarrassment, Euphoria, Forgiveness, Frustration, Guilt, Gratitude,
Grief, Hatred, Hope, Horror, Hostility, Homesickness, Hysteria, Loneliness,
Love, Paranoia, Pity, Pleasure, Pride, Rage, Regret, Remorse, Shame, Suffering,
Surprise, Sympathy

(Wikipedia, 'Emotion')

And now let's look at Wikipedia and moods. This time Wikipedia is brief:

A mood is a relatively lasting affective state. Moods differ from emotions in
that they are less specific, often less intense, less likely to be triggered by a
particular stimulus or event, however longer lasting. Moods generally have
either a positive or negative valence. In other words, people often speak of being
in a good or bad mood. Unlike acute, emotional feelings like fear and surprise,
moods generally last for hours or days. Mood also differs from temperament
or personality traits which are even more general and long lasting. However,
personality traits (eg optimism, neuroticism) tend to predispose certain types of
moods. Mood is an internal, subjective state, but it often can be inferred from
posture and other observable behaviors.

(Wikipedia, 'Mood (psychology)')

And here is part of what Wikipedia says about personality traits:

The emotions, thoughts and behavior patterns that a person has are typically
referred to as a personality... and can vary immensely between individuals.
In making the area amenable to scientific enquiry some, using the statistical
technique of factor analysis, have hypothesized that the personality contains
prominent aspects that are stable across situations called traits.

(Wikipedia, 'Personality psychology')

It should now be clear that the various terms are related, sometimes overlap,
and are ill defined by the experts. They are all words that everybody understands very well, uses freely in everyday conversations and assumes that
others also understand perfectly well.

Imagine how confused the robot rat from outer space will be after
reading this.

Does it matter?

Do these definitions really matter, and is a book about brands really the
place to debate the difference in definitions? For many years I thought that
it did not matter, and that all authors have to do is to use their own definitions and get on with the task at hand. However, it does matter. I talk at
many international conferences and lecture on the subject. Nearly always

I used to find out after such a lecture that some people had misunderstood what I was talking about because they used their own definition of what emotions are. This is not unreasonable. Everybody knows what emotions are until asked to define them, even the experts.

As I will show, the reasons why people are endowed by evolution with emotions, moods or even traits are very different. Each of these is necessary for survival, but their effects are very different. They also have very different influences on how a consumer decides on a brand or reacts to advertising. From a marketing research and planning perspective it is very important to know that when you are looking at the attention-getting ability of advertisements you are probably mainly dealing with emotions, and when you are dealing with the brand effects then you are dealing with moods, personalities, culture, etc. (I will explain this in greater depth later.) This means that you should know what you are researching when you are researching advertisements or brands, and what the influence of what you are researching should be. Literature abounds with examples where these factors are confused.

Things become very complex when one is doing research involving several cultures (multinational or even inside one country). When terminology is translated, the word in the different cultures might not have the same meaning or connotation. It might even be that the words used in the research, when translated, might change from describing an emotion to one describing a mood or even a trait. This means that the comparison between cultures of the implications of the research could become misleading.

It is especially important for account planners to plan for the emotions created by the advertisements, and then for the mood about the product that the advertisement creates – and not just as simple as stating that it creates a positive mood.

Lastly, I hope to stimulate the reader's interest in these topics, and that includes awareness of the differences in the meaning of the words, and the importance of understanding the implications of these.

Definition used in this book

By far the best book I have found about emotions is Oatley and Jenkins's *Understanding Emotions* (1996). They suggest the following relationship between the emotive terms that we all use in everyday language, but which are often so ill defined:

> Many terms have been used to indicate emotions. The term 'feeling' is a synonym for emotion, although with a broader range. In the older psychological literature the term 'affect' was used. It is still used to imply an even wider range of phenomena that have anything to do with emotions, moods, dispositions, and preferences.
>
> Part of the difficulty of answering the question 'What is an emotion?' is that 'emotion' and the adjective 'emotional' are sometimes used in the same way

as 'affect' to imply a whole range of states and conditions. But as research has proceeded it has become clear that it is merely frustrating to offer the same explanation for states that are different. It is better to use terms and concepts more selectively.

... A consensus is emerging: the term 'emotion' or 'emotion episode' is generally used for states that last a limited amount of time. Facial expressions and most bodily responses generally last from 0.5 to 4 seconds.

(Oatley and Jenkins, 1996)

I have enhanced the original schema in Oatley and Jenkins by naming it 'Feelings schema' (Figure 7.1). This division of 'feelings' is not very different from the fairly modern view of some psychologists.

FIGURE 7.1   Feelings schema

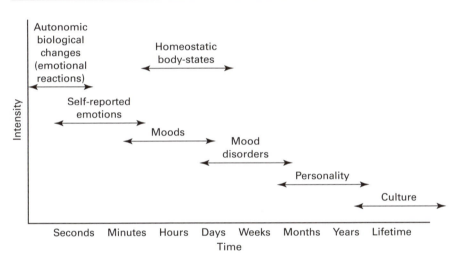

SOURCE: Developed from Oatley and Jenkins (1996).

In other words, the term 'feeling' is commonly used as a collective noun for emotions, moods, mood disorders, personality and culture.

Time

What is most important about the feelings schema above is that it relates different types of feelings to time. The reaction to the environment changes – emotions – need to be very fast, and it involves mechanisms that allow very fast reactions. It requires attention from the mind immediately.

Our reactions to changes in our bodily state (homeostasis) need to be much slower. The feeling of hunger should not be an on–off switch, but one that builds its demand for attention from the mind over time. We should start off being a bit hungry, and then slowly become hungrier, until it becomes an overriding need.

The state of our mind (moods) should not be volatile all the time. We all know that mostly moods last for quite a while.

Personality should be reasonably stable over time, as well as our reaction to values of the tribe (culture).

We know that mostly people's personalities remain fairly stable over a very long period – even a lifetime.

Next we will discuss where in the brain these feelings live and then the individual feelings themselves.

The limbic system: the oldest part of the brain

The limbic system is the oldest part of the brain in evolutionary terms. It developed to manage 'toward' or 'away from' reactions and is an evolutionary necessity for reptiles as well as humans. So how does the limbic system work to aid us in our quest for survival and procreation?

> The limbic system operates by influencing the endocrine system and the autonomic nervous system.
>
> It is highly interconnected with the nucleus accumbens, the brain's pleasure centre, which plays a role in sexual arousal and the 'high' derived from certain recreational drugs. These responses are heavily modulated by dopaminergic projections from the limbic system.
>
> In 1954, Olds and Milner found that rats with metal electrodes implanted into their nucleus accumbens repeatedly pressed a lever activating this region, and did so in preference to eating and drinking, eventually dying of exhaustion.
>
> The limbic system is also tightly connected to the prefrontal cortex. Some scientists contend that this connection is related to the pleasure obtained from solving problems. To cure severe emotional disorders, this connection was sometimes surgically severed, a procedure of psychosurgery, called a prefrontal lobotomy (this is actually a misnomer).
>
> (Wikipedia, 'Limbic system')

The term 'limbic system' implies that it is a system of parts of the brain, and that this system has a purpose and output. Brain scientists are still unsure about which parts of the brain should be considered to be part of the limbic system; the list in Table 7.1 contains only a few of those that Wikipedia lists as parts of the system and the functions ascribed to them (so far). The table highlights 'marketing words' that are implicated as the product of specific subsystems of the limbic system. It is not necessary to know which parts of the limbic system do what, but it is necessary to know what the whole system does.

TABLE 7.1 Structure and functions of the limbic system

Structure	Functions
Amygdala	Involved in signalling the cortex with motivationally significant stimuli such as those related to reward and fear in addition to social functions such as mating.
Hippocampus	Required for the formation of long-term memories.
Cingulate gyrus	Autonomic functions regulating heart rate, blood pressure and cognitive and attentional processing.
Hypothalamus	Regulates the autonomic nervous system via hormone production and release. Affects and regulates blood pressure, heart rate, hunger, thirst, sexual arousal, and the sleep–wake cycle.
Pituitary gland	Secretes hormones regulating homeostasis.
Entorhinal cortex and piriform cortex	Receives smell input in the olfactory system.
Olfactory bulb	Olfactory sensory input.
Nucleus accumbens	Involved in reward, pleasure and addiction.
Orbitofrontal cortex	Required for decision making.

SOURCE: Wikipedia, 'Limbic system'.

08

The 'feeling' brain systems and how they work

- In Chapter 5 we learned how people memorize experiences in a way that they can interpret things in the future. We discussed how everything that enters the brain becomes a developing gestalt and we hinted that the key to which of these gets attention lies in feelings.
- In Chapter 6 we described the robot rat and asked which systems it would need to be more motivated.
- In Chapter 7 we defined some types of feelings that people have, and indicated that the differences between types of feelings is related to time.
- In this chapter we will describe how each of these feelings systems works to produce motivated behaviors. We start with defining the systems in human terminology. Then we reconcile this with Damasio's views of the role of background feeling which we explained in Chapter 3, and which is the basis of his somatic marker theorem.

Let us now return to the robot rat and the systems that it would need to become a fruit fly:

- *Memory*. So we know how the 300,000 neurons of the cyber-rat lay down memories by altering the state of the synapses based on experience. This is exactly the same as for fruit flies and humans (a neuron is a neuron is a neuron, and only does this). What is lacking, as I pointed out, is motivation, ie in which direction does the robot rat want to go, and why?

- *State of body (homeostasis).* The robot rat needs to look after its body itself. The word 'homeostasis' is used in engineering to denote a feedback system like an air conditioner – the system senses that the temperature is too low, or too high, and then switches on the machine. The same word is used to describe a bodily system that serves as a feedback system about bodily conditions: hunger, cold, thirst, sexual readiness, etc. These are mostly, though not totally, driven by hormones. The advantage of a chemical system to do this is that the 'need' builds over time as more and more chemicals build up.

- *State of mind (moods).* Not only does the brain need to know what the state of the body is – especially when something is not in balance – but it needs to know whether the brain is also in balance. This especially relates to the level of arousal of the brain. Whilst it is good for the brain's level of arousal to fluctuate, it should not remain too high or too low for too long. Thus the brain needs to motivate the cyber-rat or human toward things that will increase or decrease the levels of arousal depending on the current state of the brain.

- *Environment reactions (emotions).* Not only should the cyber-rat be aware of the state of its body and the state of its mind, but it must be aware of the environment and be able to react to this. It is vital to react to changes in the environment, and an important part of the reason why we have brains. This is the role of emotions. If something in the environment changes and it is important to our survival, we will experience an emotion. This emotion will cause us to react appropriately to the change in the environment. Because a reaction needs to be fast, emotions are mostly (not entirely) caused by electronic reactions in the brain as part of the process of interpretation of the environment.

- *Evaluation/preference (dopamine).* Ultimately the robot rat, fruit fly or human will continuously be faced with choices. A decision is really just making a choice between alternatives. The best indication of which alternative would be best for you is your past experience: how did you feel last time you made the choice? If you felt bad, then it would be stupid to make the same choice; and if you felt good then it would probably be best to do this again. The system that exists in the brain to do this is called the pleasure system, and is mostly operated by dopamine and serotonin. (This is also the system that is implicated in addictions).

All of the above systems are 'feeling' systems.

Reconciling this view with Damasio's view

Does this deviate from Damasio's view? Damasio distinguishes between emotions and feelings. For him, emotions are the visceral biological reaction in the amygdala that happens first. When we become conscious of having had a reaction, we then have what he calls feelings. He uses the expression 'background feelings', and these are an important part of his theorem. He explains what he means and the relationship of this term to moods:

A note on background feelings

What little attention has been paid to the neuroscience of emotion in the twentieth century has been concentrated on the core types of emotion studied by Darwin. Fear, anger, sadness, disgust, surprise and happiness have been found to be universal emotions in terms of their facial expressions and recognizability, as shown in the work of Ekman and others.

As a result, the feelings that are most often considered are those that constitute the conscious readout of these major emotions. This would be all well and good if it would not have distracted us from the fact we continuously have emotional feelings although those feelings are not necessarily part of the set of six 'universal feelings' that hail from the six universal emotions.

Most of the time we do not experience any of the six emotions, which is certainly a blessing given that four of them are unpleasant. Nor do we experience any of the so-called secondary or social emotions, a good thing too, since these hardly fare better in pleasantness.

But we do experience other kinds of emotions, sometimes low grade, sometimes quite intense, and we do sense the general physical tone of our being. I have called the readout of this background perturbation 'Background feelings', a term I first used in *Descartes' Error*, because these feelings are not on the foreground of our mind...

In one way or another, however, background feelings help define our mental state and colour our lives. Background feelings arise from background emotions, and these emotions, although more internally than externally directed, are observable to others in myriad ways: body posture, the speed and design of our movements and even the tone of our voices and prosody of our speech as we communicate thoughts that have little to do with the background emotion.

Prominent background feelings include: fatigue; energy; excitement; wellness; sickness; tension; relaxation; surging; dragging; stability; instability; balance; imbalance; harmony; discord.

The relation between background feelings and drives and motivations is intimate: drives express themselves directly in background emotions and we eventually become aware of their existence by means of background feelings.

The relation between background feelings and moods is also close. Moods are made up of modulated and sustained background feelings as well as modulated and sustained feelings of primary emotions – sadness, in the case of depression.

It is probably correct to say that background feelings are a faithful index of momentary parameters of inner organization state. The core ingredients of that index are:

1   the temporal and spatial shape of the operations of the smooth musculature in blood vessels and varied organs, and the striated muscle of the heart and chest;

2   the chemical profile of the milieu close to all those muscle fibres; and

3   the presence or absence of a chemical profile signifying either a threat to the integrity of living tissues or conditions of optimal homeostasis.

(Damasio, 1999: 285–86)

Here Damasio mentions nearly everything that this book is about, so it is a very important passage. Oatley and Jenkins (1996) explain more about the views that different historical thinkers had.

Functions of emotions

Perhaps more than anything else the study of emotions has been put on a strong and lasting basis by the recognition of functions. None of the nineteenth century founders of research in the area thought emotions were purposeful. For Darwin, emotional expressions were patterns of action that once had functions, but in adult humans they occurred whether or not they were any use. James thought that emotions were perceptions of inner states, but with no immediate effect on action because they occurred when the real business of producing behavior was over. Freud concentrated on how emotional states could be actively dysfunctional. But within these early approaches are seeds of more recent understandings. Prompted by Darwin's work we now believe that by eliciting species-characteristic outline patterns in situations that have recurred during evolution emotions have helped adapt humans to the physical and social world. From James's thinking about emotions as perceptions of bodily processes, we can ask how they could serve a monitoring function that could be important. And by Freud drawing attention to dysfunctional aspects, we are reminded to ask about the functions of emotions in everyday life.

Functions of emotions are important not just in terms of evolutionary significance but during individual development as our actions are coordinated with those of other people... Emotions are there to modify perception, to direct attention, to give preferential access to certain memories, and to bias thinking.

(Oatley and Jenkins, 1996)

The most commonly used biological measure in neuromarketing is EEG. This measures changes in the voltage in specific spatial areas of the brain. We have seen in Chapter 7 that the best way to define feelings is with reference to time, and only one of the feelings changes quickly: emotion. Thus EEG measures mainly emotion and most of what we have in the practice of neuromarketing therefore has to do with emotion. Emotion is a foreground feeling playing off against Damasio's background feelings. This we will discuss in the next chapters.

09 The environmental awareness system: emotions

Let's go back to our cyber-rat with 300,000 neurons and the fruit fly with only 100,000. There are 120,000 species of flies, almost 7,000 in the UK alone. They are prodigious breeders. In warm weather, the life cycle from an egg through maggot to adult lasts just 8 to 12 days. Theoretically, two flies mating in April (in the northern hemisphere) could produce 191,010,000,000,000,000,000,000 descendants by August: enough to cover the earth in a blanket of horridness 47 feet deep. The main reason why we are not wading through flies is that there are many animals (and plants) that love to eat them. This means that much of a fly's life is spent dodging other hungry creatures, using its eyes and its allotted 100,000 neurons.

The robot rat might be impressive as it slowly negotiates its way around the maze it is in, but if you try to swat it with a fly swat it will just calmly sit there and allow you to destroy it! A fly's dodging ability is notorious. The problem is that the robot rat has no emotions – just memory. Emotions – especially the emotion of fear – work partly via the amygdala. How this happens is described in Joseph LeDoux's book *The Emotional Brain* (1996).

To survive, any animal must be able to avoid danger in its environment. Since every animal is food for another animal it is important to move away from danger. Danger does not come only in the form of predators. One might stumble over a cliff, a tree might drop on your head, or a car might approach you on the wrong side of the road. In all these cases it is important for the organism to prepare itself for action and to give attention to whatever constitutes the danger. Your chances of survival are dramatically dependent on how fast you react. In nature, if you get too close to a poisonous snake, your survival is dependent on who is the faster: you or the snake. I have posted a video, 'Anaconda', on my website (**www.erikdup.com**) of a snake attacking the camera. When I show this in talks some people jump out of their chairs. They feel foolish afterwards, but the fact is that if it had been a real snake they would have had a better chance of survival than those in the audience who did not move.

LeDoux describes the role of the amygdala in terms of you walking in the forest and coming across something that looks like a twig or a snake. Most people will startle. In other words you will stop walking, your muscle tone will increase, your blood pressure will increase and you will look at the object (give it attention) to see whether it is a snake or a twig. What happens in your brain is that the retina of your eye is stimulated by light from the object (snake-like twig), this stimulates neurons to the occipital region of your brain (in the back), from here the process of neuronal recruitment starts, and a neuronal cloud (gestalt) forms. Note that everything you see at that point in time, not only the twig-like snake, is triggering the same process of neuronal recruitment.

As this process moves through the limbic system the gestalts are still only half-formed, ie it is not yet clear whether you saw a snake or a twig. Because it might be a snake and you have negative feeling memories about a snake, the amygdala fires. This causes the increase in adrenalin, increased blood pressure, and 'freezing', ie an involuntary visceral reaction – even before you are consciously aware of the object.

Besides this visceral reaction the forming gestalt gets tagged with a 'priority' signal. When the gestalt arrives at the consciousness (frontal lobes), attention is immediately given to the gestalt with the priority signal for it to become a consciousness. If you had a companion you would say 'That twig gave me a fright. It looks just like a snake' or you would shout 'Snake! Watch out!'

In reality what happened is that you had a bodily reaction before you even knew what it was that caused it. We are talking milliseconds here. As mentioned earlier, some authors use the term 'emotion' to describe the visceral reaction and the resultant consciousness they then term 'feeling'. I do not believe that in common language this is the way that people use the words. People more often describe both the visceral reaction and the subsequent knowledge as an emotion, mainly because they are not aware of these as two distinct steps in their brains.

This is why I show emotion as a two-step process in Figure 7.1 (the feelings schema): 1) the biological changes that occur pre-consciousness (which I titled 'Autonomic biological changes'); and 2) the awareness (reportability) of the emotion (which I titled 'Self-reported emotions'). It makes no sense that one should have an emotion and then not be aware of having experienced an emotion.

Everything in the brain is there for survival. Consider the implication of this bodily reaction before there is even a consciousness. If the brain was so constructed that you first became conscious of the snake – and all the other developed gestalts – and then sent signals to the amygdala to ready the body for action it might be too late. Much better for survival to first ready the body (emotion) and then think about what to do about the object.

Flies seldom think about things in their environment – any sudden movement will send them flying away. In many cases the movement might not have been life-threatening and they are leaving food for no good reason. It is much better to leave your food every time for no good reason than not to leave it the once when you should. Speed of reaction to the environment is critical to survival.

The systems involved in this reaction to a threat (mostly the amygdala) are located in what is known as the human reptile brain, ie in the parts that developed early in evolution and are also present in a snake.

It is worth considering what happens during this chance encounter between human and snake from a snake's perspective, since a snake's brain is mostly just the reptile brain. Most snakes will experience a fright and slither away. Some snakes, like the puff adder, will simply lie there and, if you happen to tread on them, will strike. Some snakes, like the cobra or mamba, might even attack you. In all cases their reaction is the same as that of the human being (their amygdala firing).

LeDoux postulates that there is a circuitry in the brain where the signals from the eye go directly to the amygdala even bypassing the occipital region. We will not enter that debate here other than noting that this would make sense, because such a circuitry would increase reaction speed even more.

William James (a US psychologist, 1842–1910) asked the question: 'If I see a bear in the woods and run, do I run because I am afraid or am I afraid because I run?' In other words he wondered whether the body reacted first and then we felt the emotion, or whether we felt the emotion first and then reacted. The above description of what the amygdala does indicates that his question had much more merit than people thought at the time. Damasio talks about James in his Barcelona talk – I posted the video of this on my website (**www.erikdup.com**).

There is a lot of evidence from cognitive psychologists that the more emotional a moment is the stronger the laying down of the memory. An example that is often used is that most people can remember where they were when they witnessed the Twin Towers disaster.

An emotion is a post-rationalization

Experiencing an emotion is a two-step process. This is what I show in the feelings schema. The first thing that happens is the visceral reaction: the body readying itself not only by increased blood pressure and so on but also by giving attention to the object that created the emotion. The second step, although it happens so fast that it feels like the first step (and, in fact, should be considered to be part of the first step for all practical purposes), is that the brain becomes aware that there is something it should give attention to, ie a cognition forms. Part of this cognition is interpreting the emotion and reacting accordingly.

Imagine two infants playing next to each other. One seems to enjoy playing with a toy; the other grabs it, the first one hits the second one and the second one starts to cry. Here in a matter of seconds is a whole panoply of emotions. The parents might use words like 'jealousy', 'desire', 'possessiveness', 'anger', 'pain', 'fright' and so on. In my experience the parents themselves will also have a whole panoply of emotions when they observe this, and much of it will depend on which child's parents they are. The toddlers themselves will not have words for the emotion they experienced. Neither probably thought about the behaviour they exhibited as a result of the emotion. In fact, to them it will seem that they behaved totally rationally.

Grown-ups still experience the same emotions, often wanting what they see others have, or wanting to hurt others for perceived affronts, or feeling hurt by what others did. The difference is that they have learned words with which to describe the feelings, and they have learned not to react spontaneously to an emotion but to control it.

As we will see, moods are very different from emotions, not only in the way they are used for survival, but even in the way they are created in our minds. At the same time there is a massive interaction between moods and emotions. Emotional experience can lead to a mood, and a mood can modify an emotional experience.

One of the key differences is the speed of onset. Since emotions are caused by things outside the body and quick reactions are required, emotions have a very quick onset – milliseconds. This becomes important for marketers when they want to measure what is a mood and what is an emotion. Was it created by something outside the body as opposed to inside the body? Emotions are caused by external things that need quick reactions, whilst moods (and homeostasis) are internal and seldom require immediate action. Is the emotion mostly described in the past tense? When you get a fright in the woods as a result of a twig-snake-like object your comment to your friend will be 'That twig gave me a fright.' You might still have a raised heartbeat, but you have already processed the gestalt and you are talking about an emotion that has already passed. Maybe this thought will help researchers. Some time ago I was introduced to Johnny Fontaine of Ghent University. I took this description of who he works with from their website because I think their work is important and market researchers might want to keep an eye on their findings:

The National Centre of Competence in Research (NCCR) for the Affective Sciences is a research network financed by the Swiss government and administered through the Swiss National Science Foundation. Members of the network are the project leaders of the ten individual research projects.

In addition, a number of outstanding researchers in the area of affective sciences are Associates of the Centre. The Leading house is the University of Geneva, which accommodates the management team and a large number of the staff in its 'Centre Interfacultaire en Sciences Affectives' (CISA).

(**http://www.north-south.unibe.ch/**)

What I think they are trying to do is to identify types of feelings (or words for feelings) in different cultures. Their starting point is that one should identify whether a word is a mood, emotion, etc based on the function that it is perceived to have. A specific feeling word in English might have several equivalent words in (say) Afrikaans or Chinese. Most dictionaries will list several alternatives for any one word. By asking people questions in the different cultures about the function of the feeling state indicated by the alternative words, about its duration and its source, etc one can determine the closest alternative word in different languages.

To do advertising (and research) between language groups it is very important to use the correct words – even in terms of the brand's strategy document's translation!

Rational or emotional?

This really gets us back to the issue of emotional versus rational. It is an emotional reaction to not step on the snake. Is it therefore an irrational reaction? A snake biting a human that is about to step on it, or slithering away when the human approaches, is an emotional reaction (fright or fear). Since snakes are not seen to have a lot of rationality, is this then irrational? Is it irrational for the fruit fly to leave its food nine times in succession when it gets a fright, and not learn that it is leaving good food for no good reason?

The answer is obvious that the reaction of the human, snake and fruit fly appears to be very rational. If they behaved any differently their behaviour would be described as irrational.

Contrast this with the behaviour of our robot rat. The robot rat will not avoid the snake or anything that threatens it. This is despite the robot rat having more neurons than the fruit fly and being capable of forming memories and learning.

The point is that we should not consider emotional to be the opposite of rational, or having emotions as detrimental to rationality. Emotionality is inextricably intertwined with rationality.

But are advertisements like snakes?

In *The Advertised Mind* (2005) I told the snake story and from there expanded into the role of emotion in advertising: emotion gets attention for the developing gestalt that is the advertisement, and it sets the background against which the advertisement is interpreted. I also showed how our massive database of tracked advertisements shows that higher advertising liking scores correlate with better memories being formed, and I related the study by the Advertising Research Foundation (ARF) in the United States that found the best predictor of advertising effectiveness is ad liking. I have also heard many speakers at conferences argue the Joseph LeDoux story about the amygdala and how this means emotions are vital for advertising effectiveness. Unfortunately, all of this ignores one little detail: few advertisements are based on giving the audience a fright. Most advertisements try to create a positive emotion. Ad-liking scores are much more likely to relate to pleasant emotions being generated by the advertisement rather than fright or fear emotions.

I recently sat in an airport lounge and thought I saw a friend. My body reacted: I gave the person a lot more attention, stopped what I was doing and started to approach him, only to realize that it was someone who merely looked like my friend from the angle at which I was seated.

This was a positive approach response typical of what the amygdala generates. It makes sense that the limbic system would use emotions as a bidirectional mechanism: away from or toward. In both cases it would do this by creating attention being given to the developing gestalt. There is now brain scanning evidence that the amygdala also reacts to positive stimuli.

Culture and the amygdala

In Wikipedia, under 'Amygdala', it is reported: 'Studies in 2004 and 2006 showed that normal subjects exposed to images of frightened faces, or faces of people from another race, will show increased activity of the amygdala, even if that exposure is subliminal.'

In Chapter 14 we will discuss the effect of culture and the evolutionary reasons why culture affects our emotions. Culture has to do with the herding instinct of some animals, which is shown in the tribe forming or cultures of societies. It makes sense that, when you see somebody from your own tribe approaching, you would not have an emotional reaction involving fear, but when you see someone identifiably from a different tribe approaching you might have a reaction that prepares the body to react – or give attention at least.

Herd behaviour

We will discuss acculturation later, but first let us consider how emotion works for groups of animals (and people). Let us take LeDoux's analogy a step further. Suppose there are two people walking through the forest, talking and relaxed. One of them spots a snake and has the visceral reaction described above. The one who did not spot the snake will stop talking and direct his or her attention in the direction in which the other is looking! In other words the second person will recognize the startle and will have a similar reaction. This is a very good survival mechanism for many animals that herd or flock.

Most birds, when they find food, will sing to attract other birds. This might appear to be a poor survival strategy. After all, why share the limited supplies? In reality it is very efficient. When some have their heads down pecking the seeds, others will have their heads up. Effectively there are always some that are monitoring the environment. When any one has a fright (emotion), all will fly away immediately. The same is true for a herd of antelope on the African plains – one takes fright and all run.

One of the most beautiful sights on African plains is to see a herd of antelope grazing and one smells a lion. The body language of the smeller immediately communicates – even to a human observer – that it has smelled something dangerous. Immediately the other antelope will react and tense up, smelling the air.

Emotional reactions do not only affect the preparedness of the body (visceral), but also affect the emotions displayed. There should be no reason to display fright or fear on our faces or in our bodily posture, because this does not prepare us for flight or fight. Yet we do. The reason is that we are effectively communicating to the rest of the tribe that there might be danger.

How many emotions do we have?

This question becomes very important when we look at the brain–brand puzzle. When you want to make 'emotional' advertising for the reason that emotions are there to attract attention then you need to know what emotion you are trying to elicit in the advertising, and you need to measure whether you are successful.

The debate on the issue of how many emotions we have is confounded by people confusing emotions and moods (and sometimes other feelings). Since the consensus is now that emotions have a motivation role (toward or away from) and also urgency, it becomes easier to define what an emotion is. Thus fright would be an emotion, whereas sadness would probably be a mood.

A very good example of how the pieces of the puzzle can be viewed from different perspectives and why this is important for researchers is the use of the word 'sad'. I believe that sad is a mood because the feeling lasts quite a while. Graham Page, Millward Brown's Executive Vice President, Neuroscience Practice, points out that sad can also be an emotion if it is a fleeting feeling (in a conversation with the author). I have to agree with him. This leaves us with two interpretations for sad (emotion or mood). Generally, when we talk to each other we will deduce from the context of how the word is used whether it is meant as a fleeting experience or a longer-lasting state. However, when we design research questionnaires we might have differences between what we mean to ask and what the respondent thinks we are asking.

It also seems likely that some languages might recognize different emotions. Compare the size of the English dictionary against the much smaller Zulu dictionary. This is unlikely to indicate that people of different cultures have fewer or more emotions, but it does indicate a different richness in words for some emotions. In market research this becomes important when questionnaires are translated.

Plutchik, in 1958, differentiated between eight basic emotions and more complex emotions (Wikipedia, 'Robert Plutchik'). Unfortunately it does appear as if he includes other feelings – according to my definition – under the term 'emotions'. I am not suggesting Plutchik was wrong. He proposed his wheel of emotions (Figure 9.1) in 1958, well before the modern views of emotion.

FIGURE 9.1   Plutchik's wheel of emotions

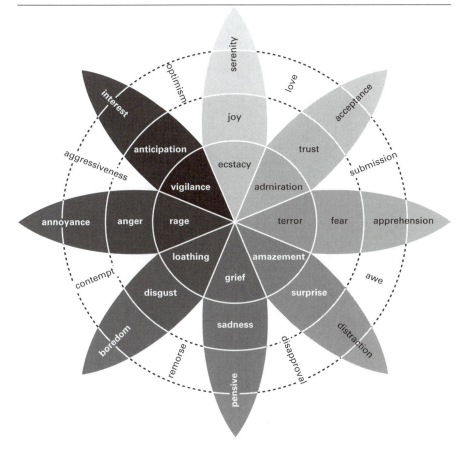

It would seem that, at the lowest level, to survive we need only two emotions: toward and away from. Flemming Hansen and Sverre Riis Christensen of Copenhagen Business School, in their 2007 book *Emotions, Advertising and Consumer Choice*, reviewed the published material on this and found that most studies that did factor analysis of the measures that they used find only two dimensions that reflect this directionality of emotions – one consisting of positive items and one with negative items. Each of these factors then might consist of several items (ie highly correlated words describing emotions or feelings). In their study they also found only two dimensions – one positive and one negative – for each of the different brands that they measured. (The items for these dimensions differ for different product types.) They deducted the score of the negative dimension from that of the positive dimension to arrive at what they term the Net Emotional Response Score (NERS). This creates an interesting conundrum. Factor analysis should yield dimensions that are not related, as shown in Figure 9.2.

FIGURE 9.2   Two-factor solution of feeling items

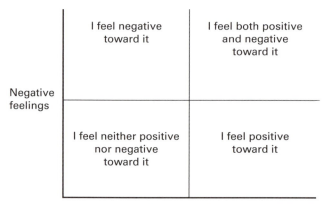

The biological problem with this is that if the brain is calculating a single-number response by deducting the negative from the positive emotion then its reaction to something it feels neither positive nor negative about might be the same number as the number for something it feels equally positive and negative about. The counter-argument is that it makes perfect sense that I might have a positive and negative feeling about something. If one measures emotions on only one scale then would such a situation lead us to add the positives and negatives and hence have no emotion?

Hansen and Christensen's work is pioneering work and the only published work I am aware of that has attempted to measure brands using exclusively emotional words. More importantly, it worked, and even changes in the way people feel about different brands over time are explainable.

I suspect this piece of the puzzle (whether measures of emotions should be viewed as one dimension with a negative and a positive pole, or whether they should be viewed as two separate dimensions) will become a part of many debates in the future (ie a piece of the puzzle that will be turned around several times to be viewed from different perspectives).

Emotions and marketing

The survival function of emotion is that it changes what we are giving attention to. In neurological terms what it does is to give a developing gestalt a priority.

I made the point earlier that all of marketing is about the brand getting attention. So emotion is involved in all that marketing is about.

I have shown that other feeling systems also cause developing gestalts to be given attention: the bodily homeostasis and the mind state, even the available size of the memory system and the size and intensity of the cause of the gestalt.

In many current marketing conferences the message is that emotions are all that matter. This is simply not true. There are many other systems in the brain that also cause attention to be given; in many cases these other feeling systems in the brain might cause attention to be given to something by way of increasing the emotion one has about it. What is true is that emotion has been seen in a new light in the past decade and is now a well-explained reason for people giving attention – and a good strategy for advertising (and brand positioning).

10 The 'state of body' system: homeostasis

The most basic reason why people buy many products is to ensure that their body is comfortable – warm, fed, etc. This statement applies to types of products rather than brands. The inter-brand decision is mostly taken after a decision was made to buy a type of product. The homeostatic system motivates people to do this. It is largely a negative motivator. By making you aware that some part of the body is not comfortable you will be driven to solve the problem for the body. This is truly where basic needs come from. This is also the lower levels of Maslow's hierarchy.

A vital function that the robot rat does not do is to look after the mechanical parts of the robot. It does not know when the battery is in need of recharging, the oil is overheating, etc. The fruit fly does this. It knows when to eat, drink, and sit in the shade or in the sun.

The consumer's brain does this seamlessly from the day he or she is born. A baby knows when it is hungry, thirsty or cold. It does not have words for these conditions, but its brain knows that there is something wrong with the body and that if the condition is not tended to it is getting worse.

The systems that do this go under the name of homeostatic systems. The word 'homeostasis' describes a system that tries to maintain a balance: an air conditioner is such a system in that it tries to keep a constant temperature in the room.

An obvious question at this stage is: 'I understand that the phrases "I feel hungry" and "I felt frightened" indicate that both of these things are feelings, but what does a description of feeling hungry do in a book about emotions and marketing?' The answer is that we are looking at how the brain decides which developing gestalt should be given attention. We have explained why an emotion will be one factor that aids the brain in this decision. We now want to show how feelings of bodily state influence this decision.

Your body's state goes out of kilter when you are hungry, thirsty, cold, in pain, uncomfortable and so on. People use brands to return their bodily state to a balance where they feel comfortable. The question becomes: how do you know that you are hungry, thirsty, in pain, etc?

Hunger is a feeling experienced when the glycogen level of the liver falls below a threshold, usually followed by a desire to eat. The usually unpleasant feeling originates in the hypothalamus and is released through receptors in the liver. Although an average nourished human can survive weeks without food intake, the sensation of hunger typically begins after a couple of hours without eating and is generally considered quite uncomfortable.

As a meal containing carbohydrates is eaten and digested, blood glucose levels rise, and the pancreas secretes insulin. Glucose from the hepatic portal vein enters the liver cells (hepatocytes). Insulin acts on the hepatocytes to stimulate the action of several enzymes, including glycogen synthase. Glucose molecules are added to the chains of glycogen as long as both insulin and glucose remain plentiful. In this postprandial or 'fed' state, the liver takes in more glucose from the blood than it releases.

After a meal has been digested and glucose levels begin to fall, insulin secretion is reduced, and glycogen synthesis stops. About four hours after a meal glycogen begins to be broken down and converted again to glucose. Glycogen phosphorylase is the primary enzyme of glycogen breakdown. For the next 8–12 hours, glucose derived from liver glycogen will be the primary source of blood glucose to be used by the rest of the body for fuel.

Glucagon is another hormone produced by the pancreas, which in many respects serves as a counter-signal to insulin. When the blood sugar begins to fall below normal, glucagon is secreted in increasing amounts. It stimulates glycogen breakdown into glucose even when insulin levels are abnormally high.

The fluctuation of leptin and ghrelin hormone levels results in the motivation of an organism to consume food. When an organism eats, adipocytes trigger the release of leptin into the body. Increasing levels of leptin results in a reduction of one's motivation to eat. After hours of non-consumption, leptin levels drop significantly. These low levels of leptin cause the release of secondary hormone, ghrelin, which in turn reinitiates the feeling of hunger.

Leptin binds to the ventromedial nucleus of the hypothalamus, known as the 'appetite centre'.

Thus, circulating leptin levels give the brain input regarding energy storage so it can regulate appetite and metabolism.

(Wikipedia, 'Hunger (motivational state)')

The important issue above is really that the homeostatic system is a 'negative feedback system'. It does not tell the brain that it is feeling good, but that something is wrong, it is feeling bad and something should be done about it (ie some plan – or decision – has to be thought of and executed). This feeling will start as mild discomfort but build in intensity over time as the chemicals signalling the discomfort build up in the brain. This happens specifically in the hypothalamus, ie the limbic system.

FIGURE 10.1 Feelings schema: homeostasis

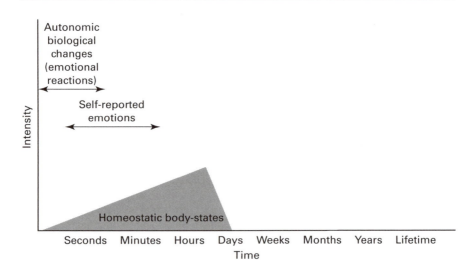

This slow build-up of a feeling makes a lot of sense, because if one ignores any of these feedback mechanisms for too long death will ensue. The purpose of these systems is to make one increasingly aware of the problem so that one will increasingly be disposed to solve the problem. As the feeling of discomfort increases so the issue becomes less which brand to use and more any brand will do! Once the feeling has been attended to, it will decrease and go away.

The speed with which the feeling builds and the speed with which it goes away will depend on many things, so the graph in Figure 10.1 is merely indicative of a build-up and decline. (The following chapters reveal similar graphs for the different feelings, all contributing to a composite graph in Chapter 16.) The very important point illustrated by Figure 10.1 is that at any point in time the emotions one experiences happen against the backdrop of the homeostatic state of the body.

Susan Greenfield describes how a consumer gets to purchase an orange (this should be read in conjunction with the description in Chapter 7 of how amines work in the brain):

> A model for the physical basis of consciousness might run something like this: A stimulus, in the simplest case an object in the outside world such as an orange, triggers a series of diverse, idiosyncratic connections in the cortex – for example eat, seeds, diarrhea, first peel.
>
> The strength and extent of these connections depend on experience. Such connections are long-lasting and not very flexible. Thus there would be a reasonable infrastructure for learning certain associations, the basis for enduring significance of objects around us – for example, the intrinsic properties relating

to the taste or the method and consequences of eating oranges. In addition, whatever degree of arousal happens to be prevalent at the time will ensure that a certain amount of particular amines is released within the cortex and that the amines modulate very large groups of neurons to be potentially more excitable. Wherever neurons are modulated, for a temporary period, to respond easily and sensitively to the corralling signals from the group of associated neurons, a gestalt forms, and a unique consciousness is generated for that moment.

If arousal is high, the gestalts forming will be small due to a rapid turnover. They will be readily formed but also easily displaced by the formation of new competing assemblies, which are themselves quickly displaced in rapid succession. Earlier news of a promotion might make me so excited that I would be barely aware of oranges in a shop window before being distracted by the sight of pineapples. On the other hand, if arousal is more moderate, a stronger epicenter, due to a louder or brighter external stimulus (a screeching cat) or a cognitive trigger (the prospect of promotion), will be needed for a gestalt to form at all.

The orange will be an effective epicenter only if it happens to have temporary significance, perhaps by my hormones signaling that I am thirsty, in conjunction with no competition plus time to recruit an increasing number of associations which would become stronger, like a flame burning out along a network of fuses.

These types of associations could include a trip to Morocco, my mother's tales of the lack of oranges during World War II, and so on. They would deepen my consciousness of the orange as I stared at it in the window. Anyone seeing me would conclude that I was concentrating on the orange.

(Greenfield, 1995: 148)

In Part 1 we described how the environment is interpreted based on memories and how these interpretations form gestalts, and ended with the question: 'So how does it happen that only one or two of these developing neuronal clouds become a consciousness?'

This story about an orange explains one way that the gestalt of an orange becomes a consciousness – based on the status of the hormonal homeostatic system, in this case thirst. This explains why something that quenches thirst becomes a consciousness, but not really why any particular brand of orange is chosen – or, in fact, why an orange is chosen when there are obviously many products in the supermarket that can quench thirst.

To understand the brand choice we need also to consider the pleasure system.

Bio-measures and homeostasis

In Chapter 17 we will discuss the bio-measurements of the brain that are used by suppliers of neuromarketing technology. The measure most commonly used and the one that is most directly linked to the brain is EEG (Electroencephalography) which measures electronic activity in the brain.

Our bodily homeostasis is not determined by electronic activity; hence it is not measured by EEG equipment.

However, as Prof Susan Greenfield explains using the example of an orange, our homeostasis does determine what we give attention to and this attention is electronic activity in the brain, and is what EEG measure.

In the most simple of terms: when a hungry respondent is wired to an EEG machine there should be more electronic activity if food related stimuli is used, as opposed to a respondent who has just had a big meal.

One way to minimize the problem would be to do a fairly large sample and spread this over the times of day hoping that we will even out homeostatic states. But, we are still just hoping.

A second alternative is to ask the respondents about their homeostatic states: are you hungry? This does mean that we need to make a prior assumption about possible homeostatic states that might affect attention.

A third alternative, and this appeals to me, is that we try to induce a homeostatic state in respondents before we measure them. This can be done by way of exposure to stimuli in the measurement process, or even in the area where respondents are waiting to be measured. As an example, if we are doing research about a food product advertisement we can in the research process show pictures of food before we measure the advertisement and get, for each respondent, a pre-measure of their response to food items. Or, we can even decorate the waiting area with food pictures hoping these will induce a state of hunger.

The main point is that in real life homeostasis influences the consumers' decision making. It influences what will be given attention to. It influences the purchase decision in the sense that people buy stuff in anticipation of future homeostatic states. This much we can learn from the neurosciences. What we do with this knowledge is part of this piece of the brain and brand puzzle.

The 'state of mind' system, or moods and arousal

11

One can include the state of mind system with the state of body system; however, they are generally seen as being different in everyday language. We have already noted that the homeostatic system motivates the purchase of many product types. The state of mind system is an important motivator for the purchase of most of the other product types – and is probably involved in the brand decisions for some of the product-type choices motivated by the homeostatic system.

Not only should the brain of the robot rat look after its body, but it should also look after the brain itself. As it stands, the robot-rat's brain is maintained by the scientists who built it; they replace the neurons regularly, feed them, give them oxygen, etc.

Mostly when we talk about the state of mind in everyday language we use the word 'mood': feeling depressed, feeling excited, feeling anxious, feeling motivated, feeling lazy, feeling sad, etc. We often simplify this to saying that 'I am in a good mood' or 'I am in a bad mood'. A mood is really just a state of mind. Like the other feelings we have described so far (emotion and homeostasis), it has a positive or negative valence.

One's mood is strongly determined by the chemical situation of the brain (although not exclusively). A lot of what people do to control their moods has to do with manipulating the chemical composition of their brain at a point in time – hence the term 'mood control drugs'. However, as I will point out, there are many ways one can manipulate the state of one's mood by non-chemical ways (yet these probably just influence the chemical composition of the brain at a point in time).

FIGURE 11.1   The arousal meter

Possibly the most important determinant of the state of mind is the level of arousal that a person experiences at a point in time. Arousal should be considered as being on a continuum varying from low arousal to high arousal. Death would be the lowest level of arousal (ie zero arousal). For consumers, the lowest level of arousal would be when they are sleeping. High levels of arousal would be described as 'being excited'.

Nearly all moods are associated with a level of arousal. In fact the mood word used is often simply a description of the reason for the level of arousal that someone is in.

> Arousal is a physiological and psychological state of being awake. It involves the activation of the reticular activating system in the brain stem, the autonomic nervous system and the endocrine system, leading to increased heart rate and blood pressure and a condition of sensory alertness, mobility and readiness to respond.
>
> There are many different neural systems involved in what is collectively known as the arousal system. Four major systems originating in the brainstem, with connections extending throughout the cortex, are based on the brain's neurotransmitters, acetylcholine, norepinephrine, dopamine, and serotonin. When these systems are in action, the receiving neural areas become sensitive and responsive to incoming signals.
>
> Arousal is important in regulating consciousness, attention, and information processing. It is crucial for motivating certain behaviours, such as mobility, the pursuit of nutrition, the fight-or-flight response and sexual activity. It is also very important in emotion, and has been included as a part of many influential theories such as the James–Lange theory of emotion. According to Hans Eysenck, differences in baseline arousal level lead people to be either extroverts or introverts. Later research suggests it is most likely that extroverts and introverts have different arousability. Their baseline arousal level is the same, but the response to stimulation is different.
>
> The Yerkes–Dodson Law states that there is a relationship between arousal and task performance, essentially arguing that there is an optimal level of arousal for performance, and too little or too much arousal can adversely affect task performance. One interpretation of the Yerkes–Dodson Law is the Easterbrook Cue-Utilisation hypothesis. Easterbrook states that an increase of arousal leads to a decrease in number of cues that can be utilized.
>
> (Wikipedia, 'Arousal')

Why the brain needs to control its levels of arousal

On the importance of the level of arousal, Susan Greenfield states:

> Strength (recruiting power) of the epicenter (of neuronal clouds) might interact with arousal to generate three different situations.
>
> For gestalt formation and for consciousness, it is very important if arousal is low, medium or high.
>
> When arousal is high and the epicenter strong then only small gestalts are formed because of the rapid imposition of new epicenters bombarding our senses due to high arousal and the constant exposure to new aspects of the external world, themselves due to the attendant high degrees of restlessness and movement.
>
> Now imagine a situation where the converse applies. We are readily distracted, less aroused, but the focus of our consciousness is still strong. In such cases, when arousal levels are more moderate, gestalt formation is larger because the epicenter acts as a raindrop in a puddle where the ripples are unopposed. We are paying attention, deeply conscious of a specific object.
>
> In the third situation arousal is low. Because we are asleep and the epicenters are completely internally driven, and thus weak, gestalts are again small. Consciousness is composed of mere fragments: We are dreaming.
>
> (Greenfield, 1995)

It is generally accepted that the brain functions best at a mid-range of arousal, but needs periods of low arousal (sleep) and periods of high arousal.

It is especially gestalt formation that is affected by the level of arousal of the brain. At low levels of arousal, gestalt formation is sluggish. It is as if one gestalt dominates the brain and competing gestalts cannot 'get attention'. Think of someone who is really drunk who seems to fixate on one idea and cannot be persuaded to think of anything else. At high levels of arousal, gestalt formation is very high and it is as if everything becomes a consciousness, making it hard to think about any one thing at a time. Anxiety would be a good example of high levels of arousal, as would the presence of danger in the environment. A good way of describing this is that one is living inside a fireworks display where every gestalt becomes a consciousness and the previous one has disappeared before one can give it any attention. It is important for the brain to be at a high level of arousal when there is danger. It needs to scan the environment for where the threat is coming from and what the response alternatives are. However, continued high levels of arousal are called attention deficit disorder (ADD), and parents of children who suffer from ADD will tell you how difficult life is for these children. Again this is because too many gestalts become a consciousness for them to be able to concentrate fruitfully on any particular one. Another good example would be anxiety attacks, which are even more debilitating.

Mood and time

I show mood as a half-circle in the schema in Figure 11.2 to denote that it develops over time and then decreases over time. However, a mood can start nearly instantaneously without any slow onset as described in the schema, or it can slowly build. A mood can disappear nearly instantaneously or slowly decrease. A mood might be fleeting or it might last for a long time. If a mood is not changed after a long period it will be considered to be a mood disorder. This might require intervention by prescription drugs to normalize the person.

FIGURE 11.2   Feelings schema: mood

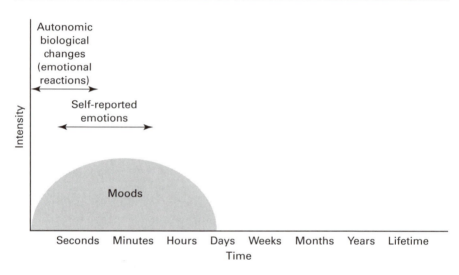

The important point for marketing is that moods form a background feeling against which emotions play. The mood that we are in will have a strong effect on our emotions: whether we experience an emotion when we see something and what form that emotion has. The emotions we experience could also have a effect on our mood. There will be an interaction between our bodily homeostasis and the mood we are in.

We continuously control our moods

What all animals do is to work continuously at adjusting their level of arousal. There are many ways that we try to calm ourselves – not only by sleeping regularly, which is hormonally induced, but also by listening to music, being in a calm environment, eating, being sociable, behaving in an introverted way, and so on. There are just as many ways that we increase our levels of arousal: playing, visiting Disney World, moving faster, having sex, behaving in an extroverted way, travelling, exploring, and so on.

Humans have the ability to make things, and we have managed to manufacture drugs that we can use to control our state of mind: tea, coffee, cigarettes, alcohol, exercise, drugs, prescription drugs and so on.

As a self-exercise, just think of how many brands use their effect on your mood (level of arousal) as a positioning: brands that will increase your excitement, brands that will make you feel calm, brands that will decrease your anxiety, brands that will make you sociably accepted, and so on. These brands are working via the brain's neurotransmitters, and they all work on the developing gestalts in the brain in the same way as the homeostatic system works to make some gestalts a consciousness. Just as consumers use brands to keep their bodily state in balance, so they use brands to keep their state of mind in balance. Not only do they use the brands that deliver chemical control, like tea and coffee, but they also use brands that have an effect on moods.

This is where things start to become interesting to a marketer. When we considered the 'bodily state' feelings, it was obvious that the feeling of hunger could be resolved with almost any food and that brands had limited ability to discriminate themselves. However, this is not true for 'states of mind'. It used to be that when I got into my Mercedes-Benz I might feel a mood of calm superiority settle on me. When my neighbour gets into his Porsche he might feel a mood of excitement settle on him. Unfortunately when my third Mercedes-Benz also gave me engine problems the mood I experienced when I got into the car was apprehension at whether it would start, and when my children ridiculed me for being a Mercedes fan despite the way the car treated me this had enough of an effect on me for me to buy a different brand. My choice was defined by the expected mood effects of the brand.

Some people listen to classical music and drink expensive red wine to relax. Some listen to Bob Dylan and drink beer to relax. Some people drink expensive bottled water to be in a good mood (some of them would be in a bad mood if they had to settle for a beer).

On my website (**www.erikdup.com**) I have a video of a genetically altered rat that became more adventurous than the rest. The point of this video is that personality can also be determined by our genes – and I address this later in this book. But the introduction of the video comments that some of us find snow-surfing exciting and others find reading a thriller exciting. Both of these are activities that increase our arousal levels. This also points toward the interactions between personalities and moods.

Marketers use moods extensively to differentiate their brands, and it works very well when done right. You need to convince the potential consumers of your brand that it is unique in creating a certain mood. This means not only stating that your brand will create this mood, but justifying why, demonstrating that it does so by being at occasions when people experience this mood, by using all the touchpoints that the brand has with the consumer, and often also ensuring that people who are not in the target market know what the brand stands for.

Going back to my experience with my Mercedes-Benz: my mood of calm superiority disappeared when my children told me they thought I was an old emotional fool for driving another one. Your mood is often determined by what others (non-users) think of your brand.

It is also worth considering the audience's mood when you do media planning. This is specially so now that time shifting of programmes is increasingly popular. It used to be that people had to watch programmes when they were transmitted. This might be just after people had arrived home from work or been obliged to explain to their children why they should do their homework, and so on. They were probably not in a good mood, and much of an advertisement might be wasted on them. Now that people can easily time-shift their viewing they do not need to watch a programme while they are in a bad mood. They can shift it to a time when they are in the mood for the programme. If they feel like a good laugh they can choose to watch a good comedy. If they feel like relaxing with a movie they can do so. If they feel like becoming aroused by some sport they can choose that (although sport programmes are less often time-shifted).

Consider these activities and work out what mood effects they have (at least just in terms of level of arousal – calming or exciting):

Drinking coffee	Bungee jumping	Smoking
Drinking tea	Flying a glider	Going to church
Driving a Harley	Flirting	Shopping
Buying a present	Visiting a Friend	Watching TV
Planning a holiday	Having a chat	Attending sports games
Eating at a restaurant	Being on Facebook	Gardening
Listening to Bob Dylan	Solving a crossword	Attending the opera
Listening to Rap	Jogging	After work drinks
Opening a saving acc.	Sunday family meal	Christmas
Buying life insurance	Drinking alcohol	Surfing the web

It is quite amazing how much we do to control our moods, or how much things we do influence our moods. In fact it is difficult to think of many things we do that don't affect our mood. But, these activities will have different effects on different people.

This is really the domain of brands: where the brand we use has a big influence on the effect on our mood.

Bio-measures, mood and arousal

We concluded Chapter 10 with a discussion of the effects that their homeostasis will have on a respondent's EEG readings. This effect will appear more as a product category effect rather than brands.

From the foregoing it is obvious that mood will have an effect on the readings for brands, and arousal will have a general effect on our EEG readings.

Arousal is easier to deal with so let's start there. Respondents at a low level of arousal will have less electronic activity and those at a high level of arousal will have more. When EEG measures are taken the researcher will, before the stimuli is exposed, measure the brain activity with no stimuli, or some simple stimuli. This is called the base level measure. Reactions to the stimuli are always taken as variations from this base level rather than the absolute reading. This compensates for the level of arousal at the time of measurement.

I have had EEG measures done on me on several occasions. I can assure the reader that when you have electrodes around your head and you are asked to do certain tasks you are not in a state of low arousal, so this should never be a problem.

The problem on the other hand, is that viewers of advertising might often be in a state of very low arousal, or in a state of very high arousal (just as bad for the advertisement's effect). This we must bear in mind when we start to flight an advertisement and when we interpret our EEG measures. I discuss (in Chapter 24) that one of the benefits that personal video recorders have for advertisers is that viewers have to give attention when they fast-forward advertisements, and they can view programmes when their level of arousal is suited to the occasion.

This brings us back to the issue that respondents in an advertising test are forcibly exposed to the advertisement – ie that the advertisement does not have to attract attention in a research project the way that it has to do in real life. I discuss this extensively in *The Advertised Mind*.

Researchers have tried to counter this problem by using show reels and then doing a recall test compensating for recency and primacy effects using norms. This does not yield anything worthwhile – in fact it just wastes the respondent's time and provides the researcher with a false sense of security.

Gordon Brown (founder of Millward Brown) was the first researcher to recognize the solution to the problem is to ask respondents introspective questions about the advertisement, and that some questions allow one to predict whether people will give the advertisement attention. In *The Advertised Mind* I explain why the most important question you can ask in this regard is whether people like the advertisement.

Whilst it is easy to discuss the effects of arousal on EEG measures, the effect of moods is really difficult to isolate.

Whilst homeostasis and arousal have a general effect on the measures, and homeostasis has a strong effect on what we buy, moods have a very big effect on our brand choices. Ultimately we are interested in brands.

I explained that we consume brands (including non-packaged goods) to influence our mood. We buy brands so that we can eventually consume them. This means that we are not necessarily in a mood that leads us to buy them at the time that we buy them. This also means that we are seldom in the mood that we will be trying to achieve by their consumption when we are exposed to their advertising!

Now this is not a problem for neuroscience or neuromarketing. It is just a simple fact of life and has always been a problem for research (and advertising, shopping science, retail, etc.). We get respondents or shoppers or clients in a specific mood which will be different than the mood effect they are consuming the brand for.

From a marketer's perspective it is mostly very important to know what mood effect the consumers are trying to achieve (bearing in mind that different people might use the same product type – or brand – for different mood effects), and then to know whether their advertising is causing the brand to be considered for that mood effect.

EEG alone is unlikely to give marketers the answer. This can only be measured by introspective questions.

The contribution from neuroscience is to make people much more aware of the importance of brands as mood moderators.

The evaluation system: pleasure

12

Brands are marketed mainly on one of two platforms: 1) the brand will make you feel less bad, ie avoid or solve homeostatic or mood problems; or 2) the brand will make you feel good, ie reward you in some way. Whilst one can philosophize about whether feeling good is just a result of not feeling bad, the biological basis for feeling good is different from the feeling bad system. This is really where we are getting to the neuroscience that will have the most impact on marketing in the future.

We have now improved the robot rat considerably – it is beginning to be able to behave like the fruit fly.

We know that with the neuronal system connected to sensors on the robot itself the brain will receive inputs in the form of electronic pulses. We know that the neurons so stimulated will recruit other neurons based on the limens of the synapses and that these limens are what memories are. This process of recruitment is really what we call interpretation. It takes the form of developing gestalts.

We know that these gestalts are developing continuously and totally involuntarily. This could mean that the areas of the brain that are supposed to think would be flooded with gestalts and not be able to do anything. Therefore the brain needs ways in which to determine which of these gestalts will be thought about (become a consciousness).

Loud and big events outside the body will create bigger epicentres and attract attention. But we are seldom surrounded by such events. If a developing gestalt includes an emotional memory then this would increase the chances of this gestalt becoming something that will be given attention to. If a developing gestalt is a solution to some bodily state problem that exists at the time, or might arise in the future, then it will be likely to get attention. If a developing gestalt is able to address a mood issue that exists at the time, or might arise in the future, then it will have a better chance of getting attention. The level of arousal of the brain at the time will also determine whether the gestalt is competing against many or just a few.

The fact that something becomes a consciousness does not mean it will be reacted to. In my talks I use a slide that reads 'Feeling Bad'; I explain the bodily state system and mention that the homeostatic system is mostly a 'negative feeling' system. I then have a slide that reads 'Feeling Good'; I explain the pleasure system and how it determines the brand choice.

In terms of the decision-making process, the 'feeling bad' system probably initiates most behaviour. This is true for not only food, water, warmth, etc but also non-consumer things like cars, banks, jobs, etc. People (as opposed to other animals) have a better ability to plan ahead, knowing that in the future the 'feeling bad' feelings will arise and they need to make plans to avoid these – a car to go to the shop, a bank to save money in, etc.

Most marketers would argue that people use their brands for the pleasure they derive from using the brand. It is probable that you eat because you are hungry, but what you eat will be the thing that gives you the most pleasure. Tap water, Perrier, Coca-Cola and beer will all satisfy the basic 'feeling thirsty'. However, people will get different degrees of pleasure from each of these, and personal preferences (the pleasure that can be derived) will even change between drinking occasions.

When making a decision, consumers will choose what gives them the most pleasure and avoid what is unpleasant. Here is another very good reason why brands exist: brands are there to give people pleasure.

The biology that underlies this system that enables the brain to make choices that will give the most pleasure is well understood, owing to re-search into drugs and addiction, which is an area of research that has been given a lot of priority. Scientists have identified several structures, mostly in the limbic system, that are now called the 'reward circuit'. This circuit involves especially dopamine and also serotonin. Opioid receptors also seem to be involved in this circuit.

On my website I have placed a link to a little game developed by the University of Utah called 'The mouse party', which allows you to inspect what different recreational drugs do inside the brain (**http://learn.genetics. utah.edu/content/addiction/drugs/mouse.html**). Recreational drugs have many reactions in different parts of the brain. However, all recreational drugs have an effect on the reward circuit and especially the neurotransmit-ter dopamine. Dopamine is released in the synapses when you 'feel good'. But after it has done its job by exciting the receiving neurons it is taken up again. Drugs interfere with this process by either blocking the re-uptake of dopamine or stimulating dopamine release or even simulating dopamine.

(In fact, this description might not be accurate: it is probably the case that we feel good because dopamine is released, rather than that dopamine is released because we feel good.)

There are many ways that consumers create a feel-good situation: not only by what they eat or drink but also by things like pleasurable social contact, receiving recognition, status and so on.

The brain lays down memories all the time, and does so involuntarily. We remember not only what we were doing but also how we felt as a result of what we were doing. This feeling good memory is created by the dopamine that is being released.

It now seems that when you see something that gives you pleasure (or just think of something pleasurable) then dopamine is released as if you are consuming the thing. In fact, the evidence is that more dopamine might be released by thinking of something than is released when you consume it.

> Dopamine's role in experiencing pleasure has been questioned by several researchers. It has been argued that dopamine is more associated with anticipatory desire and motivation (commonly referred to as 'wanting') as opposed to actual consummatory pleasure (commonly referred to as 'liking').
>
> ... Dopamine is closely associated with reward-seeking behaviours, such as approach, consumption, and addiction. Recent researches suggest that the firing of dopaminergic neurons is a motivational substance as a consequence of reward-anticipation. This hypothesis is based on the evidence that, when a reward is greater than expected, the firing of certain dopaminergic neurons increases, which consequently increases desire or motivation towards the reward.
>
> ... Clues to dopamine's role in motivation, desire, and pleasure have come from studies performed on animals. In one such study, rats were depleted of dopamine by up to 99 per cent in the nucleus accumbens and neostriatum using 6-hydroxydopamine. With this large reduction in dopamine, the rats would no longer eat by their own volition. The researchers then force-fed the rats food and noted whether they had the proper facial expressions indicating whether they liked or disliked it. The researchers of this study concluded that the reduction in dopamine did not reduce the rat's consummatory pleasure, only the desire to actually eat. In another study, mutant hyperdopaminergic (increased dopamine) mice show higher 'wanting' but not 'liking' of sweet rewards.
>
> (Wikipedia, 'Dopamine')

In other words, when I am shopping and standing in front of a shelf looking at the brands that are available, when I see a brand that I have fond memories of I actually get a dopamine release as if I am using it.

The term 'shopaholic' is probably not very far-fetched. People get dopamine experiences via the same mechanism that creates drug addictions.

It is generally accepted that your brain has an 'as if' circuitry. In other words, the parts involved in planning not only receive input from the limbic system but also send back 'thoughts' to the limbic system for interpretation. This makes it possible for me to think about things that are not in my presence and also to have a dopamine evaluation of how much these would contribute to my pleasure. (It would appear that the idea of 'thinking happy thoughts' is not ridiculous, but based on sound biology.) This 'as if' function of the brain allows me to evaluate plans I make for the future, and if these plans include a brand then obviously I will be inclined to buy the brand to execute the plan.

At this point I should make it clear that I am not suggesting some hedonistic view of irrational consumers being driven by their feelings. All that this reward system does is to include in the developing interpretation (gestalt) how people would feel. The frontal lobes will consider alternatives and how these would make you feel before they make a decision – and remember that the decision might simply be to do nothing.

'Dopaminic memories' of brands

I have structured the book to discuss the biological brain first and to discuss marketing implications (as far as I can see them arising) after that. However, I believe readers will be interested in some marketing thoughts at this first stage.

I worked for BBDO advertising well after they started the Pepsi Generation advertising campaign, but executives involved in this told me how they created the campaign that is often considered to be the start of lifestyle advertising. The challenge was to find moments that young people felt good about and that could be associated with Pepsi. The idea was to find out about such moments in their lives. I term such moments 'dopamine moments'.

As dopamine creates expectations when people consider brands, a major function of advertising is to create memories of such moments and thus keep these memories fresh. We will later consider that it is possible to create false memories, ie that people can believe that something happened to them that did not really happen to them. The key to false memories is that the event could have occurred. If it is likely that an event could have occurred to you, it is sometimes possible to convince you that it actually happened.

To my mind, dopamine moments might be one of four types:

1 pleasant things that actually happened to me as a result of the brand, or at a time when the brand was there;

2 pleasant things that actually happened to me, not as a result of the brand or when the brand was there, but that I might believe happened as a result of the brand or the brand being there (ie implantable memories);

3 pleasant things that might have happened to me;

4 pleasant things that will happen to me as a result of the brand or of the brand being there.

A major objective in research, especially qualitative research, has to be to identify such moments – dopamine-inducing moments.

Once one has a good hold on such dopamine moments and the feelings that the moment evoked one can start to build this into the brand promise and make it the basis for the creative approach. In the above four situations, such moments must be credible for the brand.

Bio-measures and dopamine

One can easily understand that the dopamine system is the most important system as far as brand marketing is concerned. All you have to do is make sure that your brand releases more dopamine when the consumer thinks about the brand than any other competing brand. In fact, this might be the best definition of the objective of all marketing activity inside this developing era of neuromarketing.

The release of dopamine is in itself not an electronic activity that can be measured by EEG. However, this is overcome by trying to measure whether the parts of the brain that are implicated in the dopamine pathways are activated by a stimulus.

In Chapter 22 I discuss Read Montague's experiment replicating the famous Pepsi Challenge of the 1970s: people were asked to conduct a blind taste test of Pepsi and Coke. In this neuro-experiment respondents did a taste test of Pepsi and Coke while they were in an fMRI machine having their brains scanned. This succeeded in showing whether the pleasure system was activated by the consumption of the brands.

Martin Lindstrom (see Chapter 20) also managed to measure the pleasure system being activated by the consumers interpreting stimuli.

Unfortunately, at this stage, it still appears as if there are insurmountable problems with measuring the dopamine effect of brands and/or advertising:

1 EEG measures only activity near the scalp and the dopamine system is deeper in the brain.

2 fMRI is unwieldy and expensive to use; it also does not measure as frequently as EEG (ie less able to measure when activations occur).

3 Whatever approach one tries the key, possibly, will have to be not whether the dopamine system was activated, but to be able to measure the extent that it was activated – ie which brand creates the most dopamine.

13 Personality

Personality is part of the feelings that people have. In this chapter I describe the evolutionary reason for personality. Personality has a major influence on brand choice, and is a major variable for marketers when they position brands.

It is obvious that we exhibit our personalities by our behaviours. It is what we do under certain circumstances that makes people ascribe a personality to us. Think of: extroverted, introverted, brave, cowardly, honest, deceitful, shy, sociable, confident, etc. We may have different personalities genetically. There is an evolutionary reason for different personalities. In the tribe there should be leaders, followers, fighters, caregivers and so on. Just as evolution does not create all of us strong and fit, but uses diversity to find the combinations that survive best in the climate that surrounds us, so it also produces different personality types.

On my website I show a video of a mouse that is genetically more adventurous than other mice of its species (see **http://www.erikdup.com/About_Personality.php**). The scientists at the Fred Hutchinson Cancer Research Center, Seattle have isolated an 'adventurous gene'. One can easily understand that this mouse is the one that will find food and lead its family to food, and hence the whole tribe. Unfortunately it might also be the one that gets killed the first. So it is not a good idea for too many of the mice in the tribe to have this gene, in the same way as it is a bad idea for none to have this gene.

Human 'personality' variation

A big question is whether one is born with a personality or 'acquires' a personality through experiences. From a marketer's perspective the issue has to be less about how personality traits originate and more about the simple fact that they exist.

Personality can be defined as a dynamic and organized set of characteristics possessed by a person that uniquely influences his or her cognitions, motivations, and behaviors in various situations. The word 'personality' originates from the Latin *persona*, which means mask. Significantly, in the theatre of the ancient Latin-speaking world, the mask was not used as a plot device to disguise the identity of a character, but rather was a convention employed to represent or typify that character.

    ... The study of personality has a rich and varied history in psychology, with an abundance of theoretical traditions. The major theories including dispositional (trait) perspective, psychodynamic, humanistic, biological, behaviorist and social learning perspective. There is no consensus on the definition of 'personality' in psychology. Most researchers and psychologists do not explicitly identify themselves with a certain perspective and often taken an eclectic approach. Some research is empirically driven such as the 'Big 5' personality model whereas other research emphasizes theory development such as psychodynamics. There is also a substantial emphasis on the applied field of personality testing.

(Wikipedia, 'Personality psychology')

There exists a body of marketing research that classifies respondents into 'personality types', and from this tries to develop marketing strategies where brands are positioned so that they meet the needs of specific types.

What is personality?

What do we mean when we say that someone is a certain personality? Generally we use words that I have classified under 'moods'. We could talk about a person as being excitable, fun-loving, depressing and so on. When we classify people as being a certain personality type we often mean that they are more prone to exhibit a specific mood than other people would be.

It is not survival of the fittest, but death to the unfit

An African story: In Africa each lion wakes up knowing it has to be faster than the slowest buck in the herd. In Africa each buck wakes up knowing it has to be faster than the slowest buck in the herd.

Darwin never said it is survival of the fittest. This was only attributed to him much later. What he said is that nature will weed out the unfit. However, fitness is very relative. There is a great survival benefit to working together, and this is the basis of herds, flocks, tribes and so on. When a species starts to form a group, then there is a greater advantage to there being differentiation inside the tribe, herd or flock. If every member of the group is an alpha male then the group will not survive. If there is diversity things might work better. A group that has a leader (alpha male), some warriors, some workers, some thinkers, some breeders and so on will work better than one that has only one type of personality. It is likely that nature has found a solution to this need for diversity by way of DNA variation and probably learning (or experience). This is what is needed in a community for it to survive. Some should go out and explore, but they run the risk of being killed. Some should stay at home and look after the group, but then the group misses out on finding richer pastures.

Whilst DNA is recently implicated in creating different personalities through genetic variation, this certainly does not imply that all, or even most, variations in personality are genetically determined. The experiences that a person has must still be the single largest contributor to personality.

Personality and time

All the types of feelings we have considered so far have an onset and an end. They all also are of relatively short duration. Personality seems to have a very long duration, and some parts of a person's personality might last a lifetime (see Figure 13.1). Similarly many elements of a personality seem to be developed at an early age (via genes or experiences). As for the other

FIGURE 13.1   Feelings schema: personality

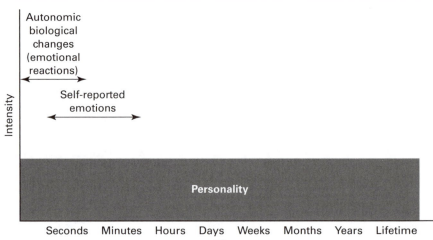

background feelings, the emotions different people will experience about the same thing in the environment will be different depending on their personalities among other things.

The difference between the influence of mood and homeostasis and that of personality is that personality is much more constant. The problem from a neuro-measurement perspective is that we measure short-term changes in the brain (emotions). The reaction that we measure will depend not only on the stimulus material used (an advertisement or logo) but also on the personality of the person being exposed to this stimulus.

What does this have to do with brands?

Personality has a lot to do with brands, and has frequently been used by marketers to position brands.

Think about the positioning of motor cars against personalities that are status conscious, adventurous or economy concerned, seek safety, and so on. A very blatant use of personality types is often the use of a spokesperson for the brand and the use of known personalities to promote the brand. It is very popular to segment markets based on personality traits and then derive strategies targeting a specific type of person.

Marketing

From a marketing perspective this is where things become more interesting.

People become hungry in the same way, by hormones affecting the hypothalamus. People will choose the way they solve this problem by way of their frontal lobes considering alternatives and setting in motion plans (choices). But this is where the similarities end. People's choices will depend on their memories (experiences). For different people the available (considered) options will evoke different dopaminic memories, and this will influence their choice. One seldom has the option of having (say) a chocolate. One can only have a brand of chocolate. This is where the dopaminic memories come into play.

This will be so for your 'solution' not only of a food type, but also of financial institution, brand of motor vehicle, brand of bicycle, brand of travel, brand of holiday and all decisions – mainly because for all decisions you need to decide on a brand.

A further influence on your decision is the type of personality that you are. There will be a big interplay between the consumer's personality type, the personality type the consumer wishes to project, the memories (experiences) that that personality type is exposed to, and the type of experiences that the specific personality type finds gratifying (dopaminic).

This all relates to 'feelings'. Some personality types (whether because of DNA or experiences) will feel better about some brands than others. This leads into market segmentation and segmentation studies, a topic I discuss in Chapter 27.

There are a multitude of personality types in reality. Not only are there many personality types, but these typologies themselves might overlay each other. As an example there is nothing that suggests an 'innovator' will also be an 'extrovert', or even that an 'extrovert' might be an 'explorer'. The problem that marketers often face is that research companies develop their 'pre-packaged' segmentation schemes and then try to sell this to all marketers. This is a 'Have tool, will travel' approach to marketing. The benefit of these pre-packaged approaches is that the research company has some theories about the personality types and probably has a lot of data about the typologies from other studies. In South Africa marketers can choose between (at least):

- the SAARF segmentation by Lifestyle Measures;
- the VALS system – people with similar values;
- an approach based on Jung's philosophies about archetypes.

All of these are well-developed segmentation schemes of the consumers, but marketers have to decide which one is most applicable to their market, and especially whether any of them are at all applicable to their market. This is discussed in greater depth in Chapter 27.

About brand personality

It is really common among marketers to talk about brands having personalities and to also discuss the desired personality for their brands.

I have moderated many focus groups leading respondents into discussions about brand personalities, and I have done many quantitative research projects using photo-sort techniques to measure purportedly brand image/personality.

The fact that these studies yield statistically stable results does not necessarily mean that brands have personalities.

I suspect that what I reproduce is a user-image. In other words: what do the respondents think the typical user of the brand is like? This will mostly be determined by their actual experiences of the users of the brands.

The fact that the respondents can easily produce a statistically stable picture means that user images are common across the population. I believe that this is often the result of advertising creating (intentionally or inadvertently) such a user image, and that often the brand is used by such stereotypes.

People often use brands to project a certain personality type. In terms of the Wikipedia definition the brand becomes part of the mask that we all have.

Bio-measures and personality

Whilst there is some speculation that personality types influence the base-level of EEG measures, there is no real reason why it should. Because personality does not change in the short term no measure that relies on measuring change will be able to measure personality.

In the introduction to the Fred Hutchinson Institutes video about the genetically altered rat, they say that for some of us skiing down a slope constitutes adventure while for others reading a thriller constitutes adventure. For those that find their adventure in dangerous skiing the activity will lead to an emotional reaction and attention, for those that find adventure in a thriller the skiing activity might also lead to an emotional reaction (fear) and then attention.

EEG measures can measure whether there is increased electronic activity in the brain; EEG can even, purportedly, deduce whether this is emotional or rational. However, EEG cannot tell us anything about the nature of the emotion that is causing this activity.

To understand the type of emotion we still have to rely on introspective questions. Since the type of emotion can be influenced by the respondent's personality we are also back to asking introspective questions. When we then analyse the EEG measure against the background of these questions we might understand what is happening in the brain – and why.

This is really a part of the brand-brain puzzle that will require a lot of reviewing by all of us before we can claim to truly understand how it fits into the bigger puzzle.

Social systems and culture

When we use the terms 'the French', 'the British', 'the Irish' and so on as generalizations we often mean a group of people with a preponderance of a certain personality type. Even when we talk about subcultures like 'accountants', 'soccer fans', 'youth' and so on we are talking about a group of people who are seen to have similar personalities. These are generalizations, but most people know what you are talking about. With culture being related to dominant personalities, and personalities to types of dominant moods, we can easily use culture as part of the feelings schema.

The neuro-basis of culture

It is obvious that a person's culture is one of the 'background feelings' that Damasio talks about. Marketers have been aware of this, and it would be a surprise if a trace of this was not found by neurologists.

Another piece of the brain puzzle that has recently emerged from brain imaging is that we possess an 'empathy circuit'. Several books on this topic have appeared recently. I recommend *Making Up the Mind: How the Brain Creates Our Mental World* (2007) by Chris Frith, a professor in neuro-psychology at the Centre for Neuroimaging at University College London. This is an easy-to-understand, well-written book. Neuroimaging has determined which areas of the brain light up when a person experiences pain. The surprise is that when we observe somebody else experiencing pain the same areas light up in our brains. But, you might say, you don't jump around in pain when someone else burns him- or herself. Frith explains:

> How is this possible? How can I experience what you are feeling? We can
> answer this question by looking at precisely which areas light up in the brain

during empathy. As we have seen, activity in some brain areas relates to the physical aspects of the pain: how hot the rod is, or where it is touching you. These areas don't light up when you know that someone else is in pain. Activity in other areas relates to your mental experience of the pain. These areas do light up in response to someone else's pain. So what we can share is the mental experience of the pain, not its physical aspect. These brain areas also become active when you anticipate pain, if you know that 5 seconds after hearing a tone you will be touched by the hot rod. If you can anticipate the pain that you will feel, is it so difficult to anticipate the pain that someone else will feel? Of course we can't experience the physical sensations that impinge on others. But we can construct the mental models based on these stimuli. It is because we make mental models of the physical world that we can share our experiences in the mental world.

Frith also reports that in conversations not only will areas in our brain that reflect the other person's movements light up, but we would often emulate the other person's body behaviour.

Whilst neuro-imaging results are very modern, the phenomenon of empathy was an important issue for Charles Darwin in his book *The Expression of the Emotions in Man and Animals*, another easy-to-read book:

> There are other actions which are commonly performed under certain circumstances, independently of habit, and which seem to be due to imitation or some sort of sympathy. Thus persons cutting anything with a pair of scissors may be seen to move their jaws simultaneously with the blades of the scissors. Children learning to write often twist about their tongues as their fingers move, in a ridiculous fashion. When a public singer suddenly becomes a little hoarse, many of those present may be heard, as I have been assured by a gentleman on whom I can rely, to clear their throats; but here habit probably comes into play, as we clear our own throats under similar circumstances. I have also been told that at leaping matches, as the performer makes his spring, many of the spectators, generally men and boys, move their feet; but here again habit probably comes into play, for it is very doubtful whether women would thus act.
>
> (Darwin, 2006 [1872])

Why do we have an empathy circuit in the brain?

For a good discussion about this system in the brain (note that it is not a unique system, but rather the ability to use a system we use for our own movements also to mirror the movements of others) see McGovern (in Baars and Gage, 2007). This discusses not only the neurological evidence and the parts of the brain involved, but also some of the evolutionary reasons for this system to exist.

According to McGovern (in Baars and Gage, 2007), the first reason is learning from peers. It is assumed that emulating the behaviour of their parents using neuronal systems that would produce a similar outcome is part of the way that infants learn from their peers. Thus, by emulating (say) the sounds of their parents and then the words of their parents children learn language.

Second is intention detection. This is where things become very interesting. It would appear that we are not merely mirroring the actions of others, but even deducing from this what they intend to do. This comes into the area that cognitive psychologists term 'a theory of mind', which roughly reduces to the fact that each of us assumes that other people have minds, and we each have a theory of how their minds work.

Based on this we can then try to deduce what they will do next. In rough terms this means that when we see someone reach for a cup on a table we not only mirror the movement of their arms, but also make suppositions about why they are doing this: to drink water from the cup, to clear the table of the leftovers from lunch, or to throw the cup at us in anger. To survive it is very important to know what others will do.

The best model we have of what others will do is ourselves. So, if our neuro-circuitry allows us to 'feel' what others feel or, rather, interpret how we would feel if we were them, then we can also know what we would do – and this is what we assume they would do.

From a brand perspective it is easy to see how, if I see somebody who is thirsty and I know Evian water would make me feel better had I been thirsty, I would offer him or her some Evian water. If, in my culture, I would feel honoured should somebody offer me the finest ground maize meal and I want to honour you, I would offer you my finest ground maize meal.

One can easily understand why tribes would do battle. We see people from a different tribe near our cattle and assume that they want to steal the cattle because that is what we would have done with their cattle. They, on the other hand, assume that we will attack them to defend our cattle and therefore they hit us before we hit them.

Prejudice

South Africa has a history of racism – which is prejudice. I have always been interested in how prejudice works and what the neurological foundation of prejudice is. Frith (2007) has the following to say about prejudice:

- 'Making guesses about what people are like before we have information about them is prejudging them. It is prejudice. Prejudice might be a dirty word these days, but it is in fact crucial for our brains to function.'

- 'We are innately predisposed to prejudice. All our social interactions begin with prejudice. The content of these prejudices has been acquired through our interactions with friends and acquaintances and through hearsay. I talk differently with my work colleagues than with non-scientists at a party.'

- 'Our prejudices begin with stereotypes. The first clue I can get about the likely knowledge and behavior of someone I know nothing about is from their gender. Even children as young as 3 have already acquired this prejudice. They expect boys to play with trucks and girls to become nurses.'

- 'Social stereotypes provide the starting point for our interactions with people we don't know.'

The important point here is not that having prejudices and stereotyping people are innate, but that they are beneficial for survival and social interactions. This stereotyping of people may lead to socially unacceptable behaviour. What is 'unacceptable behaviour' is determined by the culture itself.

Frith explains that communication is more than just speaking: 'I don't just choose my words because of what they mean; I choose my words to suit the person I am talking to'; 'The more I talk to someone, the better an idea I get of what words will suit – just as I get a better idea of how to perceive the world around me the more I look at it.' These two sentences I would consider to be the best rationale for marketers doing market research, not only when they are moving between cultures, but also inside their own countries and the subcultures that exist there. It is necessary to identify these subcultures (via segmentation studies).

The marketing error resulting from the empathy system

The marketing revolution (if there was one) came about when businesses learned that it is not enough just to produce a better mousetrap, but that it is necessary to produce what the market wants. If, in my nearly 40 years in marketing, I had received $10 for each time brand managers had explained to me why their brand is better than all the others on the market and that the consumer is an idiot, I would have been very wealthy.

The problem is that brand managers often use their empathy circuits. They assume that consumers are like them and will feel the same about the brand's benefits as they do. A similar mistake made by advertising agencies is that they assume the audience for their advertisement will feel the same as they do after viewing it. It really becomes irritating, after a pre-test, when explaining to the management team what the consumer said about the advertisement and someone chirps up that the respondents are obviously idiots.

Teaching feelings

This empathy circuit works very well when people have a lot in common. The more they have in common the more accurate they will be in their guess about what the other person will do. Unfortunately the less they have in common the more they are going to be wrong. Since nobody is exactly the same as anybody else this system has big opportunities for misunderstandings and is not as efficient for survival as it sounds. Humans have a unique ability to learn from communication by others. Frith explains not only how this works but tells the neuroimaging that supports his views:

> This sharing of experience is not just words. When I tell you of my experience, your brain will change as if you had had that same experience. We can show this using Pavlov's technique of conditioning. One such paradigm is fear conditioning. Whenever you receive a painful shock there will be an increase in activity in many brain regions. In Pavlov's terms, the shock is the unconditioned stimulus and brain activity is the unconditioned response. No learning is involved. A painful shock causes these changes in brain and body the very first time we experience it. In the fear-conditioning paradigm a visual cue (a red square, the conditioned stimulus) is presented on a screen just before the shock. After the experience of several such pairings between the red square and the shock, the subject, whether a rat or a human volunteer, will start responding to the red square with fear. One aspect of this fear response is increased activity in the amygdala. The fear associated with the shock has become attached to this arbitrary visual cue.
>
> But there is another way of attaching fear to the red square. This method works only in human volunteers. I tell new, inexperienced volunteers that the red square will be followed by a shock. Before being told this, they show no fear responses to the red square. After being told, they immediately show fear responses to the red square, including activity in the amygdala. My experience that the red square will be followed by a painful shock has created fear in another person's brain.
>
> (Frith, 2007)

This explains how a lot of advertising works. The advertiser does not have to work just with the existing knowledge structures of consumers, but also creates new knowledge structures. I see people in the advertisements using the brand to generate certain feelings, and I actually feel the feeling. But, if I had no knowledge to use, there would be physical changes in my brain that, like the red square, make me feel the feeling.

What is culture?

For all species it is important for their survival to know how to interact with others of their own species and with other species. It is important either to live as a social group or not. They must know not to eat their own kind. If they are a group they must know the social hierarchy of the group. Sometimes they must have sympathy with other members of the group.

> A society is a population of humans characterized by patterns of relationships between individuals that share a distinctive culture and/or institutions. More broadly, a society is an economic, social and industrial infrastructure, made up of a varied multitude of people. Members of a society may be from different ethnic groups. A society may be a particular ethnic group, such as the Saxons, a nation state, such as Bhutan, or a broader cultural group, such as a Western society.
>
> (Wikipedia, 'Society')

It is doubtful that one's culture is caused by the structures of the brain. It is more likely that different human cultures have similarly constructed brains but have learned to use them in different ways. For example, all humans have a language centre in their brain, but they speak different languages. People's feelings are strongly determined by their culture – and what might appear as rational behaviour for one person might appear to be very irrational to another. Once again we are looking at something that might appear to be non-rational but has a great effect on the rational output of the brain.

> Cultures are internally affected by both forces encouraging change and forces resisting change. These forces are related to both social structures and natural events, and are involved in the perpetuation of cultural ideas and practices within current structures, which themselves are subject to change.
>
> Social conflict and the development of technologies can produce changes within a society by altering social dynamics and promoting new cultural models, and spurring or enabling generative action.
>
> These social shifts may accompany ideological shifts and other types of cultural change. For example, the U.S. feminist movement involved new practices that produced a shift in gender relations, altering both gender and economic structures.
>
> Environmental conditions may also enter as factors. For example, after tropical forests returned at the end of the last ice age, plants suitable for domestication were available, leading to the invention of agriculture, which in turn brought about many cultural innovations and shifts in social dynamics.
>
> (Wikipedia, 'Culture')

Let us consider the above comment about the feminist movement in the United States.

In Africa men pay *lobola* to the bride's family when they marry. Generally this is in the form of cows. Traditionally this was because the bride's kraal was losing someone who contributed to the harvest and other hard work, while the groom's kraal gained a pair of hands. However, this system also leads to the groom feeling that he has paid for the bride and she is now his property. The *lobola* system is often blamed for female abuse.

In India marriages are often still arranged. I have heard an anthropologist explain a Lux soap campaign in India, where the bride moves into the groom's household and becomes her mother-in-law's helper with house chores. Because of the extended family situation she will have little privacy and very few 'moments of her own'. One very treasured moment of her own would be when she is taking her bath. The Lux campaign capitalized on this.

The impact of this basic cultural difference has a significant impact on how brands can be promoted in these cultures.

When marketers and researchers talk about culture they often use Hofstede's classification system, probably because no other generalized classification system has really been offered by market researchers.

Hofstede has found five dimensions of culture in his study of national work related values:

- *Low vs. high power distance* – the extent to which the less powerful members of institutions and organizations expect and accept that power is distributed unequally.

- *Individualism vs. collectivism* – individualism is contrasted with collectivism, and refers to the extent to which people are expected to stand up for themselves and to choose their own affiliations, or alternatively act predominantly as a member of a life-long group or organization.

- *Masculinity vs. femininity* – refers to the value placed on traditionally male or female values (as understood in most Western cultures). So called 'masculine' cultures value competitiveness, assertiveness, ambition, and the accumulation of wealth and material possessions, whereas feminine cultures place more value on relationships and quality of life.

- *Uncertainty avoidance* – reflects the extent to which members of a society attempt to cope with anxiety by minimizing uncertainty. Cultures that scored high in uncertainty avoidance prefer rules (eg about religion and food) and structured circumstances, and employees tend to remain longer with their present employer.

- *Long vs. short term orientation* – describes a society's 'time horizon', or the importance attached to the future versus the past and present. In long term oriented societies, values include persistence (perseverance), ordering relationships by status, thrift, and having a sense of shame; in short term oriented societies, values include normative statements, personal steadiness and stability, protecting one's face, respect for tradition, and reciprocation of greetings, favors, and gifts.

These cultural differences describe averages or tendencies and not characteristics of individuals. A Japanese person for example can have a very low 'uncertainty avoidance' compared to a Filipino even though their 'national' cultures point strongly in a different direction. Consequently, a country's scores should not be interpreted as deterministic.

(Wikipedia, 'Geert Hofstede')

Hofstede analysed country cultures of IBM employees. Marketers are very aware of subcultures and that people inside a society can associate themselves with many subcultures, and that we all have some preconceptions about these cultures. As a simple exercise think of two groups in your society: say motor bikers and accountants (I chose these because they are not mutually exclusive). Now rate them on the five dimensions above.

Hofstede said: 'Culture is more often a source of conflict than of synergy. Cultural differences are a nuisance at best and often a disaster.' His work is the only descriptive segmentation of cultures that I am aware of.

One of the main criticisms of the work is that it assumes that country and culture are the same thing, ie it ignores cultural typologies inside countries.

What makes it useful for marketers is that the descriptions of the cultures allow one to generate hypotheses about what the differences in appropriate communication styles (and brand positioning) might be.

One would expect that major marketers should be embarking on multi-country segmentation studies as a basis for how they can position brands in different countries. Such a study will have to be driven by sociologists.

I was involved in an interesting study for Coca-Cola. They had worked out what the international position for one of their brands should be and then did a lot of research in different countries to find the best way of expressing this position. As one would have expected they needed to change the positioning statement several times to find one that is workable in most countries, and then the execution was dramatically different between the US and Chinese cultures despite projecting the same positioning.

Culture and time

Culture, when we consider it at a meta-level such as country or religion, is not something that changes dramatically over time, certainly not with the frequency with which people have mood swings or become hungry and then sated. Because this is often the level at which we consider culture I have shown it to be, like personality, something that affects the consumer now, in the near future and for a long time (Figure 14.1).

When we start to consider culture at a micro-level then it is obvious that people might change between subcultures rather rapidly: you might be an accountant when among fellow accountants, but then adopt the Hells Angels culture when you drive home on your Harley. However, even at a micro-level the cultures we adopt are fairly constant. The Hells Angels culture remains similar between the times you adopt it, or even between countries.

FIGURE 14.1   Feelings schema: culture

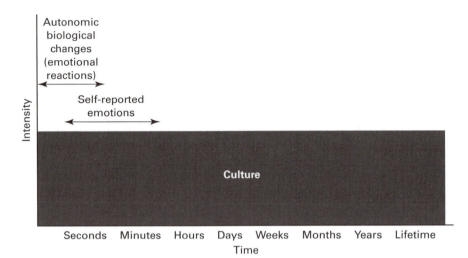

Language

Probably the most distinctive part of culture is language. Generally the definition that people use when they identify a culture in everyday language is the language that a group of people speak.

Because people's growing up, learning and social interactions all happen in a specific language, and because they probably think in that language, the language itself has a great influence on marketing and research. I told the following story in *The Advertised Mind* (2005), but it really demonstrates the problem with culture and languages.

'Black people see fewer colours than whites'

Back in the 1970s South African Breweries used a well-known psychological researcher to conduct focus groups for a label change. In his report he mentioned that he suspected black people see fewer colours than whites. South African Breweries approached me to see whether I could find a way to verify empirically this very unlikely hypothesis.

It was only a few weeks later, when my wife and I were discussing the redecoration of our living room, that I realized what the problem was. She was using terms like 'maroon' and 'beige'. These words do not exist in Afrikaans (my home language), and we would normally just use the Afrikaans words for 'yellow or brownish' and 'dark purple' to talk about these colours. In many cases we would simply use the English word, if it came to mind.

This means that, when I speak about these things (in a focus group conducted in Afrikaans, for instance), I will tend not to use these words. When the focus group is conducted in English and the respondents tend to think in Afrikaans and translate their thoughts into English when they speak the same will happen. To the moderator it might sound as if they do not know the colours or, worse, do not even see them. Whoever interprets the research could be forgiven for thinking I don't see these colours.

How big is the problem?

Webster's English Dictionary is several inches thick, compared to the Zulu dictionary, which is only one inch. There are many more feeling words in English than in Zulu. Does this mean that English-speaking people have many more feelings than Zulus?

Now consider that the 'advances' in language happen mostly when there are technological advances. The smaller language will tend to adopt the English word. The Zulus solved this problem by adding an 'i' as a prefix to the English word. Hence 'i-taxi', 'i-cup', 'i-tea' and 'i-stopstreet' are valid Zulu words. This means that there is much less space for confusion.

However, there are not many new feelings discovered these days. This means that the languages are all using the original word for a specific feeling, and their translation for it. This means that there is a much bigger chance of misinterpretations.

The problem is big not only because of the paucity of some languages to describe feelings, but also because of the size of the non-English-speaking market in the world.

Table 14.1 shows the percentage of different countries' populations who speak English as a first language, or as an additional language (often a third language). Out of the 6.7 billion people on earth only 1.1 billion speak English (17.7 per cent). This is made up of only 331 million people who speak English as a first language, and 812 million who speak English as a second language. It might be that English is the language of business across the world, but it definitely is not the language of the consumer! Even among the 20 countries that have the most English speakers, there are many where English is a very small proportion of the country's population. I was surprised to learn that Nigeria has more English-speaking people than the United Kingdom, although it is mostly only as a second language. Now consider how many cultures there are in the UK, all speaking some form of English. Even jokes do not travel across the United Kingdom.

TABLE 14.1   Top 19 English-speaking countries

Country	Percentage English speakers	Eligible population	Total English speakers	As first language	As an additional language
United States	95.81%	262,375,152	251,388,301	215,423,557	35,964,744
India	10.66%	843,900,000	90,000,000	226,449	65,000,000
Nigeria	53.34%	148,093,000	79,000,000	4,000,000	>75,000,000
United Kingdom	97.74%	60,975,000	59,600,000	58,100,000	1,500,000
Philippines	51.91%	92,000,000	48,800,000	3,427,000	45,373,000
Germany	56%	82,191,000	46,000,000	272,504	46,000,000
Canada	85.18%	33,355,400	25,246,220	17,694,830	7,551,390
France	36%	64,473,140	23,000,000		23,000,000
Australia	97.03%	21,394,309	17,357,833	15,013,965	2,343,868
Pakistan	10.36%	164,157,000	17,000,000		17,000,000
Italy	29%	59,619,290	17,000,000		17,000,000
Netherlands	87%	16,445,000	14,000,000		14,000,000
South Africa	28.63%	47,850,700	13,700,000	3,673,203	10,000,000
Spain	27%	46,063,000	12,500,000		12,500,000
Turkey	17%	70,586,256	12,000,000		12,000,000
Poland	29%	38,115,967	11,000,000		11,000,000
China	0.77%	1,300,000,000	10,000,000		10,000,000
Sweden	89%	9,215,021	8,200,000		8,200,000
Cameroon	41.51%	18,549,000	7,700,000		7,700,000

NOTE: List in order of total English speakers.

SOURCE: Wikipedia, 'List of countries by English-speaking population'.

Oatley and Jenkins's view about culture and emotions

I show the conclusions that Oatley and Jenkins (1996) come to here because I believe they have got it mostly right:

> Emotions are strongly affected by cultural ideas.
>
> In Western culture emotion is rather distrusted, as compared with reason; but at the same time it is valued as the basis of authenticity.
>
> We can recognize our own cultural ideas more acutely by making comparisons, both with historical materials, and with contemporary cultures.
>
> Historically we in the West still seem to be living in an age of romanticism, which has lasted nearly 250 years. As compared with many other cultures worldwide, present-day Euro-American culture is strikingly different in its emphasis on the autonomy of the individual, and on the individual's rights. In such a culture emotions like anger occur at the infringement of such rights.
>
> By contrast many other societies, including Japan, see the social group as the basis of selfhood. They define themselves in terms of duties, and of 'We' rather than 'I', and some emotions of togetherness are hypercognized.
>
> Many cultures stress how emotions mediate relationships – probably Westerners believe this too because we know that love, happiness, sadness, anger, all tend to concern our relations with others. But our emphasis on individuality makes us also believe that emotions are individual states.
>
> Testing the bases of cultural differences is not easy. Certainly the value placed on different emotions, the situations that cause emotions, the names for emotions, and the extensiveness of the vocabulary of emotions, all vary cross-culturally.
>
> The question of how far emotions are universal and how far they are socially constructed by cultures is more difficult. Passionate love, for instance, seems to occur in many cultures. Our own Western culture has a form of it which is not only distinctive, but has particular functions just in our kind of society.
>
> (Oatley and Jenkins, 1996)

This explains very clearly why we should study the effects of culture in this book: culture affects our emotions, even to the extent that we express them and admit to having them.

Oatley and Jenkins also discuss the problems that you encounter when you want to do research about feelings as they relate to your brand and your advertising. First you need a working theory on what emotions, moods, personality and so on are and then how these are affected by culture:

> One of the unresolved issues in emotion research is what emotions are made up of.
>
> One view is that they are made up of components that are not themselves emotions, such as appraisals and pieces of expression. If this were the case it would help understand how different cultures prioritize and name different bundles of such components.

The other view is that there is a small set of biologically given basic emotions, and that these are elaborated by culture to produce the large set of emotions that people experience.

(Oatley and Jenkins, 1996)

The global brand

In 1983 Theodore Levitt published a paper that became famous, 'The globalization of markets', in the *Harvard Business Review*. In essence he argued that the world is becoming flat and that the future of brands lies in globalization. Pankaj Gemawat of the Harvard Business School referred to this as 'globaloney', writing: 'It took Coke the better part of a decade to figure out that globaloney and its strategic implications were hazards to its health – in the course of which its market value declined by about $100 billion, or more than 40% from its peak' (in Hollis, 2008). One might argue that that was 1980 and now is 30 years later, with the internet happening in between.

Since 1998 WPP has conducted a worldwide survey for its constituent companies every year based on the Millward Brown BrandDynamics model. This measures the extent to which consumers are bonded to a brand.

Nigel Hollis, Millward Brown's Chief Global Analyst, analysed the 2008 database to identify which brands have truly succeeded in becoming global, and also what strategies worked for them. He calculated a 'global brand power score'. The highest scores were for Pampers (42.8), Nokia (37.5) and Microsoft (33.0). One can see already how big the distance is between even the top three brands. Among the top 25 brands is Toyota (number 21, with a score of 7.5), HP (number 22, score 7.5) and Vodafone (number 23, score 7.0).

Hollis's book *The Global Brand* (2008) is highly recommended, because it analyses the problems that brands have when they attempt to cross country borders, shows how few are really successful and also makes many suggestions as to what should (not) be done.

Culture is much more than countries

Whilst a lot of my examples here relate to countries, we must be aware that cultures stretch deeper than countries, and culture can be across many countries. Certainly some cultural aspects will transcend different countries, not only in terms of language or religion but in many other respects (level of development, dress code, freedom of personal expression, etc). On the other hand, inside countries there will be many local cultures based on a multitude of things. We mentioned accountants and Hells Angels, but the list goes on and on.

One might have thought that the internet and television would have homogenized cultures. They appear to be doing the opposite in many ways. Subcultures are arising via the social media, and these are seldom bound by physical boundaries to any specific region. The internet has opened new potential disasters for marketers. Different internet social groups might adopt or knock a brand and have an effect on other groups, and this might easily spread worldwide. Certainly the internet messages are not limited to the brand's area of distribution, and therefore damage cannot be contained to a region.

Bio-measures and culture

I am not aware of any neuroscience that indicates differences in brain structures based on cultural differences (even for different nationalities). Because culture does not change while bio-measures are taken techniques that rely on measuring change (EEG) will not measure it directly. This is especially true when comparing Hells Angels and accountants!

However, since our culture has a strong effect on our emotions EEG will measure whether there is an emotional reaction to a stimulus. But, as for many of the background feelings' effects on emotions, one will have to rely on introspective questions to determine the reason for the emotional reaction as well as its valence.

Let us go back to the example of South African biltong (dried meat). Hypothetically, one might get a strong positive emotion from a South African, a strong negative emotional reaction from a Brit, and a neutral reaction from an American (used to jerky). If one was basing your advertising campaign purely on EEG measures of emotional reactions you might conclude that you are getting a reaction from South Africans and Brits and can use the campaign in both countries.

15 Gender differences

I do not include in my feelings schemata gender as a feeling despite it obviously having a big influence on emotions. One might argue that gender is a determinant of personality.

I include a discussion of gender and the brain in this book because gender obviously relates to hormones (at least). Plus the work by Brizendine gives a beautiful insight into how similarly structured organs are used differently.

Some suppliers of neuromarketing equipment argue that one can get away with smaller samples when using these techniques. There is no logic to this: if variation in the universe exists then the sample needs to be bigger. Certainly this chapter shows how big a variation there could be between the genders.

Enjoy.

A major part of what this book is about is the piece of the brain puzzle relating to what hormones do to the brain, and the fact that this is largely ignored in pop-neuromarketing.

Obviously we cannot ask market research respondents to donate blood for analysis to see what their hormonal levels are when being scanned (they might be willing to donate spit?). However, we know that for some hormones there are differences between men and women, and maybe this will help us understand that piece of the puzzle better.

This was part of a study done in 2007:

What influence does the variation in estrogen level have on the activation of the female brain? Using functional Magnetic Resonance Imaging, Jean-Claude Dreher, a researcher at the Cognitive Neuroscience Center (CNRS/Université Lyon 1), in collaboration with an American team from the National Institute of Mental Health (Bethesda, Maryland) directed by Karen Berman, has identified, for the first time, the neural networks involved in processing reward-related functions modulated by female gonadal steroid hormones. This result, which was published online on January 29, 2007 on the PNAS website, is an important step in better comprehension of certain psychiatric and neurological pathologies.

... Estrogens and progesterone are not just sex hormones that influence ovulation and reproduction; they also affect a large number of cognitive and affective functions.

(**ScienceDaily.com**, 11 February 2007)

These observations show that gonadal neurosteroids modulate the female dopaminergic system, but the question remains as to whether these hormones modulate the reward system neuron network.

In order to answer this question, the team developed an experiment using functional Magnetic Resonance Imaging (fMRI). The brain activity of a group of women was examined twice during their menstrual cycle. Each time they went into the MRI, they were presented with virtual slot machines showing different probabilities of winning.

When women anticipate uncertain rewards, they activate the brain regions involved in processing emotions, particularly the amygdala and the orbitofrontal cortex, to a greater extent during the follicular phase (4 to 8 days after the start of the period) than during the luteal phase (6 to 10 after the LH(7) hormone surge).

These results demonstrate increased reactivity of the female recompense system during the follicular phase, which is also the phase in which the estrogens do not oppose the progesterone.

In order to determine the gender-related differences of reward system activation, the same experiment was carried out on a male group. Result: when men anticipate rewards, they mainly activate a region involved in motivation for obtaining rewards, the ventral striatum, whereas in women, it is a region dealing with emotions, the amygdalo-hippocampal region, which is the most highly activated.

(**ScienceDaily.com**)

The difference between men and women was also the topic for a 2008 study, this time considering reactions to stress:

Functional magnetic resonance imaging of men and women under stress showed neuroscientists how their brains differed in response to stressful situations. In men, increased blood flow to the left orbitofrontal cortex suggested activation of the 'fight or flight' response. In women, stress activated the limbic system, which is associated with emotional responses.

(**ScienceDaily.com**, 1 April 2008)

The way that the scientists introduced stress in this experiment was to ask the respondents to count backward from 1,600 in steps of 13.

Marketers sometimes try to induce stress in the advertising by way of telling people what would happen if they are not insured, or if they use cheap tyres, or if their toilets smell, or if their children are not being given the best, and so on. All of these messages are professionally executed and likely to be more stressful than counting backwards. Advertisers should be aware not only that their audiences might respond differently, but also that they might be using different areas of their brains. For marketers who are using biological response measures of reactions to advertising and brands this becomes very important.

Mostly what is measured is emotions, and here I am using the definition I set up for the book. These are measured by EEG methodologies reliant on electrodes measuring electronic activity in the brain. These activities occur against the backdrop of the background feelings (hormonal, cultural, etc). This will lead to different responses by different people depending on the state of the background feelings at the time of measurement.

From a technical perspective neuromarketers will need to know what the background feelings are that they should monitor before the experiment, and this will probably have to be done using introspective questions of respondents. Some of these questions might even be the type that respondents consider personal, for example 'At what stage of your menstrual cycle are you today?'

It goes without saying that a marketing message never finds a respondent with no background feelings at the time. In fact, in my experience, it is often the case that a marketing communication is designed to work better on a consumer who is in a certain mood or hormonal state (eg hungry, relaxed, excited).

This implies that market researchers will need to know, from the client briefing, whether there is a specific set of background feelings that the advertiser hopes to find the respondent in, and then to induce this into the research design. This we seldom do at this stage.

The male/female brain

Many people told me that they enjoyed reading *The Advertised Mind* not only for what it taught them about the consumer, but also for what they learned about their own brain. I hope that readers of this book have a similar experience. Two books that gave me such an experience are *The Female Brain* (2007) and *The Male Brain* (2010) by neuro-psychologist Louann Brizendine. Both books are a combination of psychological observation studies and neurology, and move easily between these. They are both designed to be easy reads.

Brizendine considers two dimensions: the differences between male and female brains; and the changes that occur to these brains over time (age).

Being a recent grandfather of boys and girls, I really enjoyed learning why they behaved differently from each other, and also comparing the differences between the life stages of the grandchildren, the children and my wife and me.

Brizendine's books did not get past without receiving some heavy criticisms on **amazon.com** from readers, but then that is the nature of the site. This did not make me feel that anything Brizendine said was really wrong.

Anybody in the marketing communication business will benefit from reading these books for ideas on how to create communications that are more effective.

The following quotes are all from *The Male Brain* (Brizendine, 2010).

> As a medical student I had been shocked to discover that major scientific research frequently excluded women because it was believed that their menstrual cycles would ruin the data. That meant that large areas of science and medicine used the male as the 'default' model for understanding human biology and behavior, and only in the past few years has that really begun to change.

This quote, with the 2007 and 2008 studies quoted above, should lead us all to think carefully when we read about the conclusions of neuromarketing studies. Respondents are different, except when they are the same.

> Male and female brains are different from the moment of conception. It seems obvious to say that all the cells in a man's body and brain are *male*. Yet this means there are deep differences, at the level of every cell, between the male and female brain. A male has a Y chromosome and the female does not. That small but significant difference begins to play out early in the brain as genes set the stage for later amplification by hormones. By eight weeks after conception, the tiny male testicles begin to produce enough testosterone to marinate the brain and fundamentally alter its structure.
>
> ... In the female brain, the hormones estrogen, progesterone and oxytocin predispose brain circuits towards female-typical behaviors. In the male brain it's testosterone, vasopressin, and a hormone called MIS that have the earliest and most enduring effects. The behavioral influences of male and female hormones on the brain are major.
>
> We have learned that men use different brain circuits to process spatial information and solve emotional problems.
>
> Their brain circuits and nervous system are wired to their muscles differently – especially in the face.
>
> The female and male brains hear, see, intuit, and gauge what others are feeling in their own special ways. Overall, the brain circuits in male and female brains are very similar, but men and women can arrive at and accomplish the same goals and tasks using different circuits.

Brizendine and some reviewers of her book note that many said that a book about the male brain would be a very short book:

> We also know that men have two and a half times the brain space devoted to the sexual drive in their hypothalamus. Sexual thoughts flicker in the background of a man's visual cortex all day and night, making him always ready for seizing sexual opportunities.

... Men also have larger brain centers for muscular action and aggression. His brain circuits for mate protection and territorial defense are hormonally primed for action starting at puberty.

Pecking order and hierarchy matter more deeply to men than most women realize.

Men also have larger processors in the core of the most primitive area of the brain, which registers fear and triggers protective aggression – the amygdala. This is why some men will fight to the death defending their loved ones.

What's more, when faced with a loved one's emotional distress, his brain area for solving and fixing the situation will immediately spark.

We all are aware of these male behaviours. A lot of brands and advertising are specifically based on them.

Brizendine spells out one of the basic arguments that I have extensively explained in this book:

Our understanding of essential gender differences is crucial because biology does not tell the whole story. While the distinction between boy and girl brains begins biologically, recent research shows that this is only the beginning. The brain's architecture is not set in stone at birth or by the end of childhood, as was once believed, but continues to change throughout life.

Rather than being immutable, our brains are much more plastic and changeable than scientists believed a decade ago. The human brain is also the most talented learning machine we know. So our culture and how we are taught to behave play a big role in shaping and reshaping our brains.

Earlier I mentioned how dopamine is an important neurotransmitter that influences what we decide to do. I also mentioned how our brain actually makes use of circuitry related to muscular actions when we think about doing something. Here is Brizendine's version: 'Research from Stanford shows that playing Wii activates parts of the male brain linked to dopamine production. Boys get rewarded by this feel-good brain chemical, just as they do when roughhousing. The more opponents they conquer, the more stimulated their male brain becomes, and the more dopamine their brains release' (Brizendine, 2010, *The Male Brain*). I never quite understood why I played computer games till the early-morning hours, as did my sons, and neither my wife nor my daughters showed any interest in such games. Yet they did play Sims.

My intention is not to plagiarize *The Male Brain*, which would in any case deny the reader the pleasure of reading it. I want to use it to demonstrate the role of background feelings and how they potentiate certain things for attention.

However, since I started research for this book I have become interested in the biology of love. Whilst it is common to view love as an emotion, it did not appear to me as if it really fulfils the role as an attentioning feeling – at least not all the time. I also could not quite define it as a hormonal thing or as a homeostatic feeling.

The Male Brain does a very good job of explaining the process of falling in love and staying in love. The author uses the hypothetical situation of

Ryan and Nicole, falling in love at the age of 28:

> As Ryan watched Nicole, he was practically oblivious to everyone but her.
> His brain's sexual-pursuit area, in his hypothalamus, lit up like a slot machine.
> Suddenly all he could think about was how to get her attention. Without being
> conscious about it, Ryan was following the commands of his ancient mating
> brain.
>
> The men alive today have been biologically selected over millions of years
> to focus on fertile females. What they don't know is that they've evolved to
> zoom in on certain features that indicate reproductive health. Researchers have
> found that the attraction of an hourglass figure – large breasts, small waist, flat
> stomach, and full hips – is ingrained in men across all cultures. This shape tells
> his brain that she is young, healthy, and probably not pregnant with another
> man's child. Like all men's, Ryan's visual cortex is prewired to notice women
> who are shaped like Nicole.

I would be hesitant to use the words 'visual cortex is prewired', but
certainly there will be much more attention being given to such a figure.

Following the story of flirting between Ryan and Nicole, the two are
seated next to each other:

> Now that Ryan was sitting next to Nicole, he was close enough to take in
> her sweet scent, and his nose instantly messaged his subconscious brain that
> she not only smelled good, but was also potentially a good genetic match.
> Our pheromones – odorless 'smells' detected by our noses – carry genetic
> information, according to researchers...
>
> Ryan's mating brain was giving him encouraging hormonal signals, and
> Ryan thought Nicole seemed interested.

Their flirtation continues, and Ryan drives Nicole home, where they kiss.
(Women reading this book will say that I skipped over the 'important bits';
men will know that I am telling just the important bits.)

> In the mating game, a kiss is more than a kiss – it's a taste test. Saliva contains
> molecules from all the glands and organs of the body, so a French kiss serves
> up our signature flavor. As soon as Ryan's tongue touched Nicole's, information
> about each other's health and genes was collected and secretly sent to their
> brains. If Nicole had genes that were too similar to his and the kiss tasted sour,
> it could have been a sexual deal-breaker.

The story continues with Ryan wanting to have sex as soon as possible, but:

> In the bases of way, to a man, winning the mating game means getting his DNA
> and genes into the next generation. Even though he isn't consciously thinking
> this, the instinctual part of his brain knows that the more women he has sex
> with, the more offspring he is likely to have. Meanwhile, the female brain is
> trying to discern whether a man has what it takes to be a good protector and
> provider. Researchers find that this holds true regardless of a woman's level of
> education or financial independence.

One can easily see how this works in evolutionary terms. Promiscuous males would end up with more descendants, and if promiscuity is genetic then the offspring will be more inclined to promiscuity. A female who has help from her mate to raise children will be more likely to have children live long enough to enter the gene pool. The author explains that studies with voles show that some are monogamous and some not. The monogamous vole's vasopressin receptor gene is longer than that of the promiscuous vole:

> Although the brain biology in men may turn out to be more complicated than it is in voles, humans have this vasopressin receptor gene too. Some men have the long version, while others have the short one. A study in Sweden found that men with the long version of the vasopressin receptor gene were twice as likely to leave bachelorhood behind and commit to one woman for life.

The story continues to where Ryan and Nicole are having sex on a daily basis – or more:

> Ryan's brain on sex was producing chemicals that create a blissful euphoria, similar to being high on cocaine. He couldn't figure out why, when he was away from Nicole for more than four or five hours, he started getting a primitive biological craving. If we could travel along Ryan's brain circuits in a miniature train as he was falling in love, we'd begin in an area deep at the centre of his brain called the VTA, the ventral tegmental area. We'd see the cells in this area rapidly manufacturing dopamine – the feel-good neurotransmitter for motivation and reward. As the train was being filled with dopamine at this VTA station, Ryan was starting to feel a pleasant buzz.
>
> Filled with dopamine, the train would speed along his brain circuits to the next station, the NAc, or nucleus accumbens, the area for anticipation of pleasure and reward. Because Ryan is a male, we'd see the dopamine from the train being mixed with testosterone and vasopressin. If you are a female, it gets mixed with estrogen and oxytocin. Mixing dopamine with these other hormones was now making an addictive, high-octane fuel, leaving Ryan exhilarated and head over heels in love. The more Ryan and Nicole made love, the more addicted their bodies and brains became.

From a marketing perspective there are great similarities between the Ryan–Nicole story and how consumers start to use brands because these brands meet their hopes for the future and attract attention.

It is unlikely that brands have the same 'high-octane fuel' effect, but that this is happening at a lower level seems reasonable. What is even more reasonable is that this process may be different for males than for females. Or maybe it is just different for different product types.

Here we are discussing another piece of the puzzle, and hoping that we will learn about it. As we learn about these processes for brands and product categories among people of different genders and cultures we will also be learning a lot more about the brain.

What we have described above is really the brain on infatuation. The ideal for marketers is to learn about the brain in love – brand loyalty. Whilst this might have to do with the vole's vasopressin receptor gene it is unlikely. Monogamy is a more serious issue in life than brand loyalty. I am also not aware of any market research that shows some people are more brand monogamous in general than others.

But let us continue with what one could consider 'true love', because a lot of how Brizendine describes this resonates with what marketers call brand loyalty:

> As the train sped into the final station, the caudate nucleus, or CN, the area for memorizing the look and identity of whoever is giving you pleasure, we'd see all the tiniest details about Nicole being indelibly chiseled into his permanent memory. She was now literally unforgettable. Once the love train had made these three stops at the VTA, the NAc, and the CN, we'd see Ryan's lust and love circuits merge as they focused only on Nicole.

16

Let's put it all together

We have now described:

- how neurons lay down memories and use these to interpret things;
- how events outside the body are interpreted and lead to emotions;
- how the states of the body and mind are created and, if needs be, rectified;
- how our personality and culture influence how we interpret things;
- how we identify that something or some course of action will make us feel good based on these systems.

What is left is to explain how these interact in the making of decisions – deciding between alternatives.

The problem with finding a book that makes the mind simple enough to understand is that the authors mostly make it too complicated. Edward de Bono (1969) said: 'It may be the brain is not too difficult to understand, but too easy. Matters are often made more and more complex by the ability of man to play elaborate games that feed on themselves to create bewildering structures of immense intricacy, which obscure rather than reveal.' At the moment the pieces of the puzzle are lying all around us, and we are just in the process of putting them together.

So how do we think we think?

There is little debate that we 'think' with our frontal lobes, and that this is where what we call consciousness resides. In the modern view this is supported by fMRI studies where, when people are given tasks that involve thinking, the frontal lobes are active. If we are idly watching things on a screen or listening to words there is little activity in the frontal lobes. When we are asked to 'do things' with the images or sounds there is a lot of activity in the frontal lobes. This we sort of knew long ago – before brain scanning techniques. We knew that the major difference between humans and other animals is the relative size of the frontal lobes, and we believed that humans were the species that 'think' the best.

The question then becomes: what do we mean by 'think'? At this stage it seems as if the best way to approach this problem is to break it into two parts: 1) planning actions: basically deciding what to do and making plans for the future; and 2) creativity: making unusual connections between things in the mind. Creativity is an area that is not understood, and filled with a lot of pop psychology books that are mostly well worth not reading. At least the good news is that Antonio Damasio is now turning his attention to this aspect of the human brain.

There are only a few animal species that show evidence of creativity – like using objects as tools. Nearly all animals, other than the most basic ones, show evidence of 'planned behaviour', even if this is at a very basic level for some very basic animals. At its most basic, planning is seen as the ability to make choices between alternatives. The cow chooses between different areas at which to graze, or whether to stand in the shade or the sun, or walk toward the dam for a drink or continue grazing or simply stare at the hill contemplating its future. The fruit fly chooses which fruit to fly to, or whether it should have sex rather than eat, or go somewhere to drink water rather than just bask in the sun.

It might mistakenly be thought that the survival model set out above is a basic process that is not really part of higher mental processes where brand decisions are made. This is not so. The output of the human brain's survival process (monitoring the environment and the body, reacting to environmental and bodily changes, etc) is simply a choice between alternatives. The brain considers some alternatives in terms of how they would change the body's homeostasis or the mind's mood now or in the future and then chooses the one that will make the person feel best.

For a person to decide on a specific brand there should be awareness of the brand as one of the alternatives at the time when a choice is being made. The choice will be made based on memories about the brand or, if there are no memories to rely on, the mere presence and awareness of the brand being in the environment of the consumer. The final choice can take a long time to be made after a lot of consideration, or nearly instantaneous with little consideration being given.

'Thinking' involves a lot of brain process

The brain is like an orchestra playing a symphony. All the parts have roles to play, each acts independently, but all act in concert. Studying the score sheet of any one instrument tells you nothing about the symphony, but studying all the score sheets simply confuses. Yet each instrument playing off its own score sheet makes the symphony. Further, the conductor makes no music, yet makes the symphony.

This might be an analogy that explains what the frontal lobes do. All the sounds of the different sections of the orchestra and even individual instruments come to the conductor, who will pay attention to some of these to the exclusion of the others. The conductor will send messages back to the different sections during the performance as to what he or she would like them to do and when. The sections of the orchestra, and the individual members of each section, have been trained by years of rehearsal as to what they should be doing and will be playing their score sheet even when the conductor is not giving them attention.

This is really the way of the brain. Specialist parts are all working in harmony to produce something that is much greater than any part. Studying and measuring one part make little sense in terms of understanding the whole, but not understanding the individual parts means we cannot understand the whole. (I mention this merely as a criticism of articles suggesting that measuring one part of the brain gives an understanding of the whole, or even the output.)

Making a choice

It seems that the essence of making a choice involves a feedback system from the frontal lobes to the limbic system. In other words, when the frontal lobes 'think' of something they send signals back to the limbic system, which then feeds back memories of how it feels about this 'idea' (or concept).

Some evidence for this is that there are fewer neurons leading from the frontal lobes to the limbic system than there are leading the other way. Remember that gestalt formation means we need only a few inputs to generate a bigger output – one that includes 'feelings'. When the frontal lobes become conscious of things in their environment, they will be receiving from the limbic system indications about the desirability (dopamine levels) that these gestalts involve and can use this in their 'deliberations'. As the frontal lobes evaluate alternatives, even these can be fed back (by the process of neural recruitment – not consciously sending things back to the limbic system), and they will return to the frontal lobes with a 'feeling' connotation included. This 'feeling' will be based largely on previous dopamine levels (memories) invoked by the thought. In other words the frontal lobes are simply making 'decisions' or choices between alternatives based on the feedback from the limbic system based on dopamine levels (and other hormones) evoked by the memories.

A 'new' thought

We all have experiences of starting off to do something and then doing something different. I go to the supermarket to buy things to make a steak barbecue and come back with the ingredients for a chicken stir-fry. Of course there would be the obvious reason that there was a promotion for chicken stir-fries in the store. But, more often than not, there would be no great reason for me to leave the house telling my wife what I am going to buy and then to come back with something else. This is the beauty of the brain. Gestalts form. Earlier I described the formation of gestalts as analogous to a handful of stones being thrown into a pond and the concentric waves that emanate from this.

I have a house on the river, where people play with jet-skis. A jet-ski creates a wave, as a gestalt would. A favourite trick of the drivers is to drive in a tight circle, and the waves run into one another, creating a new wave that has no relation to the original waves. This also happens when a few speedboats cross and the waves hit each other, creating a new mini-tsunami that has no relation to the creating waves.

The same happens in the brain. As the gestalts are forming by the initial recruitment of neurons, so 'unexpected' neurons are recruited, which might form their own 'wave of recruitment'.

Thus, whilst I was shopping for my steak barbecue, I might have been thinking about many things, one of which might have started a memory of having a wok on the patio, and when this thought entered the limbic system it might have returned a more positive dopaminic memory that would then influence my choice – in buying not only steak but also all the necessary condiments and spices. My wife would say that I am irrational and unreliable. Presumably so would the market researcher who did an entrance interview with me. Factually I behaved totally reasonably, because I bought what I believed would make me feel best in the future.

Feelings and time

We're now in a position to 'improve' the feelings schemata in Figures 10.1, 11.2, 13.1 and 14.1. They are all put together in Figure 16.1.

FIGURE 16.1   Feelings schemata

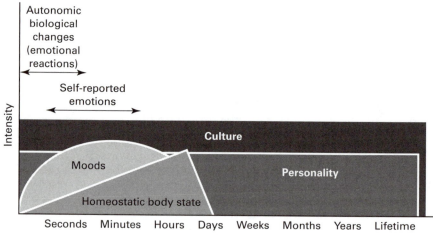

Measuring the brain

17

There are by now more than 100 companies offering brain scanning to marketers. Many are not explicit about the methodology used, nor about what the measurements will really reveal. In other words, there are some snake oil salesmen out there. It is not the intention of this book to educate marketers to become neuroscientists, but I do believe that marketers will benefit from understanding what the mines are when they walk the minefield of neuromarketing – which can be a very expensive exercise.

When we talk about brain scans we are really referring to a collection of techniques that exist for the physical measurement of the brain. Each of these has its own strengths and weaknesses. If you read articles about the result of brain scans and the implications for marketers, you should be very aware of the methods that were used and what their weaknesses are. An excellent book in this regard is *Cognition, Brain, and Consciousness: Introduction to Cognitive Neuroscience* (Baars and Gage, 2007). I have used Chapter 4, 'The tools: Imaging the living brain', by Bernard J Baars and Thomas Ramsoy (2007) as the basis for my description of the methodologies.

The speed at which neurons fire and propagate a signal is very fast. To measure brain activity the measurement technique needs to measure very fast activities. When, on the other hand, the objective is to see whether some region in the brain has been damaged (say by a stroke) then the measurement has to be high resolution of a specific area and the speed of measurement is really secondary. The most important differentiation between the methodologies is the accuracy of their spatial resolution versus the accuracy of their temporal resolution.

Single-cell measurement

It is possible to measure whether a single neuron fires or not. In 2005 Quiroga at Caltech found a single cell that was activated by photos of Jennifer Aniston but not other photos (Baars and Gage, 2007). This was done by inserting a needle in the cell (or next to it) and measuring whether there was electrical activity. Such measurements are done only during brain surgery and are of little relevance to marketers. Although this neuron became known as the 'Jennifer Aniston neuron' it does not mean that memories about the actress are stored in the neuron. We explained that neurons work as a whole network. The so-called Jennifer Aniston neuron is only part of a big neuronal network that becomes active when the patient is presented with her picture. In fact, this neuron might also be part of other neuronal networks.

Electroencephalography (EEG)

EEG was discovered in 1929. Electrodes placed on the scalp can measure electric activity when groups of neurons fire. Electromagnetic waves propagate nearly instantaneously in the brain, which means that EEG is very sensitive temporally.

The spatial ability of EEG is dependent on the number of electrodes used, but even units with 64 electrodes can pinpoint a signal coming from only a fairly gross area in the brain. Baars and Ramsoy point out that:

> EEG is quite selective being more sensitive to neurons near the surface than to the deeper neurons. EEG is picked up through layers of moist tissue, so that the original activity is attenuated and distorted by the shape and conductive properties of the intervening cells. Some researchers believe that EEG is largely sensitive to the first layer of the cortex...
>
> With tens of billions of cortical neurons firing at about 10Hz, we have several trillion electrical events per second. The raw EEG was therefore difficult to interpret before the advent of powerful computerized analysis...
>
> This event-related potential is sensitive to large neuronal population activity that characterizes visual auditory and even semantic processes [note that these are processes that happen very close to or in the surface of the brain]...
>
> It is very difficult to locate the electrical source of the EEG signal. It helps to increase the number of electrodes and to use sophisticated analytic methods. However, EEG gives us little information about brain regions deep beneath the cortex. Since sub-cortical regions such as the hypothalamus are very important, EEG seems to have inherent limits.
>
> (Baars and Ramsoy, 2007)

When marketers embark on a neuromarketing study or read about the results of such a study, they should be very aware of this weakness in the methodology. This is especially true when the study purports to be measuring emotion in the limbic system (which is a deep-brain measure). However, since the reason for these deep-brain activities is to guide the frontal areas, EEG can pick up the signals. There are distinct and well-documented EEG signals for positive and negative feelings.

Besides these problems for marketers, there is also the inconvenience that most systems require conductive jelly to be applied to the scalp, leaving respondents with jelly in their hair. However, there are now dry systems that have many advantages in terms of market research, not least that they allow much larger samples to be measured.

Currently there is a lot of debate about the number of electrodes needed for EEG measures that are useful for neuromarketing. Neurofocus – a leading supplier of this technology – markets a set with 16 electrodes. In his book *The Buying Brain: Secrets for selling to the subconscious mind* (2010), AK Pradeep argues that this is what is needed because the US legal system requires that readings from equipment with at least 16 electrodes are required before somebody can be declared legally dead.

AK Pradeep claims that Neurofocus produces seven readings of the brain when they evaluate advertising. However, what they do is produce three readings of the brain from the 16 electrodes. They then combine these readings in pairs so that this produces another three measures, and then they combine all of the measures to produce a seventh.

This argument will dominate the neuromarketing industry for a long time.

Magnetoencephalography (MEG)

Whilst EEG measures the electric fields that are produced in the brain, MEG measures the magnetic fields that result from these electric fields. MEG yields about the same temporal resolution as EEG (milliseconds) and a much better spatial resolution (a few millimetres) at parts of the cortical surface.

MEG does not, in itself, produce an image of the brain. However, MRI produces such an image, and the activity can then be superimposed on this picture.

Baars and Ramsoy (2007) note: 'MEG has advantages, but also limitations. Because of the direction of the magnetic fields produced by the cortical neurons, MEG is strongly affected by the hills and valleys of the cortex... And, like EEG, MEG does not pick up subcortical activity.'

MEG is often used before brain surgery to determine areas that should be avoided. This process requires that the respondent come to the machine, is prepared for the machine and is then inserted into it.

Transcranial magnetic stimulation (TMS)

By applying brief magnetic impulses over the scalp we can now excite or inhibit activity of small areas of the brain briefly. For example, stimulating the motor area that controls the subject's hands will move them involuntarily, and an inhibitory impulse will cause subjects to have problems moving their hands.

Whilst this leads to some very important experiments by brain scientists it is unlikely to be used by marketers.

Indirect measures of neural activity

All the above methods measure the electronic activities of neurons directly. There are other measurement methods that measure brain activity indirectly. When the brain is active it consumes energy, and these techniques measure the blood flow and oxygen levels in parts of the brain.

Positron emission tomography (PET)

This is not only expensive but also requires the patient (respondent) to be injected with a radioactive tracer. The flow of this tracer and areas that it builds up in are measured. This is used less often in research today, and is unlikely to be used in market research.

Functional magnetic resonance imaging (fMRI and MRI)

These are the most often used brain imaging methodologies, and probably what the layperson understands as brain scans. Basically what is measured is the blood oxygen demand in certain brain areas.

The machine into which the person is inserted generates a magnetic field about 600,000 times that of the earth. With this the blood oxygen atoms are stimulated to line up instead of spinning randomly. This is then picked up by sensitive coils surrounding the subject's head. This allows very accurate measures of where there has been activity in the brain, but because it takes several seconds for the blood oxygen demand to be established and for blood to arrive there is a built-in time lag in fMRI measures.

These machines cost at least $4 million, weigh more than six tons and, because of the high magnetic fields (which attract any metal in their vicinity), need to be housed in special areas – much like old computers before the arrival of laptops. This raises issues about the ethics of using the machines for non-medical purposes, and limits the sample sizes that can be studied.

Very indirect measurements of brain activity

There are several measurement technologies that do not measure the brain, but are gaining in popularity. These techniques were mostly developed by psychologists and are now finding a new lease of life as the understanding of the way the brain works increases.

Some of these are based on measuring the skin's electro-conductivity, and are basically lie detector tests. They reveal when the patient is stressed or excited and can be related by implication to the functions of the amygdala. Some of these measures are based on recording eye movements. Again this can reveal whether the respondent is excited.

For this book I will not delve into these, partly because they are based on assumptions that are contentious.

'Reading' the measures

None of the direct or indirect measures deliver the pretty pictures that we see of brain scans. These pictures suggest a situation where the brain is a blank slate before the respondent is exposed to some material and then the material causes some areas in the brain to light up. The fact is that even the resting brain is never silent. When we are asleep the brain is active, and some areas in the brain seem to be more active when we are asleep than when we are aroused. What the neuro-measures produce is a picture of all the noise in the brain.

Neuroscientists collect data about the brain in two states: a resting state and then a state where the brain has been stimulated by some material. One measure will be overlaid on the other; then the resting-state picture is subtracted from that of the stimulated state. The assumption is that the difference is due to the stimulation. This is done for both EEG and MRI scans.

However, the same areas in people's brains do not light up each time the material is presented. To overcome this the experiment not only takes several measures of one patient, but also takes measures of many patients. These measures are then averaged. Baars and Ramsoy (2007) demonstrate the above processes well in pictures.

Understandably there is a whole literature and debate about what 'resting state' really is, what happens in people's brains during the resting state (ie what they really think about), and whether there is a contamination between the experiment and its results, or even contamination between subsequent exposures to stimuli.

Creativity in designing brain scanning experiments

Probably the worst way to do brain scanning experiments for neuro-marketing is to push someone into an fMRI machine asking them to think of something and hoping you will learn something. It is much better to have a hypothesis about which brain areas will respond to the stimuli and, especially, why we would expect those areas to respond. Where it is possible to use more than one technique this should be done.

Baars and Ramsoy give the example below in *Cognition, Brain, and Consciousness*:

> The best science is done by combining imaging techniques with genuine creativity. A lot of creativity goes into the selection of functional variables. What is the best way to understand vision? Selective attention and conscious cognition? A great deal of ingenuity has been devoted to those questions.
>
> For example, taxi drivers are well known for their ability to know their way around a city. They know not only how to get from A to B, but also the most efficient way to get there. Such ability to navigate through a complex road system depends on our spatial ability. Studies have shown that the hippocampus, a part of the medial temporal lobe, plays an important part in the navigation and memory of places and routes. Rats with lesions to the hippocampus have been known for decades to perform disastrously on spatial tests. Birds and other animals that bury or hide their food at multiple places have larger hippocampi than non-storing animals. Therefore, one question that arises when we think about taxi drivers is, are the brain regions responsible for spatial navigation more developed in taxi drivers than other people? Indeed, it has been found that part of the hippocampi of taxi drivers was larger than the same region in a group of people with a different background. OK, you might question, but what if people with large hippocampi choose to be taxi drivers, and not vice versa? Here, the study showed that the size of the hippocampus depended on how long people had been working as taxi drivers. In other words, the longer you work as a taxi driver (and use your spatial navigation ability) the bigger your relevant part of the hippocampus will become.
>
> Notice how imaginative the taxi driver was. It is usually easier randomly to select human subjects (usually undergraduate students!) to stand for the entire human population. But the fact is that there are differences of age, particular abilities and talents, and other cognitive capacities between 'average' subjects. London taxi drivers are highly experienced experts (they are required to pass tests on the geography of the city), and they can be compared to a plausible control group. One important implication is that the sheer size of brain structures may change with specific experiences (Maguire et al., 2000). That claim has now been supported for other brain regions as well. The taxi driver study is therefore an excellent example of creative selection of comparison conditions, leading to new insights.
>
> (Baars and Ramsoy, 2007)

Increasing our brainpower – using neuroscience effectively

18

GRAHAM PAGE

Executive Vice-President, Consumer Neuroscience,

Millward Brown

> The previous chapter reviewed some of the methodologies that can be used to obtain bio-measures of the brain, but is only a discussion from the perspective of neuroscience. To get a real perspective of what neuromarketing is like in practice I asked Graham Page to write a chapter on what Millward Brown is doing in this field, and why, with some case studies.

Erik's book illustrates both the complexity of neuroscience as a field, and the crucial implications it has for brand owners as they seek to make their brands more desirable to consumers, and win in the marketplace. It is, therefore, unsurprising that marketing and advertising conferences now incorporate a strong neuroscience emphasis, and many recent papers and articles maintain that scientists' increased understanding of the brain will change marketing and the way we measure it. *Buy-ology*, by Martin Lindstrom, makes similarly strong claims: that neuroscience will play a revolutionary role in research and marketing in future. As a result, many marketers challenge accepted modes of brand and advertising development and research on the grounds that 'neuroscience says' that what we've done before is wrong.

Similarly, we now see neuroscience being cited in many brand and advertising decisions. The phrase 'neuroscience proves...' is increasingly being used to justify a new model of advertising response, brand strategy or advertising research tool (though it's often useful to examine just how much actual proof follows such statements). Most crucially, over the last few years there has been a blossoming of neuromarketing agencies who claim to deploy the methods used by neuroscientists to answer marketing questions in a way that conventional research cannot.

So we'd be forgiven for believing that traditional qualitative (focus group based) and quantitative (survey-based) techniques are not sufficient anymore, and that we need to turn to the methods used by cognitive neuroscientists, such as brainwave measurement (EEG), brain scanning (fMRI) and other biometrics, to really understand how consumers will respond to marketing.

However, despite all the discussion about neuroscience, the vast majority of brands and ads are still researched using traditional methods. Likewise, over the last few years, papers have periodically emerged that question the value of the whole area. So who's right? Are we poised at the start of a revolution or is neuromarketing overhyped wishful thinking?

The current state of play

Millward Brown conducted its first neuroscience project in 2004, and since then we have reviewed all the key methodologies available in this area, working with our clients, neuromarketing practitioners and academics. Our experience is that marketers are increasingly turning to neuromarketing, and they will continue to do so more and more in future. But this has been a gradual process for several reasons:

1 Marketers are rightly being cautious. Neuromarketing is new and to some people controversial. So they are working with partners who they trust to do their homework before adopting more widely.

2 There are still significant practical hurdles. The technologies are not available everywhere, and the logistics of brainwave measurement or brain scanning are not trivial. Testing robust numbers of participants is often expensive – or worse, not done.

3 The extreme claims of some of the early practitioners in the field have inspired some scepticism.

4 Many of our clients believe their work in this area has the potential to generate significant competitive advantage, and so are understandably coy about sharing too much publicly.

5 Most marketers quickly realise that neuroscience methods in isolation can be hard to interpret and don't stand alone.

This last point is crucial. Over the last six years we have examined all the main techniques in the area and compared them to the existing qualitative and quantitative work we do to ensure a realistic perspective on what the science can and can't say. We've seen that there is clear and significant value in certain neuroscience methods, but only when used alongside existing methods rather than as a replacement, and only if interpreted with care by people with experience in the field. To this end, in 2010 we created a dedicated Neuroscience Practice to ensure that, as a business, we would implement neuroscience-based approaches in a realistic manner that added to our insights about consumers.

Key questions to ask

When deciding which methods to use, we have applied the following tests:

1 Does the method tell us something meaningful about brands or marketing?
2 Does the method tell us something we don't already know (and enough to justify the costs)?
3 Is the method practical and scalable?

There are neuroscience-based methods that meet all three of these tests. These are: implicit association measurement, eye-tracking and brainwave measurement.

Implicit association measurement

While not strictly speaking a 'neuroscience' technique, what it shares with more biometric methods is the principle of inferring consumers' responses rather than asking direct questions. The approach measures consumers' reaction times or accuracy on tasks that are systematically biased by their reactions to brands or ads. At first this sounds strange, but the approaches capitalize on the way the brain stores information – as a network of connections rather than isolated units. It is for this reason, that, for instance, thinking about the idea of a 'doctor' means you will tend to respond faster to a related idea like 'nurse' than an unrelated one like 'plumber'. Similarly, if you feel positive you will tend to respond faster to positive words and slower to negative ones, but this is reversed if you feel negative. Implicit association methods therefore have a long history of use in cognitive psyhology to infer unstated processes and responses, especially in researching socially sensitive areas, such as people's biases towards different races or genders. They offer market researchers a window to the 'raw' ideas and feelings stirred up by brands and ads, prior to any filtering for 'sense' or social desirability, which still may play a role in shaping consumers' responses.

We have used these methods in a variety of markets and with a diverse range of clients to understand the implicit associations activated by brands, by ads, and by hard-to-discuss stimuli such as brand logos. For instance, we recently used this approach to research an award-winning Australian TV ad for Allens (a confectionery brand). The spot featured a giant doll walking the streets, blowing bubbles which turn into the product and rain down onto a crowd of children and parents. The ad was designed to reinvigorate the brand, which although a long-time favourite had lost some relevance and presence in the market, by reminding consumers of the magic of childhood. The ad proved to be hugely engaging, but the implicit association test clearly identified that the ad works in a somewhat way different from that expected. While explicitly consumers played back messages of fun and happiness, implicitly, the spot also communicated irresistibility and playfulness. Also while explicitly the ad was not directly 'persuasive', the implicit measures revealed that it strongly reawakened the emotional connection to the brand. Therefore rather than being a simple nostalgic look at a trusted favourite, the ad functioned very strongly as a modernizing ad, while still highlighting the playfulness of childhood, and reinvigorating the emotional resonance of the brand. The creative device is clearly 'childish' but it's a more modern take on childhood – so it updates the brand rather than simply exploiting its past memories.

Similarly, in Poland we recently conducted some logo research for a financial services client. Logos are a topic that consumers find difficult to talk about as they are not usually subjects of much thought, but they are full of nuance and symbolism. Although the results from explicit ratings correlated with results from this implicit test, the implicit method pulled out a much clearer winner (see Figure 18.1), suggesting that this is a useful approach for this type of research.

On the whole, we've found this type of approach allows us to see in more depth whether a brand is achieving its desired positioning, or if a campaign or logo has the potential to shape a brand's perceptions in the intended way.

Eye-tracking

Eye-tracking technology is now widely used, partly because it has become simpler to implement and cheaper than in the past. The benefits are clear: eye movements indicate the focus of visual attention with more detail and accuracy than self-reported answers. However, the method doesn't reveal why a particular area of an ad catches the eye, or how people respond to it, which is why it can be difficult to interpret in isolation.

FIGURE 18.1 In a recent logo test, implicit results showed a clearer winner

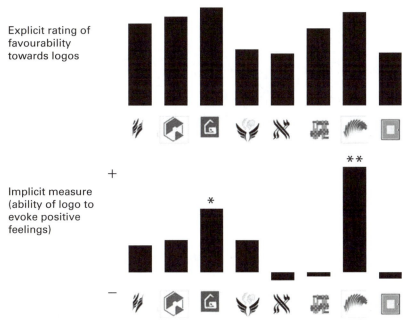

Note: logos here are dummies to protect client confidentiality

We have used this approach in a number of markets, and have found it a useful additional diagnostic technique that helps explain advertising or packaging performance as measured via conventional survey methods. Figure 18.2 shows the results from a particular scene from the Skoda *Car bakers* ad, a very well known UK ad from 2007/8, in which the car is built entirely from cake. This ad was shown to be powerfully branded to Skoda in our Link survey work, and eye-tracking helped illustrate why. Visual attention is clearly focused on the Skoda badge when it is affixed to the front of the cake-car. However, this contrasted with dispersed visual attention at the end of the ad when the Fabia nameplate is mentioned, which was a useful diagnosis of the weaker nameplate-branding we saw in the survey results. In a similar project for RoC skincare, we found a powerful illustration of a communication barrier due to misdirected attention during a key scene. Using this information the client was able to re-edit the ad and generate a much stronger final film.

FIGURE 18.2   Good Skoda branding in 'Car bakers' is supported by tight attention when badge is on the screen

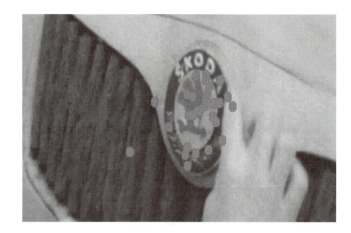

Brainwave measurement

Brainwave measurement is perhaps the most complex area in neuromarketing, due to the variety of systems and companies offering them. Millward Brown conducted one of the first large-scale commercial EEG projects in the UK for the Newspaper Marketing Agency, in 2005. Since then we have partnered with US-based EmSense to integrate EEG and other biometrics with survey tools. We chose EmSense because the company's technology is far more scaleable and cost effective than conventional EEG methods. Using a simple headband with dry electrodes, EmSense collect EEG and secondary biometric data, such as heart rate, respiration, blink rate and body temperature. This method not only makes the equipment less intimidating for participants and simpler to apply, it is also more cost-effective than conventional EEG equipment, which tends to use full-head skullcaps and gel to make connections with the scalp. Consequently, it enables fully robust quantitative testing (eg samples of over 100 versus the 20 or so typically used in conventional EEG), and so allows cross-analysis with explicit questions and metrics. We have therefore deployed this technology in a significant number of countries across the globe, and it has become an important component of the ad development work that we do. This is because brainwave data can provide a powerful diagnostic of people's reactions to an ad or brand experience on a moment-by-moment basis, revealing responses that are so quick or fleeting that respondents may not even remember them, let alone be able to objectively report them. This is also particularly powerful in markets such as India, China, and Latin America, where the tendency for research respondents to be positive on surveys is stronger, and where we may miss some negative responses as a consequence.

FIGURE 18.3 Emsense biosensory results for Dove 'Evolution'

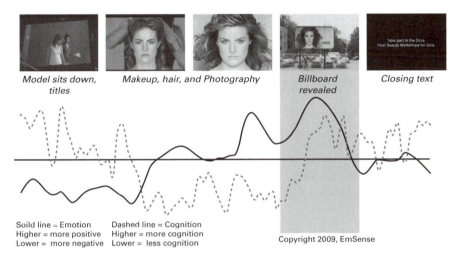

Both positive emotion and cognition peak at the 'reveal' moment
– then emotion becomes more negative as message sinks in

Model sits down, titles   Makeup, hair, and Photography   Billboard revealed   Closing text

Soild line = Emotion   Dashed line = Cognition
Higher = more positive   Higher = more cognition
Lower = more negative   Lower = less cognition

Copyright 2009, EmSense

For instance, Figure 18.3 shows the results of this approach for the well-known Dove 'Evolution' film. In Link survey-based research this film is a hugely powerful performer – engaging, emotionally resonant, and a powerful communicator of the core idea of encouraging a portrayal of real beauty. The EmSense data provides a powerful illustration of the journey consumers take to get to that set of responses, and which creative elements are driving this response. As Figure 18.3 demonstrates, while the model is being 'made-up', positive emotion actually rises (which is not something viewers report verbally). There is also a crescendo of both positive emotion and cognition at the moment it is revealed the film is about the making of an ad; as understanding blossoms and the cleverness of the idea is apparent. This is crucial to the overall positive reception the film generates. However, it is also clear that as the implications of this moment sink in, positive emotions decline as the point of the ad is considered, which is what gives the communication such power.

Work using this form of EEG with other clients has helped reveal and address issues such as weak communication, branding, or disengagement with key protagonists. It has also evidenced which elements of an ad should be retained in cut-downs of long-form ads, and which elements to pull out for use in other parts of campaigns.

While we have focused on these three approaches, it is important to remember that there is no one-size-fits-all neuroscience-based technique; depending on the individual client issue one approach will be better suited than another. fMRI, for instance, is hugely powerful, and we have used it with the Royal Mail in a groundbreaking project about the effect of 'physical' versus 'virtual' media in marketing effectiveness. However, it is limited in its scalability so we have used it less extensively than the other methods outlined above. It is important, however, that marketers use the right tools for the issue they face, rather than treating 'neuroscience' as a single entity, and trying to use one tool to do everything.

Will neuroscience replace conventional research?

It is a misconception, and a scary one, that marketers will be able to (or want to) just measure people's responses to brands via electrodes, and work out what they really want. There is still no substitute for talking to people, as this is the only way we can understand the whole meaning of their relationships with brands and products. The point of market research is to generate insights that lead to more desirable brands, rather than to use the latest methods for the sake of it. For this reason we don't believe neuroscience methods can ever replace the need for conversation with consumers, though we do believe they can be a powerful complement to it.

In addition, on a practical level, survey-based techniques have been shown over many years to have a demonstrable link to consumer behaviour — and such linkages are still being forged for neuroscience methods. For instance, Figure 18.4 shows the behavioural validation of the Link advertising development system. This is a survey-based approach that has been validated

FIGURE 18.4   Behavioural validation of the Link™ advertising

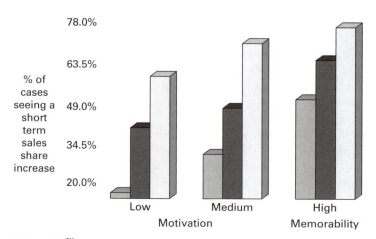

SOURCE: Link™ ad development research database, 872 cases

against in market consumer behaviour, as evidenced by sales effects. As performance on two independent dimensions (expected memorability and rated persuasiveness) increases, so does the probability of observing a sales increase when the ad goes to air. This sort of evidence is crucial for methods to be credible in the ad development space, and is an additional reason why we think it would be unwise to abandon conventional research. Survey-based work has a proven link to behaviour. It may not tell the whole story, but to abandon it in favour of neuroscience would mean abandoning methods that have demonstrable meaning and insight.

The future: integration

We don't believe that marketers need to turn their backs on tried-and-true research techniques in favour of neuroscience, but we do believe that neuroscience can offer an additional perspective on consumer responses and motivation. Therefore, the approach we've taken at Millward Brown has been to roll out neuroscience-based methods alongside, and integrated with, existing tools, rather than as a replacement. Each method is used when it will add value, and when it is relevant to the client issue.

When should neuroscience-based techniques be used?

Neuroscience-based techniques will tend to add the most value under certain circumstances:

1 *Dealing with sensitive material.* This is when qualitative/survey methods are most vulnerable to distortion, so methods that don't rely on explicit questions can reveal unstated attitudes more effectively.

2 *Dealing with abstract or higher-order ideas.* Consumers face challenges when trying to talk about the often complex ideas at the heart of many brands' positioning. Implicit Association methods, in particular, are useful at probing for ideas that participants think sound strange or overblown in black and white on a survey, or which they might discount as irrelevant when answering explicit questions.

3 *Probing for transient responses to ads or brand experiences.* Consumers are great at talking about the gist of an ad or brand, or experience, but they may not be able to articulate all the steps in the process that got them there. Biometric methods, such as EEG, can add value in pinpointing the emotional or cognitive highlights and low points in a piece of creative, or the focus of attention,

which can provide powerful insights for developing more effective campaigns for brand experiences.

4 *Giving more detail on consumers' feelings.* Feelings can be difficult for people to talk about, though, qualitative and survey-based methods can help people do this. However, neuroscience methods can add a powerful additional level of detail here, about the depth of emotional response, the timing of these responses, and the elements of an ad or brand that are driving the way consumers feel. Given the importance of emotion in motivating behaviour, these methods have a powerful role to play here.

In terms of specific research applications, the differing advantages of each method mean they lend themselves to different areas of research. Implicit association measurement is well-suited to brand strategy work, product testing, concept testing and assessment of communication from marketing campaigns. Eye-tracking is strong on in-store and online marketing optimization, and advertising development. Brainwave measurement adds greater detail in these areas, especially regarding emotional and cognitive responses, and so in addition strongly lends itself to advertising optimisation.

Getting the best out of neuroscience

Based on our experience researching and implementing these methods, we suggest the following best practices:

1 **Be critical.** The technology can be alluring, but the same questions (detailed above) that would be asked of any conventional research technique should be asked of these methods. Ask for proof.

2 **Look for experience.** This is a complex area, so familiarity with the approaches and a scientific perspective is important to understand what is claim versus reality, and when neuroscience adds most value. Likewise, experience in drawing together neuroscience and conventional research is key to maximizing the value.

3 **Integrate.** Neuroscience-based methods do not reveal the inner truth, rather they provide additional perspective on consumers' responses to brands and marketing, which needs interpretation in the light of other information. A holistic approach reveals greater insight than conventional or neuroscience methods alone.

Our experience suggests that in the future, neuroscience-based research will be a standard tool in the researcher's toolkit, but it won't be the only tool. Neuroscience techniques on their own can't fully explain consumers' responses. The most complete understanding will come from integrating information rather than looking at one perspective alone, and using the right tool at the right time.

PART THREE
Creating mischief

On creating mischief

19

My three most powerful reasons for writing this book were:

1 to explain that the modern insights into the brain should not be limited to measuring the short-term effects of emotions, which are largely restricted to implications for advertising;

2 to extend the 'feelings model' beyond emotions, which has not really been done explicitly by anyone writing about neuromarketing before (and in fact has been treated with little regard by neuroscientists);

3 to make marketers and neuroscientists aware that a very useful tool for marketing (brain scanning) could lead to mischief along the lines created by *The Hidden Persuaders* (Packard, 1957) in the 1960s.

When a statement is couched in terms such as 'Neuroscience proves that...', it gains a lot of credibility, even if it is total rubbish. We are living in the 'age of the brain', when major discoveries are made, and often these get reported on in the popular press. Invariably reporters look for a catchy line, and mostly will include that they are reporting on something that 'neuroscience has now proved'. A good example is a heading talking about a 'buy button', which leads to a wrong interpretation by laypeople of what the neuroscience experiments are all about or, more specifically, what neuromarketing is about.

The Hidden Persuaders

At conferences I take great delight in telling the audience that the book that had the most influence in advertising was written not by an advertising practitioner but by a journalist, Vance Packard. His book, *The Hidden Persuaders* (1957), deals with subliminal techniques.

A subliminal message – sub-liminal, beneath a limen (ie a threshold) – is a signal or message embedded in another object, designed to pass below the normal limits of perception.

These messages are indiscernible by the conscious mind, but allegedly affect the subconscious or deeper mind.

Subliminal techniques have occasionally been used in advertising and propaganda; the purpose, the effectiveness and the frequency of the application of such techniques are debated.

During World War II, the tachistoscope, an instrument which projects pictures for an extremely brief period, was used to train soldiers to recognize enemy airplanes. Today the tachistoscope is used to increase reading speed or to test sight.

In 1957, market researcher James Vicary claimed that quickly flashing messages on a movie screen, in Fort Lee, New Jersey, had influenced people to purchase more food and drinks. Vicary coined the term subliminal advertising and formed the Subliminal Projection Company based on a six-week test. Vicary claimed that during the presentation of the movie *Picnic* he used a tachistoscope to project the words 'Drink Coca-Cola' and 'Hungry? Eat popcorn' for 1/3000 of a second at five-second intervals. Vicary asserted that during the test, sales of popcorn and Coke in that New Jersey theatre increased 57.8 percent and 18.1 percent respectively.

Vicary's claims were promoted in Vance Packard's book *The Hidden Persuaders*, and led to a public outcry, and to many conspiracy theories of governments and cults using the technique to their advantage. The practice of subliminal advertising was subsequently banned in the United Kingdom and Australia, and by American networks and the National Association of Broadcasters in 1958.

But in 1958, Vicary conducted a television test in which he flashed the message 'telephone now' hundreds of times during a Canadian Broadcasting Corporation program, and found no increase in telephone calls. In 1962, Vicary admitted that he fabricated his claim, the story itself being a marketing ploy. Efforts to replicate the results of Vicary's reports have never resulted in success.

(Wikipedia, 'Subliminal stimuli')

Even today the practice of subliminal advertising is explicitly banned in many countries. No advertiser has had such a big influence on advertising, and it all based on a fabricated claim.

It can be argued that the book had a big effect because of the environment in which it was published: the Cold War, Freud's subconscious and lots of talk about brainwashing. It might also be that people were disposed to believe negative things about advertisers, especially in connection with a seemingly neurological claim.

Much of what one reads about neuromarketing has the same potential for mischief as Vicary's fabrication and its popularization by Vance Packhard. Already the claims that are made are very similar to the claims made for subliminal advertising, and these often involve distortion of the facts. In Chapter 3 I already quoted how Damasio is upset by what some people say he said.

When I started working in an advertising agency in the 1980s, a popular joke doing the rounds was: 'Please don't tell my mother I am working in an advertising agency, she thinks I am a piano player in a whorehouse.' This public skepticism about what advertising does has not changed much over the intervening decades. It still does not take much for the public to read sinister ulterior motives into what advertising is trying to achieve.

'The seductive allure of neuroscience explanations'

This is the title of a paper by Weisberg *et al* (2008), and here is their synopsis:

Abstract

Explanations of psychological phenomena seem to generate more public interest when they contain neuroscientific information. Even irrelevant neuroscience information in an explanation of a psychological phenomenon may interfere with people's abilities to critically consider the underlying logic of this explanation. We tested this hypothesis by giving naive adults, students in a neuroscience course, and neuroscience experts brief descriptions of psychological phenomena followed by one of four types of explanation, according to a 2 (good explanation vs. bad explanation) × 2 (without neuroscience vs. with neuroscience) design. Crucially, the neuroscience information was irrelevant to the logic of the explanation, as confirmed by the expert subjects. Subjects in all three groups judged good explanations as more satisfying than bad ones. But subjects in the two non-expert groups additionally judged that explanations with logically irrelevant neuroscience information were more satisfying than explanations without. The neuroscience information had a particularly striking effect on non-experts' judgments of bad explanations, masking otherwise salient problems in these explanations.

(Weisberg *et al*, 2008)

Table 19.1 shows the statements that Weisberg *et al* used in their experiment. The statements that the respondents saw did not have the neurology words highlighted. As the article was a very scientific paper aimed at a scientific audience, they discuss the results in great detail, but the end result is that everybody rated the explanations with neuroscience wording as being much better than those without – whether they were bad explanations or not. Here is the final paragraph of this paper:

Regardless of the breadth of our effect or the mechanism by which it occurs, the mere fact that irrelevant information can interfere with people's judgments of explanations has implications for how neuroscience information in particular, and scientific information in general, is viewed and used outside of the laboratory. Neuroscience research has the potential to change our views of personal responsibility, legal regulation, education, and even the nature of the self. To take a recent example, some legal scholars have suggested that neuroimaging technology could be used in jury selection, to ensure that jurors are free of bias, or in questioning suspects, to ensure that they are not lying. Given the results reported here, such evidence presented in a courtroom, a classroom, or a political debate, regardless of the scientific status or relevance of this evidence, could strongly sway opinion, beyond what the evidence can support. We have shown that people seem all too ready to accept explanations that allude to neuroscience, even if they are not accurate reflections of the scientific data, and even if they would otherwise be seen as far less satisfying. Because it is unlikely that the popularity of neuroscience findings in the public

TABLE 19.1   The statements that Weisberg *et al* used in their experiment

	Good explanation	Bad explanation
Without neuroscience	The researchers claim that this 'curse' happens because subjects have trouble switching their point of view to consider what someone else might know, mistakenly projecting their own knowledge on to others.	The researchers claim that this 'curse' happens because subjects make more mistakes when they have to judge the knowledge of others. People are much better at judging what they themselves know.
With neuroscience	**Brain scans indicate** that this 'curse' happens because of the **frontal lobe brain circuitry known to be involved in self-knowledge**. Subjects have trouble switching their point of view to consider what someone else might know, mistakenly projecting their own knowledge on to others.	**Brain scans indicate** that this 'curse' happens because of the **frontal lobe brain circuitry known to be involved in self-knowledge**. Subjects make more mistakes when they have to judge the knowledge of others. People are much better at judging what they themselves know.

SOURCE: Weisberg *et al* (2008).

sphere will wane any time soon, we see in the current results more reasons for caution when applying neuroscientific findings to social issues. Even if expert practitioners can easily distinguish good neuroscience explanations from bad, they must not assume that those outside the discipline will be as discriminating.

(Weisberg *et al*, 2008)

The buy button

There have been a number of reports in the popular media and even respected magazines like *Newsweek* about the aim of neuromarketing being to find the buy button. There is an example on the *Newsweek* website (**www. commercialalert.org/issues/culture/neuromarketing/pushing-the-buy-button**). This story states that consumers are not able to tell you why they make a certain choice when you ask them, but that neuroscience can now look into the brain and get at the truth. The article also mentions that Gary Ruskin (executive director of Commercial Alert) had sent a letter to the university where the study was performed asking it to stop using its equipment for this. In fact, he has subsequently approached the US senate and asked it to stop funding the university unless it desists.

I am not questioning the facts in the article, but they are presented in such a way that the layperson would probably interpret them as implying that there exists a buy button in people's minds ready to be discovered – and then exploited. Certainly the title of the article, 'Pushing the buy button', would not have convinced Commercial Alert that there are no dangers in neuroscience.

At first I thought that the reaction by Commercial Alert was very much along the lines of the 'my-mother-thinks-I-am-a-piano-player-in-a-whore-house' syndrome. However, their website puts foward the argument that advertising is to blame for American obesity because it promotes fast food – naïve, but convincing. One only needs to make it sound more convincing by adding the words 'neuroscience', 'buy-button' and 'McDonalds' to create a really irrational reaction among the general public. Or, as I have seen recently, use the same type of sensationalism tied to elections.

Sensationalism will increase

Just as it is true that adding the words 'Neuroscience has proved...' to a statement lends credibility to it, it is also true that converting what was apparently proved into a sensationalistic heading will attract attention and sell.

Here is an example I have come across, on the CNN website ('Men see bikini-clad women as objects, psychologists say', **http://edition.cnn.com/2009/HEALTH/02/19/women.bikinis.objects/index.html**, 2 April 2009):

> It may seem obvious that men perceive women in sexy bathing suits as objects, but now there's science to back it up.
>
> New research shows that, in men, the brain areas associated with handling tools and the intention to perform actions light up when viewing images of women in bikinis.
>
> The research was presented this week by Susan Fiske, professor of psychology at Princeton University, at the annual meeting of the American Association for the Advancement of Science.
>
> 'This is just the first study which was focused on the idea that men of a certain age view sex as a highly desirable goal, and if you present them with a provocative woman, then that will tend to prime goal-related responses,' she told CNN.

The report itself seems scientifically factual to me, but starts off with claiming neuroscience foundations, and leads to the sensationalistic heading 'Men see bikini-clad women as objects, psychologists say'. I have seen the same report quoted on sites less reputable than CNN as 'Men see bikini-clad women as tools'. The heading and introductory sentence seem to me to have very little to do with the rest of the article. The same neurological evidence could have been reported as 'Men see hammers as bikini-clad women'.

20

Buy-ology

There are really only two major published neuromarketing experiments to date: 1) Read Montague's Pepsi Challenge; and 2) Martin Lindstrom's *Buy-ology* (2008). The styles of the experiments and the reporting of the results cannot be more different. In Chapter 22 I will give my views of the Pepsi Challenge.

Martin Lindstrom is the author of *Brand Sense* (2005), which I believe is one of the best modern marketing books. The more I learned about the brain the more impressed I became with what Lindstrom propagates in *Brand Sense*: the brand should be identifiable to all senses.

The one area where this makes particularly good logic is the sense of smell. This is the only sense that goes directly to the limbic system and therefore the sense that can raise very strong emotions. It is also very difficult to find ways in which to market the fragrance of a brand. This creates great opportunities for creative marketing. I recently spoke at two conferences of people who market flavours and fragrances to marketers, and I can really recommend such events to marketers as sources of new ideas of how emotions can be created.

Lindstrom's book, *Buy-ology*, is based on a $7 million experiment in which 2,081 volunteers' brains were scanned. The book is promoted as: 'How everything we know about how we buy is wrong'. In Chapter 3 I explained that when there is a paradigm shift it means that the measurements we have taken of reality are still valid, but the way that we look at these measurements has changed. I doubt that our perspective of buying behaviour will change as much as the subtitle of *Buy-ology* suggests.

The book is described on Amazon:

How much do we know about why we buy? What truly influences our decisions in today's message-cluttered world? An eye-grabbing advertisement, a catchy slogan, an infectious jingle? Or do our buying decisions take place below the surface, so deep within our subconscious minds, we're barely aware of them?

In *Buy-ology*, Lindstrom presents the astonishing findings from his groundbreaking, three-year, seven-million-dollar neuromarketing study, a cutting-edge experiment that peered inside the brains of 2,000 volunteers from all around the world as they encountered various ads, logos, commercials, brands, and products. His startling results shatter much of what we have long believed about what seduces our interest and drives us to buy. Among his findings:

- Gruesome health warnings on cigarette packages not only fail to discourage smoking, they actually make smokers want to light up.

- Despite government bans, subliminal advertising still surrounds us – from bars to highway billboards to supermarket shelves.

- 'Cool' brands, like iPods trigger our mating instincts.

- Other senses – smell, touch, and sound – are so powerful they physically arouse us when we see a product.

- Sex doesn't sell. In many cases, people in skimpy clothing and suggestive poses not only fail to persuade us to buy products – they often turn us away.

- Companies routinely copy from the world of religion and create rituals – like drinking a Corona with a lime – to capture our hard-earned dollars.

- Filled with entertaining inside stories about how we respond to such well-known brands as Marlboro, Nokia, Calvin Klein, Ford, and American Idol, *Buy-ology* is a fascinating and shocking journey into the mind of today's consumer that will captivate anyone who's been seduced – or turned off – by marketers' relentless attempts to win our loyalty, our money, and our minds.

Let us take, as an example, the conclusion that 'Gruesome health warnings on cigarette packages not only fail to discourage smoking, they actually make smokers want to light up.' This is based on people who are smokers, who have not been allowed to smoke for two hours, lying in the fMRI with anti-smoking warnings being flashed at them; the areas in their brains that are associated with desire then react. As these messages are interpreted via neuronal recruitment and this process goes through the limbic system, the parts of the brain that have to do with desire, it would be very surprising if these areas of the brain did not light up when the word 'smoking' was interpreted.

My view

I do not doubt that the experiments reported in *Buy-ology* were conducted to the highest standard. I have my doubts when any study concludes that neuroscience has now proved that <u>everything</u> we knew about behaviour is wrong. Martin Lindstrom is not the only author I would criticize for popularizing his findings. There are a number of books that have appeared in the last few months of 2010 that seem to echo this approach towards sensationalism.

The elusive subconscious

The use of neuroscience instead of established research techniques is often justified on the basis that it will reveal what is happening in people's subconscious. However, in reality there is little scientific evidence or agreement that such a thing as the subconscious exists. We may make a decision without fully appreciating all the influences that cause that decision but that does not mean we can accurately reflect on why we chose what we did. Another rationale for using neuroscience is that respondents lie. But respondents only lie when they believe the truth will reflect badly on them.

The *big* subconscious

My working career has been spent in advertising agencies, and I have often heard: 'More than 90 per cent of what we do is driven by the subconscious, so consumers cannot tell you why they buy brands.' This is often an argument used to dismiss research findings, or especially as a reason to discard research findings that are not popular, eg advertising tests that criticize the creative product.

I wanted to know more about the subconscious, because I would like to offer research that can tell my clients more about this subconscious (and apparently very important) part of consumer decisions. The logic appears to be: because the respondent is not aware of the subconsciousness it cannot be researched. This raises the question of how the agency then can make an advertisement that will influence this thing that we don't know anything about and cannot be measured but that has such a big influence on what we do.

These easy generalizations about the subconscious influence on behaviour invariably imply that the subconscious is not rational. Therefore we should not make advertising that appeals to rationality (notice how the argument easily shifts into rationality = consciousness and subconscious = creativity).

Whilst I am happy to accept that there is a consciousness and therefore something that is the opposite, what I wanted to know was 'Where is the boundary?' If we have some idea about where the boundary might be then we can also decide what is researchable, and therefore what can be consciously taken into account by brand strategists (who are presumably also using their subconsciousness to make strategic decisions that they do not understand).

The subconsciousness and religion

I thought that the real problem is me: I have not studied psychology and therefore I know very little. I approached my friend Eddie Wolfe (then the Dean of Psychology at Johannesburg University) with my problem. Over lunch we discussed the items we ordered. How much did the subconscious influence our decisions and in what way? Eddie gave me an insight that has helped me understand things a lot better: the subconsciousness is a closed system. All the evidence for the subconsciousness is inside the theory of subconsciousness.

He explained that this is like religion: if you believe in God then you see God's hand in everything. If you do not believe in God then you see God's hand in nothing. He explained the analogy: If you believe in the subconscious then the evidence is in all decisions, if you don't then the evidence is in all decisions. The analogy goes further: debates between people who believe in God and those who don't generally lead to nothing because the starting points are different. The clergy, by the very nature of their job, expand the area that they have influence over as much as possible. Similarly psychologists will try to expand the area covered by the subconscious as far as possible. This alone made it difficult for me to find the borders that I was looking for.

I decided to have an open mind and admit there is a subconsciousness, but that its influence might not be as big as claimed by some. Interestingly one should note on Wikipedia that scientists nowadays prefer not to use the word 'subconscious' but rather 'non-conscious' or 'pre-conscious'. If we consider our discussion of the brain and how things are interpreted (including how we feel about these things) then the terms 'pre-consciousness' and 'non-consciousness' make sense. Unfortunately most non-scientists are not aware of these subtle distinctions and 'hear' 'subconsciousness' when the newer terms are used. Here is what I found in Wikipedia:

> The term subconscious is used in many different contexts and has no single or precise definition. This greatly limits its significance as a meaning-bearing concept, and in consequence the word tends to be avoided in academic and scientific settings.
>
> In everyday speech and popular writing, however, the term is very commonly encountered. There it will be employed to refer to a supposed 'layer'

or 'level' of mentation (or/and perception) located in some sense 'beneath' conscious awareness – though, again, the notion's dependence upon informal 'folk-psychological' models that remain vague means that the precise nature and properties of this 'underlying' layer are either never made explicit or possess an ad hoc quality.

At different times, references to the 'subconscious' as an agency may credit it with various abilities and powers that exceed those possessed by consciousness: the 'subconscious' may apparently remember, perceive and determine things beyond the reach or control of the conscious mind.

The idea of the 'subconscious' as a powerful or potent agency has allowed the term to become prominent in the New Age and self-help literatures, in which investigating or controlling its supposed knowledge or power is seen as advantageous.

The 'subconscious' may also be supposed to contain (thanks to the influence of the psychoanalytic tradition) any number of primitive or otherwise disavowed instincts, urges, desires and thoughts.

The word 'subconscious' is an anglicized version of the French *subconscient* as coined by the psychologist Pierre Janet. Janet himself saw the *subconscient* as active in hypnotic suggestion and as an area of the psyche to which ideas would be consigned through a process that involved a 'splitting' of the mind and a restriction of the field of consciousness.

Though laypersons commonly assume 'subconscious' to be a psychoanalytic term, this is not in fact the case. Sigmund Freud had explicitly condemned the word as long ago as 1915: 'We shall also be right in rejecting the term "subconsciousness" as incorrect and misleading.' In later publications his objections were made clear: 'If someone talks of subconsciousness, I cannot tell whether he means the term topographically – to indicate something lying in the mind beneath consciousness – or qualitatively – to indicate another consciousness, a subterranean one, as it were. He is probably not clear about any of it. The only trustworthy antithesis is between conscious and unconscious.'

Thus, as Charles Rycroft has explained, 'subconscious' is a term 'never used in psychoanalytic writings'. And, in Peter Gay's words, use of 'subconscious' where 'unconscious' is meant is 'a common and telling mistake'; indeed, 'when [the term] is employed to say something "Freudian", it is proof that the writer has not read his Freud.'

Freud's own terms for mentation taking place outside conscious awareness were *das Unbewusste* (rendered by his translators as 'the Unconscious') and *das Vorbewusste* ('the Preconscious'); informal use of the term 'subconscious' in this context thus creates confusion, as it fails to make clear which (if either!) is meant.

The distinction is of significance because in Freud's formulation the Unconscious is 'dynamically' unconscious, the Preconscious merely 'descriptively' so: the contents of the Unconscious require special investigative techniques for their exploration, whereas something in the Preconscious is unrepressed and can be recalled to consciousness by the simple direction of attention. The erroneous, pseudo-Freudian use of 'subconscious' and 'subconsciousness' has its precise equivalent in German, where the words inappropriately employed are *Unterbewusst* and *Unterbewusstsein*.

(Wikipedia, 'Subconscious')

The confusion that arises when people willy-nilly talk about the subconsciousness

I have described how you have systems that look after your heart beating, your breathing and so on that you actually cannot experience working. You have neurons doing interpretation that you cannot feel working. When you are walking this happens without you thinking or without this disturbing your thoughts about what to say. When you reach out for a cup you do so without thinking about the muscles you move, or even your arm. So there is a lot that you are doing at any point in time without consciously thinking about it. The pyramid in Figure 21.1 demonstrates this.

Against this background it would be fair to say that only a small part of your brain is involved in conscious decisions. I certainly get the impression that when many people talk about 'consciousness' their audience hears the word 'rational'. Because emotionality is seen as being the antithesis of rationality this leads to the model in Figure 21.2 being very popular.

Firstly, equating rationality with consciousness is not acceptable. Damasio's point is exactly that there should not be distinctions between rational and emotional in decision making; they are inextricably intertwined.

Things get worse when people talk about brand positioning and advertising styles. Somehow the model in Figure 21.2 gets extended into one that looks like that in Figure 21.3.

Advertising philosophers talk about rational appeals being out and emotional appeals being in. What they seem to imply is that emotional appeals are creative. When they talk about 'rational advertising' they imply that they mean boring advertising about the functionalities of the brand. This jump in logic is not realistic.

Further mischief is created by confusing the consciousness with awareness in terms of what I can report on about my decisions, as shown in Figure 21.4. (This becomes an issue in market research.)

In many papers I have read the authors seem to make a logical jump that our consciousness is also our awareness, and therefore we are not aware of what happens outside our consciousness. Also they often make the jump that everything that is not conscious now never was or never can be again. Now this is also pushing things very far. I might not, at the time that I make a decision to choose a brand, be aware of all the considerations that have gone into the decision over many years of experience. But I can mostly think about why I did what I did and find reasons in memory that I might not have considered explicitly at the time I made the decision. So, when you ask me why I did this, I can mostly give you a reason. That reason might not have been explicitly considered at the point of purchase, but I can tell you why I did this.

I am a smoker and have changed brands three times in my life. I will walk into a store and buy my brand without thinking about the other brands on display. If you stop me and ask me why I bought this brand my answer will

FIGURE 21.1 Pyramid 1: consciousness

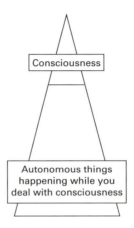

FIGURE 21.2 Pyramid 2: rationality–emotionality

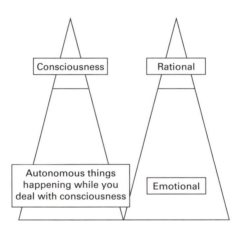

be: 'Because I always buy this brand.' This is an honest and truthful answer and accurately reflects my purchase decision. But, because I have changed my brand three times, there were at least three occasions in my life when I thought about the brand I smoked and the other brands that were available. There had to be three times that I was uncomfortable with the brand I was smoking. In Damasio's terminology, the soma when I thought about the brand was negative. If you asked me why I changed from one brand to the other I am able to give you cogent reasons. In terms of the triangles in Figures 21.1 to 21.4, when I buy a packet of cigarettes the only thing that is a consciousness is my decision to buy cigarettes. The brand choice is so

FIGURE 21.3 Pyramid 3: functionality–creativity

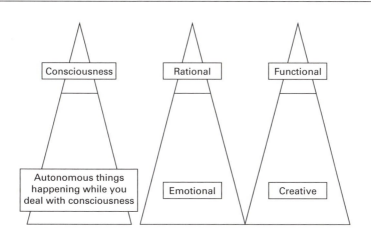

FIGURE 21.4 Pyramid 4: awareness

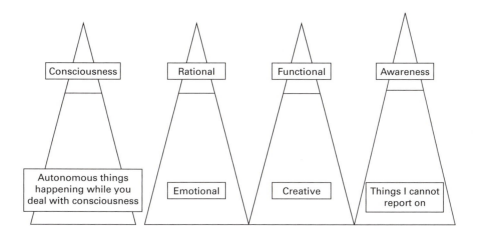

automatic that it can barely be called a consciousness. This is until the person at the counter tells me they are out of stock. My considerations about which brand I will buy do then become a consciousness. If this replacement brand makes me feel good it is possible that next time I buy I will consciously decide between my usual brand and the one I have now tried.

This is a personal belief

When Freudian and other psychologists debate the differences between consciousness, pre-consciousness and unconsciousness they are not really concerned about how we make brand choices or respond to advertising or even economic theories. They are mainly interested in bringing things that we might not be aware of at the time to our consciousness by way of hypnotism or other techniques. They want to do this to rectify our behaviour, which has presumably become so deviant from normal that we had to visit them.

There are few marketers or consultants who have Freudian training, and the use of the word 'subconscious' does give them away – as do the logical jumps they make into simply using the word to find an excuse for making things non-measurable.

Eddie Wolfe's description that views about the subconscious are like a religious system where the evidence is based on one's beliefs is pertinent. I am sure that there will be many pop psychologists, and even real psychologists, who will disagree with the view I express above.

A justification for brain scanning projects?

I have encountered some of the proponents of brain scanning techniques arguing that respondents do not tell you the truth because they cannot, but 'with fMRI we will get behind the real truth'. In fact, see the definition of 'neuromarketing' used in Wikipedia, where this statement is made:

> Marketing analysts will use neuromarketing to better measure a consumer's preference, as the verbal response given to the question, 'Do you like this product?' may not always be the true answer due to cognitive bias.
>
> This knowledge will help marketers create products and services designed more effectively and marketing campaigns focused more on the brain's response.
>
> Neuromarketing will tell the marketer what the consumer reacts to, whether it was the color of the packaging, the sound the box makes when shaken, or the idea that they will have something their co-consumers do not.
>
> The word 'neuromarketing' was coined by Ale Smidts in 2002.
>
> (Wikipedia, 'Neuromarketing')

If you Google the word 'neuromarketing', you will see how many bloggers and journalists are on this bandwagon. They are making the direct jump from the triangle on the left in Figure 21.4 (ie some things happen autonomously in the brain) to the triangle on the right (ie I cannot tell you why I bought the brand I did). This is really a massive jump in logic, and a vast over-claiming of what fMRI can do.

What Freud said

Whilst Freud did not coin the term 'subconscious' he is credited with it by most people. He had a patient who had an unreasonable (illogical, non-rational) fear of horses which he could not explain to anyone. In the early 1900s this was disabling, because horses walked the streets in Europe's major cities and towns. Freud hypnotized the patient and discovered that, when the patient was a small boy, a horse had bitten him, an incident that he did not remember until hypnotized. By making the patient aware of the incident, Freud could discuss this with him and work through his fears until they were resolved. From this grew a booming business – analysis and treatment of people with such problems (Freud called it 'repressing memories').

Freud said about his theories that they were stopgaps until we found ways to explore the human brain better. Maybe this is happening now.

If we consider this story against the background of what we now know about the brain then it is obvious that the boy, having been bitten by a horse, would have a fear of horses. Every time he saw a horse (and this would have happened a lot) his amygdala would fire, warning him of imminent danger. Over time he might have forgotten about the biting incident itself, but the fear would remain as a conditioned response – and the synapses involved would be activated every time he saw a horse.

There was nothing irrational about the boy's fear. If you had a fear of snakes after you had been bitten by one you would not be considered irrational. The emotion would be seen as evidence of your rationality.

Respondents lying and our ethics

Another urban myth that students raised in my class at Copenhagen Business School is that respondents lie. It would be very interesting to know where students got this story from. It came to light when we discussed the idea that with brain scanning we would be able to get more 'truthful' responses from respondents.

This book is as good a place as any to explain that respondents seldom lie, and if they do then it is due to poor design by the researcher inviting a situation where respondents feel they must lie to hide something.

Consider why people become respondents in research projects. Millions of people all over the world do this willingly. Their daily life is interrupted, they are asked a lot of questions, they get no feedback about what happens as a result of the survey, they are seldom paid, and when they are paid it is a pitiful amount. People mostly do it because their opinion is sought. They love to feel important and to give their opinions. Witness the numbers of people who phone in to radio programmes on any subject. Consider the number of blogs out there. These are people spending time and money just to hang their opinion out there, with no indication that others will read it. Think about the numbers who publish their photos and activities and opinions on Facebook and join forums on the internet. Why would people who are giving up their time to answer research questions lie? That would be the greatest waste of their time.

It requires a lot more mental energy to lie than it does to tell the truth. Why bother unless the research topic is one that causes people to lie – or the design of the questionnaire is such that respondents feel compelled to make jokes?

There are situations where people might lie, for example when you ask them about embarrassing personal things like their sex life, whether they are AIDs risks, and their financial position. If you are doing research in this area you are doing so at your own risk. People have a right to privacy. If you transgress the boundaries then you are inviting them to lie. But, rather than lying, it might be easier for them to refuse to partake in the survey. An unscrupulous researcher might try to disguise the purpose of the survey, but this should not be done.

So, yes, in some extreme circumstances people will lie. But, if you are now going to put them into scanners in these circumstances, to get past the lie, then you are treading on very thin ice as far as ethics (and probably the law) is concerned.

PART FOUR
Towards insights

As for any new science there will be those that over-claim what it can achieve because they are excited, and there will be those that over-claim because they have a financial motive to do so.

In Part 3 I tried to caution the reader about the over-claiming that appears to be happening, and also that such over-claiming is strengthened by the claims being made under 'neuroscience has proved that …'.

In Part 4 I will discuss some of the good science that has appeared in the area of marketing.

I started this book with good intentions to publish some case studies, and ended with only one: Read Montague's Pepsi Challenge experiment. He did not do this as part of a neuromarketing experiment, but rather a neuro-economics/psychology study.

Graham Page mentions some examples; and in the section about the media implications repeat exposures I mention an interesting result by Ron Wright, but he did not publish it as having implications for media planners.

This paucity of case studies could be due to the newness of what is known as neuromarketing and due to clients keeping their results confidential (although there is a possibility that this is overstated as a reason).

This really left me with the excellent work of Read Montague and some general comments of my own.

Read Montague's Pepsi Challenge

22

In Part 1 of this book I explained how neuroscience – especially Damasio – has led us to a new paradigm about the role of emotions. I concluded Part 1 with a discussion of how different sciences are now converging in their view of how the brain works and how some of these bring neurological insights to the party, some bring databases from psychology, sociology and marketing to the party.

In Chapter 20 I was critical of the contribution made by the *Buy-o-logy* experiment. In this chapter I will discuss the contribution of Read Montague, which stands in stark contrast to the contribution by Martin Lindstrom.

During the 1970s and 1980s Pepsi ran a campaign where a representative set up a stand in a shopping mall and invited people to do a blind taste test of two colas (Pepsi and Coca-Cola), indicating which one they preferred. This was carried into a television campaign showing Coca-Cola drinkers preferring Pepsi. (The last such test was apparently done in 2001.)

In a study from the group of Read Montague, the director of the Human Neuroimaging Lab and the Center for Theoretical Neuroscience at Baylor College of Medicine, published in 2004 in *Neuron*, 67 people had their brains scanned while being given the 'Pepsi Challenge', a blind taste test of Coca-Cola and Pepsi. Half the subjects chose Pepsi, and Pepsi tended to produce a stronger response than Coke in the brain's ventromedial prefrontal cortex, a region thought to process feelings of reward. But when the subjects were told they were drinking Coke three-quarters said that Coke tasted better. Their brain activity had also changed. The lateral prefrontal cortex, an area of the brain that scientists say governs high-level cognitive powers, and the hippocampus, an area related to memory, were now being used, indicating that the consumers were thinking about Coke and relating it to memories and other impressions. The results demonstrated that Pepsi should have half the market share, but in reality consumers are buying Coke for reasons related less to their taste preferences and more to their experience with the Coke brand.

(Wikipedia, 'Neuromarketing')

This book covers a lot of the area that marketers need to be aware of to put such research findings in a realistic perspective.

It is easy to sensationalize such experiments and their outcomes, which could also lead to groups like Commercial Alert creating problems for the whole developing science of neuromarketing and even for advances that could benefit medical research.

To appreciate the above developments we need to appreciate that Read Montague did not decide to randomly measure brain activity and thought he might use Pepsi and Coke. He based his whole design on a well-researched area in marketing, one where he had a hypothesis about which areas of the brain should react, etc.

What happened in the brain was a process of interpretation. The subjects had stimuli enter their brain via nerves not only from the mouth as they tasted the products but also from their ears when they were told which brands they were tasting. These sensations were interpreted in a process called 'neural recruitment'. This process of interpretation is based on memories. Not only the memory of the word 'Coke' but everything they knew about Coke and all their experiences about Coke were being evoked by the simple use of the word 'Coke'. This would include all the marketing activities that had gone into Coke and Pepsi.

This process of interpretation works its way through the limbic system to the frontal lobes of the brain. The limbic system is especially involved in adding 'feeling memories' to the developing interpretation. This is so that when the interpretation reaches the frontal lobes (where it can be used for thinking about actions) the person not only knows what it is but also how he or she feels about it.

Damasio calls this 'feeling' part of the interpretation the soma. It is called the brand soma when it has to do with a brand. Brands are just a sub-part of the things that the brain needs to interpret. It is this brand soma that allows the person to make decisions that rely on knowing what the brand is and how he or she feels about the brand.

From a marketing perspective what Read Montague measured was really the end product of a lot of marketing activities (and other things that happened in the lives of the respondents) that resulted in brand memories. This we would call brand equity.

About Read Montague

Read Montague is the author of *Your Brain Is (Almost) Perfect: How we make decisions* (2007), which was previously published as *Why Choose This Book?* He is a scientist in the field of computational neuroscience, which is a discipline that stands on the shoulders of evolutionary biology. I mention this because in Chapter 4 I explained that there are now many sciences that contribute to understanding the brain, each explaining the brain from a different perspective and all building on each other's insights.

Montague describes his area as the field that studies the actual information processing supported by our brains. What computational neuroscientists are especially interested in is finding efficient ways that the brain should work. Many aspects of the brain appear to have inefficient designs, but when one truly considers how the brain handles information it is (almost) perfect:

> The average 100 watt light bulb costs about a penny an hour to run, at the average market rates for electricity in the USA in 2005: around ten cents per kilowatt-hour. Go ahead and check your monthly bill.
> A human being sitting comfortably in a chair consumes energy at the rate of about 100 watts, roughly equivalent to the average light bulb! And this consumption is running literally everything – digestion, blood pumping, breathing, mental function, and a myriad of other processes. The brain consumes about a fifth of this rate; therefore, while sitting, the brain costs about a penny every 5 hours to operate, less than a nickel a day – now, that's an efficient machine.
>
> (Montague, 2007)

While Damasio was not interested in the efficiencies of the brain's information processing and Montague was not really interested in emotions, their conclusions are very similar: you use 'feeling good' as an input in your decision making.

The contribution of other sciences

The reader would by now have gathered that I believe neuroscience has contributed to marketing at a macro level. It has taught marketers about the importance of emotion in creating attention, and that there exists a soma that sets the background for brand decisions, ie the role of feelings in brand choice. And, at a micro level, it has given us the ability to measure arousal levels when people watch advertisements – although this has been available since 1929.

I believe that a lot of the hype about neuromarketing and discussions about buy buttons are just that: hype. Presumably a lot of this is driven by commercialism. I also believe that marketing can contribute to neuroscience in that it can lead the thinking of experimental designs based on marketers' empirical databases and years of experience studying how people make brand decisions. I find it rewarding to hear another discipline echoing the same thought.

> As modern neuroscience continues to deliver on its promise of understanding the biology of the nervous system, it's very clear that neuroscience is not equipped on its own (or on its own terms) to comprehend fully how to connect its vast physical understanding of the brain to our mental software. Psychology, cognitive sciences, and formal theoretical work will always be needed for this job. Software problems are not always directly related to hardware problems

– biologically or otherwise. In many ways, psychology may have more to teach the physical scientist of the brain than the other way around.

(Montague, 2007)

Montague on culture

At Baylor College of Medicine Montague's team set up an experiment that has received a lot of mentions in the popular press – especially with the recent recession in the economy. They built a hyperscan fMRI. This is a device where two (or more) fMRI machines are connected via the internet so that two people's brains can be scanned simultaneously. They were researching the feelings of trust and regret, especially trust as a feeling that underlies the formation of cultures. You need to trust the other people in your tribe, your spouse and so on.

They played economic games with the subjects being scanned, including one where investors played the stock market without knowing that the games data were those of the 1929 crash. This is where regret comes in: as a player invests money in the growing market he or she regrets not having invested more when the investment grows, so invests more, and a bubble is formed.

The initial experiment was carried out in the United States. Some of Montague's student co-workers were Chinese, and they suggested that the results would be different for China. Montague then set up an experiment with volunteers in China. Again the machines were linked via the internet. The Chinese subjects received their instructions in Cantonese. The results were still pending at the time he wrote his book:

> Many answers are still out, but the group recruited and instructed in Chinese uses a different strategy, especially in the role of trustee, and we believe that there are a couple of different brain activations that correlate with this different style of play.
>
> It's pretty clear that I need to add a cultural anthropologist to the lab's intellectual fabric, since questions about how to analyze these kinds of data are not separate from an understanding of how cultural influences may act as brain-changing inputs.
>
> (Montague, 2007)

Of course, I am glad that he reached a similar conclusion to that of my feelings schema where I added personality and culture as feelings (Figure 16.1).

From a much broader perspective, Millward Brown is the company that does the most advertising measurement in the world. It has offices in 49 countries, doing work for all the major multinational companies. The advertising measures used by Millward Brown are standardized as much as is reasonable, which means that comparative data are collected in all these countries. One can only imagine the benefit to any neuroscience team of all these data and the massive experience that Millward Brown has developed in communications research.

Science: models and measurements

23

The homunculus

We have mentioned Descartes, the amazing scientist-philosopher of the 17th century who said 'I think, therefore I am.' One of his amazing insights was that our muscles are controlled by our nerves. He believed that the juices of life (*vitae*) are pumped via the nerves into the muscles to make them contract and hence control movement. This was quite an insight given that electricity was still to be discovered.

His explanation was that we had a little man (homunculus) in our head. He would watch through our eyes and hear through our ears. He would then decide what we should do and pull levers to manipulate our movements. We might now laugh at the idea of a homunculus, because the obvious question is 'What makes the homunculus move? Is there a homunculus inside the homunculus?' Yet many explanations of the brain still sound suspiciously as though they rely on a homunculus. They end with: 'Well, there is this funny thing in your head that makes you behave in ways that you cannot control.' This is then just a homunculus in another guise. Certainly theories about the subconsciousness and theories about us not knowing why we make decisions are all really just postulating the existence of a homunculus in disguise.

I am not suggesting that the way I described the brain working in this book gets us to the final answer, but it certainly avoids some of the traps that some theories head toward.

Decision making

Philosophers of old kept themselves occupied answering questions like 'Who are we? How do we know who we are? How do others know who we are?'

These questions evolved into questions about the consciousness. Psychologists developed the issue further into debates about the consciousness and the subconsciousness (and then the pre-consciousness and unconsciousness). Economists, marketers and other disciplines concentrated on decision making, especially in so far as it results in behaviour. To some extent this meant that they did not have to involve themselves in the debates of psychologists.

With the advent of neuromarketing this luxury of ignoring other disciplines is no more. We are all researching the brain, trying to learn more about the same thing, whether we call it 'decision making' or 'consciousness'. I have found that when I read books (psychology, marketing, etc) that refer to the 'consciousness', I am well served if I replace the word by the term 'decision making'. Mostly it helps me understand what is being said better.

At Copenhagen Business School I was asked by Flemming Hansen to start a course in neuromarketing, although we called the elective 'Emotions in Advertising'. This became a very popular elective within three years. During this time Hansen started a unit headed by Thomas Ramsoy, a neuropsychologist, with access to all the important brain measurement equipment. Wisely they decided to call this unit the Neuro-Decision Making Unit. This stresses what we are really looking at among all the disciplines that contribute.

Models and measurement

If we ultimately want to understand the brain and how we make decisions then we need to be in a situation where we have: 1) models (or theories) of how the brain works, supported by measures of behaviour that confirm the model; and 2) measures of the brain, which we understand against the background of our model.

We are now entering the era where we can take biological measures of the brain in ways that we have never been able to do before, and this should help us to understand which models of the brain making decisions we should accept. A very big step has already been taken by scientists like Damasio, LeDoux and Read Montague.

There are two dangers that face us: 1) models that do not explain the measures that are taken; and 2) measures that do not lead into existing or new models.

The term 'neurobullshitting' has appeared on the web and seems to have all the potential to become a popular derogatory term for what we are attempting to do. In this section of the book I have shown some examples of where I believe a lot of measures have been taken with the findings not explained by the researchers, ie creating opportunities for neurobullshitting.

FIGURE 23.1   Models and measurement

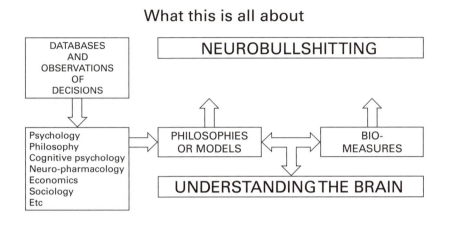

Models: the future

Should the measures lead the models, or the models lead the measures? In Part 1 I explained that this area of neuro-decision making is attracting the attention of many disciplines, and for the first time they do have a common biological measurement to work toward. Most of these (described as working 'from the outside in' and from the 'top to the bottom' in Figure 4.1) are disciplines that consider behavioural data and develop models about the decision-making processes that underlie the behaviour. These disciplines have substantial databases measuring behaviours and have debated the underlying models in academic papers for many decades.

Ultimately what we are facing now, in the quest to understand decision making, is marrying the databases of behavioural data with the developing databases of biological measures.

For marketers there is a really exciting time lying ahead. Economists have generally accepted Adam Smith's *Homo economicus* without doing research to explain this model. Psychologists have collected either data about abnormal behaviour or small samples consisting of students for academic papers. Marketers have used large samples, studying normal decision making over a massive number of product categories and brands in multiple countries. Companies like Millward Brown have compiled databases for their standardized research methodologies that span all continents and all product types.

In many respects we are now at the threshold where we need to consider how the databases of behaviour and the models/theories of behaviour align with the bio-measures of neuroscience.

We can decide to ignore the bio-measures and continue with our pet theories about behaviour, or we can reject our models/theories of behaviour based on databases and accept the bio-measures as new truth. Lindstrom certainly seems to have done the latter when he states that 'everything we believed about why people buy is wrong'. Both of these actions lead to neuro-bullshitting.

On the other hand, if we really work at resolving the differences that are emerging, we are working toward a much better understanding of the brain/ brand puzzle.

PART FIVE
Some marketing implications

At the turn of the century four things that affected our lives as marketers happened simultaneously and independently:

1 The paradigm of why people have emotions changed totally from what it was since Descartes, and even Freud. This is largely ascribed to Damasio, but as I indicated there are several thinkers from different disciplines that had the same thought at about the same time.

2 fMRI became a reality, and brain scanning pictures flooded the media.

3 Bio-measures, like EEG and eye-tracking, despite being very old techniques became popularized in market research.

4 The term neuromarketing came into vogue, partly because of the marketers of bio-measures, against the background of fMRI's popularity and Damasio's theorem.

Unfortunately very few marketers realized that these four are largely totally uncorrelated and occurred reasonably independently (ie each would have happened without any of the other three occurring). However, their futures will be increasingly intertwined!

Damasio came to his conclusions largely by observation of patients, possibly assisted a bit by fMRI. This led to a paradigm shift.

fMRI has actually contributed very little to neuromarketing. Most of what was contributed was by way of sound experimental design based on pre-existing knowledge leading to good hypotheses about how the brain could work being confirmed.

Bio-measures have existed for decades before. They have achieved new interest because of the insights of Damasio, and the fact that these measures have become more economical and practical to apply.

It is easy to understand why the simultaneous occurrence of these events gave rise to marketers, researchers and teachers being confused. It is also easy to see how over-claiming for the achievements of neuromarketing will happen.

However, if one takes the four points above in isolation then it is a lot easier to make sense of what is happening today.

The marketing implications I chose

Marketing can be discussed under many headings. To the students and practitioners of marketing it often appears like a *capita selecta* ('issues I'd like to discuss') when reading marketing books. The fact is, that if one reads the topics that I discuss in the next few chapters then it could really appear like 'Erik's Random Thoughts'.

There is, however, a very solid foundation and continuity to the topics that I have chosen to discuss:

1 They are all grounded in the neuroscience that I have discussed in the book.

2 They form a continuum – they do lead into each other from the very basics of marketing tactics to the ultimate of strategy: the budget.

The build-up of the next five chapters

1. Attention

It should not be a surprise that at the lowest level of this discussion I talk about attention. Some readers might be surprised that I see the issue of attention being at the lowest level of discussion as far as marketing is concerned, but then, without attention and memory nothing happens.

Without a memory you cannot interpret and without interpretation you cannot decide.

I started this book with a description of how neurons, synapses and neural networks form memories and are used to interpret gestalts. I kept referring back to this throughout the book as we built our way into the more meta issues like Damasio's somatic marker theorem.

A very real application of what neuroscience has taught us is in the way that Digital Video Recorders (DVRs) actually might be improving advertising efficiencies – despite billions of dollars being moved away from television mistakenly.

I also mention Robert Heath's work in this area, providing a direct contradiction of my views.

2. Brand soma

Much more important to us, in my mind, is Damasio's somatic marker theorem. This is where we start to understand the new paradigm of 'feelings' where feelings are not bad things, but things that drive decision making.

Simplistically Damasio states that people use emotions as an input to rational decision making, and that these emotions play off against the background of background feelings.

Brand choice is simply another decision in the consumer's life. Sometimes an important one, sometimes one that is inconsequential. But it is still just another decision.

Like all decisions the somatic marker theorem applies. I simply created the term: brand soma, to differentiate between brand decisions and others. There is really no difference as far as the consumer is concerned.

I argued in *The Advertised Mind* that mere ad-likeability is the best measure of advertising effectiveness based on the fact that when people talk about advertising they use this terminology, and that we then see this in all the measures of the advertisement that we are measuring.

I argue that we see the effect of the brand soma in all our data, we just call it the halo effect.

Ultimately the brand soma is merely how I feel about the brand, or, more specifically, how I think I would feel about using the brand.

I chose to discuss this because this is one of the true contributions to marketing from neuroscience, but not by way of fMRI or even bio-measures, but from the philosophical insight of Damasio.

3. Decision making heuristics

It is a fallacy that consumers spend a lot of time thinking about all aspects of a brand every time they make a choice (decision).

It is also amazing how often one hears speakers at conferences announce this as if they discovered a new truth. We all knew this.

Consumers use simplified decision rules called heuristics for most of their decisions. A major part (input) of these heuristics is the brand soma. However, not everybody has the same heuristic for a brand and not everyone has the same brand soma. This makes it very difficult to generalize about a brand's soma or its users' heuristics (or those of its non-users).

It is a lot easier if one can find ways to group users into groups that have similar heuristics for their brand choice and then also those that have similar brand somas. This is generally attempted by way of segmentation studies.

4. Market segmentation

I have always been intrigued by, what appeared to me, the fashions of new segmentation schemes that emerged in marketing.

Of course there are the demographics, lifestyles, life stage, values, etc. but then there was also Freudian, Personalities, Educational, Media Imperatives, Jungian, etc. At a stage I considered asking people their star signs to see whether this helps to predict their brand preferences.

Not surprisingly there is an anti-segmentation lobby building arguing that segmentation has been disproven.

Yet, it is fairly obvious that for many markets there exists a segmentation based on age, gender, life stage, income, etc.

There is now evidence emerging that, at least, personality and culture are differentiators in terms of decision making, and for good Darwinian reasons.

Neuroscience's contribution to this is even more far-reaching explaining the effect of moods and homeostasis on our decision making.

This brings us back to Damasio's background feelings. It is these background feelings that determine our decision making heuristics at any point in time that also have an effect on our attention.

Market segmentation is really the most important thing that a marketer can do, not because it is a sexy research exercise, but because it is based on real neurological differences among people. The issue is that it has to be done multidimensionally.

5. Budgets and life cycles

Right at the top of marketing decisions that have to be taken is the marketing budget.

Obviously when these decisions are taken no one thinks about the neurons of the consumer. But, it is what happens in the consumers' memories that actually determine these decisions.

For most established brands there is a surprisingly simple relationship between their advertising share and their market share (at least for 70 per cent of the brands on the market). Few marketers realize this, and even fewer use it for sensible marketing decisions.

This relationship has been established in many studies by some of the biggest brains in marketing since as far back as the 1960s to as recently as 2009. Marketers, and accountants, just prefer to ignore the evidence. This might be the single driving factor behind brand life cycles.

Ultimately the biggest decision that marketers have to take involves how much money to invest in marketing a brand.

This decision hinges on the brand soma and the advertising leverage among the market segments based on their heuristics, which, as background feelings, will also contribute to the attention that they pay to the advertising and the brand, etc.

Ultimately it all comes together. The marketer's understanding of people's memories of his brand and the feelings about the brand this results in and how these are used by the different segments to decide on a brand comes together in the composition of the marketing budget.

Attention

24

Why it is an important topic

We have discussed how feelings lead to one developing gestalt being given more attention than the other developing gestalts. We can define attention in this sense as being a temporary stable dominant gestalt – albeit that this could be for just a very brief moment.

In *The Advertised Mind* (2005) I explained how we have emotions because they cause us to give attention to things. I also explained what is needed in advertisements that lead to ad liking (ie emotions). In that book I criticized Robert Heath's low attention processes model. This led to Heath conducting two experiments that support his views. One won the best paper award at the British Market Research Conference. During this time, because of the speculations about the effect of DVRs giving people the ability to time-shift programmes and the developing belief that as a result television advertising effectiveness would decline, I conducted an experiment to see whether this was so.

I found that the opposite is true, even to the extent that DVRs might improve television advertising effectiveness. I then found data in Millward Brown's Adtrack database that corroborates this finding. I published this in *Admap* (du Plessis, 2007), calling the phenomenon 'inadvertent attention': in the process of trying to avoid advertising, people actually give the advertisement attention. Resulting from this I was asked to talk at the Wharton Business School's Future of Advertising conference in December 2008 (**http://www.scribemedia.org/content-libraries/empirical-generalizations/**), which led to a shortened version of the paper being published in the *Journal of Advertising Research* (du Plessis, 2009). This was picked up by an editor of the *Harvard Business Review* producing an even shorter article in the April 2010 edition (O'Connell, 2010). Quite clearly there is a lot of interest in this topic, and it is seen to have real business applications.

The issue

One of the most important issues facing marketers is attention. You want your brand to get attention when people are standing in front of the shelf.

You want your communication to get attention when people are exposed to it, and the brand to get attention when people are exposed to the advertisement.

> Attention is the cognitive process of selectively concentrating on one aspect of the environment while ignoring other things.
>
> Examples include listening carefully to what someone is saying while ignoring other conversations in a room (the cocktail party effect) or listening to a cell phone conversation while driving a car. Sometimes attention shifts to matters unrelated to the external environment, a phenomenon referred to as mind-wandering or 'spontaneous thought'. Attention is one of the most intensely studied topics within psychology and cognitive neuroscience.
>
> (Wikipedia, 'Attention')

Most advertising exposures occur in situations where people are giving attention to something other than the advertisement and we hope they will shift their attention to our advertisement. TV viewers are giving attention to programmes or their meal, or talking to other people; we hope they will give attention to our advertisement when it appears. Newspaper readers are reading what is on a page; we hope they will shift their attention to our advertisement on the page. Internet surfers are giving attention to what is on the screen; we hope they will look at the banner advertising our brand. It is the shift in attention that matters. This is why we spent a lot of space in the earlier part of the book explaining how gestalts form via neural recruitment and how it then happens that a specific gestalt is given attention owing to a variety of factors, including feelings.

Some advertising practitioners argue that what cognitive scientists have learned about 'learning' is irrelevant to advertising. The argument is that when you learn for an exam you are giving a lot of attention, but people seldom want to learn from an advertisement. It is true that people do not sit in front of a TV set anxiously waiting for advertising. It is also true that when they see an advertisement they seldom concentrate on the advertisement. Nearly always advertising works at a low level of attention. This should not be a concern to an advertiser, because advertising has always worked at a low level of attention. I stress the word 'worked' in the previous sentence, because some advertising works, and when it works it works very well – as proved by John Philip Jones (1995).

Some people debate whether we can give attention to only one thing at a time or possibly a few things. This views attention as an on–off switch: 'I am giving something attention, or not.' It is much more likely, as I will show, that what we really have is a situation where there is a 'degree' of attention. Hence we can talk about low levels of attention and high levels of attention, and degrees of attention in between. High levels of attention are given when we are concentrating on something. This something might be something in the environment, or it might just be something we are thinking about.

When we are trying to learn something we force our attention toward it. We try to exclude other distractions; we might repeatedly give it attention.

Students trying to learn something will reread the text several times. When people try to memorize a number they will repeat it several times. We might do this when we are reading the small ads in a newspaper when looking for a used car. When people watch TV they do not do this – except, sometimes, when there is a call to action in the advertisement that is very relevant to them.

Consider the quotes from Greenfield (1995) (see Chapters 7 and 10) about how things become a consciousness. Among her examples is how even a soft whisper in a library can become an irritating consciousness or how a soft stroking on the skin by a lover can become a consciousness. Her point is that in the absence of competing stimuli small developing gestalts can become a consciousness. So, if you sit in front of a TV and there is little else competing for your attention, the chances are better that the advertising on TV is your consciousness at that point in time, even if you are not concentrating on it or you will subsequently say that you were not really looking at the advertisement. This statement is important: when in research people are asked about advertising they will often report that they do not watch advertising. The fact is that they do not consciously watch advertising. However, even being exposed to advertising at a low level of attention means that people are physically giving it attention.

For most of the time we are not consciously giving attention to anything very important. We sit in the train to work. We drive somewhere. We do the couch-potato bit. We surf the internet with no great intent. This is when advertising can create a consciousness.

The issue of whether advertising relies on a low level of processing or a high level of processing is really just a red herring. What does matter is whether the advertisement has the ability to attract attention (at whatever level of attentioning it finds the viewer).

Studying for an exam or giving attention to an advertisement

In the first instance we must recognize that the memory formation in both cases uses the same neurons. The brain does not have different neuronal structures with which to remember things. It especially does not have a specific memory structure for advertising or brands and another for things that are important for it to know about.

The difference between memories from studying processes and those from advertising processes lies in the way that attention is given – ie how the memory was created – rather than the form of the memory or where it is stored in the brain.

The following is about the experiment that I described in the article in the *Harvard Business Review*. It demonstrates not only inadvertent attention, but also how exposures to an advertisement once it has been given cognition lead to re-cognition and can happen at a very low level of exposure.

Death of the 30-second ad?

A major debate (in the United States and then the rest of the world) was started when Joseph Jaffe published his book *Life after the 30-Second Spot* in 2005. In this he suggested that the 30-second ad had lost its effectiveness, and he suggested using other ways to talk to the consumer.

Mostly the death of the 30-second advertisement is blamed on the advent of the digital video recorder (also called the personal video recorder). This is the device that you hook on to your television that records programmes for later viewing and allows you to fast-forward through advertisements. This resulted in many advertisers moving billions of dollars out of television advertising into other media like sponsorships.

Here are quotes from the internet suggesting the extent of the effect of the book:

- 'Accenture have a new report out, estimating the effect of DVRs to be a reduced growth in US TV ad revenues to just 3% by 2009 – versus other analysts' predictions of between 6% and 10%, leaving a $27 billion hole in the industry bank account' (**http://adage.com/images/random/accenture041405.pdf**).

- 'Heineken have pulled out of TV advertising in the UK; their £6.5 million budget will go on sport sponsorship and POS in 2006' (**http://www.brandrepublic.com/news/526361/Close-Up-Live-Issue--beer-brands-need-TV-advertising/**).

- Quoted in *The Times*: 'Rob Marijnen, managing director of Heineken UK, said that a number of factors had prompted it to put its money elsewhere, including the rising cost of buying airtime and the advent of Sky Plus, which enables viewers to skip ads' (**http://business.timesonline.co.uk/tol/business/industry_sectors/consumer_goods/article581094.ece**).

- 'Following on from P&G and Unilever switching money out of TV, Carat forecast a $40 billion switch' (**http://simonandrews.typepad.com/big_picture/2005/10/carat_forecast_.html**).

It makes for some scary reading.

The book resulted in a conference at Wharton Business School at the end of 2008 to discuss the implications of the death of the 30-second ad. All the evidence for the death of the 30-second ad is based on research, and makes clear that 'Research proves...'. The research that is quoted just asks people what the major benefit of these recorders is, and most people state that the benefit is that they can fast-forward through the advertising breaks. The assumption is that when people fast-forward through an advertisement it will have no effect.

Some empirical data

It is often easy to build arguments by heaping assumption on to assumption. Marketers and advertisers are prone to this – probably because they are very clever people. However, they very seldom spell out what the assumptions are, and very seldom then try to verify these assumptions.

The whole scenario about the death of the 30-second ad is based on two assumptions: 1) the major benefit of these machines to the consumer is that they can fast-forward through the ad break; 2) an ad that has been fast-forwarded has no effect. These assumptions might appear to be reasonable at first glance.

Millward Brown conducted two experiments – one in the United States and one in South Africa. At the time neither of the groups was aware of what the other was doing.

In the United States Millward Brown did a survey among 2,000 people of whom 1,200 owned DVRs. They were asked ad recall and ad recognition questions for 16 advertisements in different product categories. There was little difference for both measures between owners and non-owners. In fact the owners of these devices scored higher on both measures than the non-owners, admittedly not statistically significantly so. (See Figure 24.1.)

The reason for there being little difference is explained by a second experiment that Millward Brown did in South Africa.

I realized when I was given a DVR for Christmas that fast-forwarding requires a lot of attention. Once you have pressed the fast-forward button you have to concentrate on the screen to stop at the right point. Generally you overshoot a bit. Thus whilst the ads are appearing at double speed on the screen, you are really paying attention.

To see how this works in real life the Millward Brown team recorded a normal advertising break of advertisements at triple-fast-forward speed. We showed this to people in a cinema environment (we wanted to have complete control of the setting and their attention). Then we asked them to write down the advertisements (recall), whether they had seen them before (recognition) and how much they liked the advertisements.

In our Adtrack system we had measured all the advertisements used in the test among an independent sample, where we had obtained like-ability scores.

- The ads in the show reel were recalled by 40 to 90 per cent of the audience. This is very high for such a memory task.

- Most of the people who recalled an advertisement claimed that they had seen the advertisement before.

- The liking scores given in the cinema were highly correlated with the liking scores given in the independent Adtrack system.

These results are on my website (**www.erikdup.com**) with the full presentation I did at the Wharton Business School conference.

FIGURE 24.1 Ad recall and ad recognition

Ad recall results for the respective 16 brands based among those asked the category. Average base: DVR owner 400; non-DVR owner 600. Results then aggregated to create an average score.
- There are no significant differences between DVR owners and non-DVR owners for the 16 individual brands.

Ad Recognition results for each of the 16 ads based upon those asked about the ad. Average Base: DVR owners 100; non-DVR owners 150.
- There are no significant differences between DVR owners and non-DVR owners except for one ad which has significantly higher recognition among DVR owners.

Total average across categories	DVR owners %	Non-DVR owners %	Index of DVR owners against non-DVR owners
Ad recall (aware of TV advertising for specific brands)	43	42	102
Prompted ad recognition (recognized ads based upon six unbranded ad frames)	44	43	102

Movie average	DVR owners %	Non-DVR owners %	Index of DVR owners against non-DVR owners
Ad recall (aware of TV advertising for specific brands)	32	30	107
Prompted ad recognition (recognized ads based upon six unbranded ad frames)	50	47	106

Car averages	DVR owners %	Non-DVR owners %	Index of DVR owners against non-DVR owners
Ad recall (aware of TV advertising for specific brands)	41	38	108
Prompted ad recognition (recognized ads based upon six unbranded ad frames)	27	25	108

Fast food restaurants	DVR owners %	Non-DVR owners %	Index of DVR owners against non-DVR owners
Ad recall (aware of TV advertising for specific brands)	45	46	98
Prompted ad recognition (recognized ads based upon six unbranded ad frames)	49	46	107

Cell phones average	DVR owners %	Non-DVR owners %	Index of DVR owners against non-DVR owners
Ad recall (aware of TV advertising for specific brands)	53	53	100
Prompted ad recognition (recognized ads based upon six unbranded ad frames)	49	52	94

When I present this study to South African marketers I show the reel we used in the experiment at the triple-fast-forward speed we used for the experiment. This contains two humorous advertisements, and when these appear the audience laughs. It took me several presentations to realize that they are each time confirming my interpretation of the results of this study – not only does my audience recognize the advertisements at speed, but they also react emotionally to them by laughing.

When people see an advertisement they have seen before they recognize it. The word 'recognize' means exactly that: re + cognize. The process of re-cognition not only involves interpreting what is on the screen, but includes how people feel about it. In other words, what we saw in this experiment is exactly the Damasian processes we described earlier. Isn't it great to see how marketing contributes to neuroscience by proving things?

The audience were interpreting their environment – in this case the screen. The process of interpreting involves recruitment of neurons based on previous experiences. If an advertisement has been 'cognized' before this experience then this is what the recruitment of neurons is based on. The gestalt that forms is more than the mere flickering fast-forward images with no sound. The gestalt that comes to mind includes how the advertisement made the people feel before. This process of neurons being recruited, as we know, increases the limens of the synapses, ie reaffirms the memories themselves.

Take note that this experiment does not show how attention has an effect. It shows that the high attention resulting from fast-forwarding has an effect if the advertisement is recognized. The description of the brain process above does however give insights into understanding low attention effects.

Why is this in a book about neuromarketing?

The main reason is that it is an example of what neuromarketing is about. Because I have studied things about the brain and how neurons work and how synapses lay down memories I had a fairly good idea of what to look for.

I mentioned that in my presentations at conferences I show people pictures of cats and dogs at the rate of up to one-tenth of a second. I then later show them pictures that they have seen before and some they have not and they have to identify which were part of the first showing. They mostly get it 100 per cent right. The objective of showing this to the audience is to demonstrate the amazing abilities of memory and attention.

Having done many talks showing the cats and dogs slides and therefore being hyper-aware of how fast people can classify pictures between cats and dogs, I was also aware that there might be effects from fast-forward advertisements, ie as we understand the brain better we will also understand our research better and make better marketing decisions.

Inadvertent attention

I published a paper in *Admap* (2007), which reported on an amazing pheno-menon that the Millward Brown team measured in South Africa because of very unique circumstances. Because these circumstances are unlikely to have occurred in any other country, and because the phenomenon demon-strates an important point about advertising attentioning, I'd like to repeat it here.

Our Adtrack system measures the recall of every television commercial in the country; we do this once two weeks after they are launched. In other words it is a census of all advertising. Quite simply, we are notified of all new advertising on television, we wait two weeks for some media pressure to build up, we then do a telephone survey of 200 people asking them whether they have seen an advertisement for the brand in question and, if they did, we ask them to describe it. If the description is correct we ask the people to give the advertisement a rating of points out of 10 for how much they liked it.

We obviously know how long the ad was, what the media pressure behind it was, and so on. It is this database that allowed us to 'discover' the power of ad liking as a simple emotional measure. This confirmed the ARF Copy Validation Project and led to the book *The Advertised Mind*.

What we have not shown before is what happened to the average recall of advertisements over time. In Figure 24.2 I have highlighted how the aver-age recall of TV advertisements has decreased at the rate of 4 per cent per annum. In *The Advertised Mind* I show that this is not just a South African phenomenon but that it has happened to all media in all countries where such information is available. We were just in the fortunate situation of capturing the data as a census of all ads over time for a long period. However, there is a very obvious break in the trend line in 1994, after which the 4 per cent decline re-emerged, but just from a higher starting point.

What happened was that in the racial South Africa – pre-1994 – separate channels were used to transmit programmes, ie white vernacular pro-grammes were on channels 1 and 2 and black vernacular programmes were on channels 3 and 4. Post-1994 the channels were all mixed-language. This meant that, on channel 1, which used to carry only English programmes, there was now a multi-language offering, and an English programme was followed by a Zulu programme. The same was true for the other channels. This meant that English-speaking people watching an English programme would find themselves next exposed to a Zulu programme – a language they did not understand. They would then channel-hop to find an English programme.

Most advertisers thought that this would lead to audience loss – and it did. Yet measures of ad recall increased dramatically, as shown above. What happened was that people were low-attentive in front of their TVs and advertising noting decreased at about 4 per cent per annum, as I have shown. But when the channel changed its language they started to change channels.

FIGURE 24.2 Average recall of TV advertisements

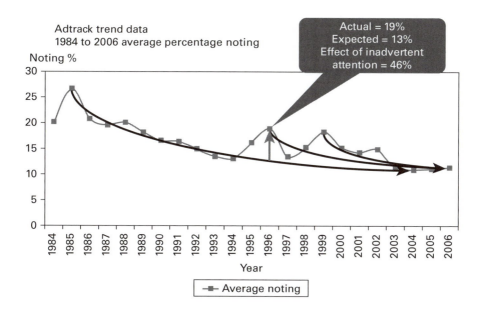

To do this they had to give attention to the television screen, and 'inadvertently' saw the advertisement.

This story fits with the story of the fast-forwarded ads. When people give attention to anything for any reason this will reinforce the memory of the ad.

Is this a neuromarketing story? Of course it is.

We know from neuromarketing that memories are laid down by experience and reinforced by experience. We know that the memory laying down happens because of interpretation of the environment and that the mere interpretation reaffirms memories. Am I suggesting that any exposure is good? No. Any memory laid down in a situation where the body feels negative will create a negative soma.

The 1998/99 increase in average noting is generally believed to be due to the better use of black actors in television advertising. Before this the bulk of television advertisements were produced in two formats: one with white actors and one with black actors. Because the channels were racially targeted this did not cause problems with scheduling the advertisements or even mixing an advertisement's race and the audience's race.

From 1998 marketers had to use mixed models in their advertising because the channels were not racially targeted. It is generally assumed that because this was 'new' (to both cultures) the audiences gave more attention to the advertising. Again one can classify this as a sort of inadvertent attention because in many cases people were probably not intending to give the advertisement itself more attention.

The response curve and re-cognition

One of the most hotly debated topics even today is how often the audience should be exposed to an advertisement, and inside what time. If people are seldom exposed to the advertisement it cannot be expected to have an effect; if they are overexposed to it the advertiser wastes money.

In *The Advertised Mind* I spend a lot of time explaining the debate and also the history of the debate – so I will not repeat it. It is enough to say that this is a debate about whether there exists a threshold effect, a sort of 'aha' effect. In other words, do audience members see the advertisements a few times and then react, or do they react from the first exposure? Proponents of both views agree that after the audience have had this 'aha' effect the effect of the advertisement is still increasing but at a decreasing rate. Figure 24.3 demonstrates the two views.

FIGURE 24.3   Response curves

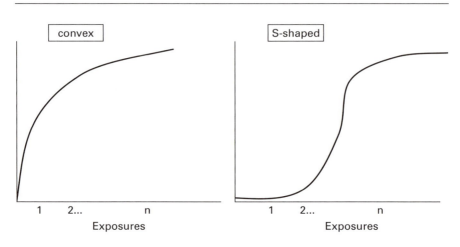

In *The Advertised Mind* I argue that the convex curve is just a special case of the S-shaped curve with an inflection point at one exposure. In both cases there appears to be a further increase in response after the critical point, but at a decreasing rate. However, the issue is not what happens at the top end of this hypothetical curve, but what happens at the bottom. If an inflection is not achieved then nothing good will happen.

What I did not realize before I did the DVR experiment is that the inflection point in these graphs is really just the point where cognition (memory formation) happens. This might be after one exposure or several exposures, as Krugman (1972) argued.

Once the advertisement has been 'cognized', a whole new process is in place in the brain: re-cognition.

Re-cognition in non-fast-forwarded advertisements

It was quite a surprise to see, in the DVR experiment, that the fast-forwarded advertisements not only are recognized (ie would have increased the limens of people's memories) but also carried a similar ad liking to that which they had in the Adtrack system. However, when we view these results against the background of the neurology explained earlier in the book it should not have been a surprise. This did, however, explain to me something that I had always found interesting (and had chosen not to think about too much).

In all the arguments about media strategy it is assumed that after an advertisement has 'entered the mind' it has an effect that increases with each exposure, but at a decreasing rate. In other words the ends of the graphs in Figure 24.3 show a convex curve. This is in line with nearly all empirical evidence I have ever seen (Millward Brown tracking, Adtrack, journal papers and John Philip Jones's work): once an advertisement has established a measurable level of effectiveness this does not decrease in the short or medium term owing to the number of exposures.

I have read as much as I can about wear-out (and very little is written about it). Most research papers, when they talk about wear-out, lament that advertisers change advertisements before there is any real evidence that they have worn out. I was really expecting that somehow when people have seen a lot of a commercial they would just screen it out and therefore the effectiveness would dramatically decrease! Yet there is no empirical evidence of this happening.

The DVR experiment really provides a lot of insight into this:

- When people see an advertisement they have seen a lot of times before they do not look at it.
- To recognize the advertisement they must have 'cognized' it before.
- The process of recognition stimulates the synapses, resets the limens, and involves recalling the 'feelings'.
- This makes later exposures nearly as effective as the exposures that created the cognition.
- If cognition has never happened, then because advertisers seldom will have a higher level of frequency of exposure after launch the effect also remains the same, just at a lower level, ie the impact rate of an advertisement is unlikely to increase over time.

Media strategy implications

There are a number of research studies that conclude that advertisements that are fast-forwarded have the same effect as those viewed at normal speed

– provided they have been seen before. From a media planning perspective the optimal approach would be:

1 Launch the advertisement on channels that are not fast-forwarded (sports, news, etc).

2 Monitor whether people have 'cognized' the advertisement (is there a memory?), using an advertising tracking system.

3 Once cognition has been achieved, move the advertisement to cheaper fast-forwarded channels (the repeat exposure might even be better than on a non-fast-forwarded channel, as I will discuss next). A major benefit of moving the advertisement to fast-forwarded channels is that then the audience will watch it when they can give attention, are in a positive viewing mood, and have to give attention when they fast-forward the advertisement.

Neuroscience and re-cognition (or repeat exposure)

The issue about repeat exposures to an advertisement is one of the important issues of marketing – specifically media planning – and is a vital determinant of the size of the advertising budget. The issue about re-cognition and how this works in terms of the audience's memory and media planning, especially in the environment of DVRs and cross-media planning, arose from other evidence which goes back to Krugman's work in the 1970s.

New evidence recently appeared on the CNN website, and it was not in itself published as evidence for the issue about what happens with repeated exposures in media plans. Yet it addresses this fundamental issue of media planning and marketing budgets. It quotes Ron Wright, President and CEO of neuromarketing firm Sands Research Inc.:

> We have found that in the first 800 milliseconds of every participant watching television commercials there is a spike in activity ... This is the viewer's brain, specifically the frontal lobe, deciding 'Have I seen this before, do I continue to watch the material and how much of my brain resources do I allocate to continue watching this commercial?'
> (**http://edition.cnn.com/2010/TECH/innovation/10/05/neuro.marketing/**)

Figure 24.4 shows this effect.

In other words, what we measure is increased cognitive activity at the start of people being exposed to a commercial, and if they have seen it before (cognized it) then they do not waste much time giving it further attention.

Graham Page reminded me that this is probably the P300 effect seen in EEG measures. I must admit that I did not think of this effect when I read the Sands Research, but since this effect has been well studied since the 1960s it is a very useful insight from Sands Research.

FIGURE 24.4   Neurophysiological analysis

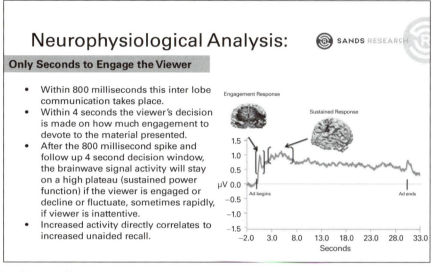

(Sands Research)

The **P300** (P3) wave is an event related potential (ERP) elicited by infrequent, task-relevant stimuli. It is considered to be an endogenous potential as its occurrence links not to the physical attributes of a stimulus but to a person's reaction to the stimulus. More specifically, the P300 is thought to reflect processes involved in stimulus evaluation or categorization. It is usually elicited using the oddball paradigm in which low-probability target items are inter-mixed with high-probability non-target (or 'standard') items.

When recorded by electroencephalography (EEG), it surfaces as a positive deflection in voltage with a latency (delay between stimulus and response) of roughly 300 to 600 ms. The signal is typically measured most strongly by the electrodes covering the parietal lobe. The presence, magnitude, topography and timing of this signal are often used as metrics of cognitive function in decision-making processes. While the neural substrates of this ERP still remain hazy, the reproducibility of this signal makes it a common choice for psychological tests in both the clinic and laboratory.

Early observations of the P3b were reported in the mid-1960s. In 1964, researchers Chapman and Bragdon found that ERP responses to visual stimuli differed depending on whether the stimuli had meaning or not. They showed subjects two kinds of visual stimuli: numbers and flashes of light. Subjects viewed these stimuli one at a time in a sequence. For every two numbers, the subjects were required to make simple decisions, such as telling which of the two numbers was numerically smaller or larger, which came first or second in the sequence, or whether they were equal. When examining evoked potentials to these stimuli (ie ERPs), Chapman and Bragdon found that both the numbers and the flashes elicited the expected sensory responses (eg visual N1 components), and that the amplitude of these responses varied in an expected fashion with the intensity of the stimuli. They also found that the ERP responses to the numbers, but not to the light flashes, contained a large positivity that peaked around 300ms after the stimulus appeared. Chapman and Bragdon speculated that this differential response to the numbers, which came to be known as the P300 response, resulted from the fact that the numbers where meaningful to the participants, based on the task that they were asked to perform.

... Since the initial discovery of this ERP component, research has shown that the P300 is not a unitary phenomenon. Rather, we can distinguish between two subcomponents of the P300: the novelty P3, or P3a, and the classic P3, or P3b.

The **P3a**, or novelty P3, is a component of time-locked (EEG) signals known as event-related potentials (ERP). The P3a is a positive-going scalp-recorded brain potential that has a maximum amplitude over frontal/central electrode sites with a peak latency falling in the range of 250–280 ms. The P3a has been associated with brain activity related to the engagement of attention (especially orienting and involuntary shifts to changes in the environment) and the processing of novelty.

The **P3b** is a subcomponent of the P300, an event-related potential (ERP) component that can be observed in human scalp recordings of brain electrical activity. The P3b is a positive-going amplitude (usually relative to a reference behind the ear or the average of two such references) peaking at around 300ms, though the peak will vary in latency from 250–500ms or later depending upon the task. Amplitudes are typically highest on the scalp over parietal brain areas.

The P3b has been a prominent tool used to study cognitive processes for several decades. More specifically, this ERP component has played a key role in cognitive psychology research on information processing. Generally speaking, improbable events will elicit a P3b, and the less probable the event, the larger the P3b.[3] However, in order to elicit a P3b, the improbable event must be related to the task at hand in some way (for example, the improbable event could be an infrequent target letter in a stream of letters, to which a subject might respond with a button press). The P3b can also be used to measure how demanding a task is on cognitive workload.

(Wikipedia, P300, neuroscience)

Since we are considering, in this book ways that the pieces of the brain and marketing puzzle are being shifted it is noteworthy that this information has been lying around since the 1960s and only now is becoming an insight about how advertising works, and when one combines this with the DVR experiment about how repeat exposures work.

Krugman, in his 1972 paper *Why Three Exposures May Be Enough*, described the process that audiences go through with subsequent exposures to an advertisement as three steps:

1 What is this?

2 What of it?

3 I have seen this.

This was really based on a sort of cognitive psychological view of what happens with subsequent exposures to an advertisement. Most importantly, his third phase of exposures was described by him as: 'thereafter the process of disengagement begins'.

He does make the point that the first two steps might happen at the first exposure a consumer has to the advertisement, or the 21st (in his words). In other words, the giving of attention (cognition) might happen at any stage – or even never.

It is this process of disengagement (his words) that produces the convex effect at the end of the response curve.

A lot of media planning philosophy – including the issue of continuity planning – suggests that you should try to schedule your media so that you operate in the early part of the curve rather than the later, which is seen as an area of diminishing returns.

Figure 24.5 shows what would happen to the response curve of a advertisement that has the ability to make 10 per cent of the people that are not aware of the advertisement aware of the advertisement.

Not surprisingly, when 100 per cent are not aware of the advertisement, the advertisement makes 10 per cent aware; and then when only 90 per cent are not aware, the advertisement makes 9 per cent aware; when 81 per cent are not aware, the advertisement makes 8.1 per cent aware. In other words: seemingly diminishing returns.

The fact is that the advertisement does not suffer from diminishing returns. It still makes 10 per cent of the people that were not aware of the advertisement aware of the advertisement.

If you want to get to a stage where 60 per cent of people are aware of the advertisement, you have to go through the steps of increasing diminishing returns to get to that level!

This is why in tracking studies the impact rate of advertisements, measured in terms of their ability to make people aware as a percentage of those that are not aware, remains fairly constant over long periods (years).

What underlies this, neurologically, is the process of cognition and re-cognition. Re-cognition is not a bad thing; in fact, it is a very good thing because it lowers the limens of the advertisement's memories.

FIGURE 24.5 Awareness

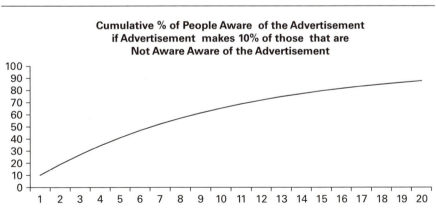

Why repeat exposures to an advertisement?

A lot of advertising papers and talks about advertising debate whether an advertisement should form a memory, whether this should be related to the brand, whether this should be functional or emotional, etc.

In general, one gets the impression from all these papers that the issue is whether consumers should notice (or not notice) the advertisement, and thereafter everything will be fine. Or, let's make it very simple: when the consumer has noticed the advertisement and knows the benefits of the brand, then no more advertising is needed.

It is as if the view expressed is that all that is needed is to create a memory once, and thereafter everything will be OK.

Even the proponents of continuity planning tend to fall into this trap by arguing that the objective of such a media schedule should be reach, not frequency. In other words, keep exposing new people to the advertisement.

The obvious question then is: Why do big brands have big budgets that obviously mean high frequency, and small brands have small budgets (mostly aimed at specific sub-markets) which imply high frequency against these sub-markets? Why does what marketers tend to do in practice not tie up with the theories of continuity planning and a quest for reach rather than frequency?

Let's simplify the question: Why would you aim for re-cognition (frequency) rather than mere cognition (new reach) in your media schedule? Especially since this makes a very big difference to your advertising budget and the way it is implemented.

For many years I believed that the answer lies in the fact that people forget your advertisement. In all tracking studies this would be reflected by the estimates for the retention rate of your advertisement's awareness. I discuss this in depth in *The Advertised Mind* (2005), and point out that there exists no empirical research into this aspect of advertising.

I also recognized that, as the proponents of continuity planning argue, you get more improvement in ad awareness (or anything else) by spreading your media over time. But this is merely because you are allowing the base level of awareness to go as low as possible before advertising again. Or simply, in terms of the diminishing returns model, you get more immediate returns if the existing awareness is zero than when it is at a higher number.

But why does the level of awareness matter?

In *The Advertised Mind* I explain that you get different research readings when you use a recall versus a recognition (prompted awareness) measure for an advertisement.

In this book I want to point out a very important neurological implication for marketers.

We have spent quite a bit of time on Susan Greenfield's beautiful book *Journey to the Centers of the Mind* (1995), in which she not only talks about the gestalts that are formed in the brain as being like waves in a pond. We have also explained how the direction of these waves is formed by the state of the limens in the synapses that comprise the memories of what is being perceived and how these determine which next neurons are being recruited.

This is really the issue. When I am thinking about buying a brand, what comes to mind?

In this book we discussed feelings and emotions. We discussed expectations and dopamine. We discussed brand soma and functionality. Ultimately the question is: What comes to mind?

We know from a neurological perspective that what comes to mind will be the brand's functionality and the brand soma. We know that what comes to mind will be determined by our emotions at the time. We know that these emotions will be playing off against the background feelings of homeostasis, moods, personality and culture (at least). But none of these explains why you need repeated exposure (frequency) in your advertising once a memory has been established – ie when cognition has occurred.

The answer lies in two areas, and I believe that many empirical marketing databases point toward this, and that this will guide some neuromarketing research into even better neuroscience research:

1 When gestalts are developing in the brain, one of the determinants of how they do so is the status of the limens in the synapses – ie the development of the gestalt takes the path of least resistance. This fits with Susan Greenfield's model. The objective of repeat exposure to an advertisement is to lower the limens involved in re-cognizing the advertisement and, included in this, the brand.

2 The process of frequency of advertising exposure does not rely on the advertisement having the same effect on each exposure. In fact, it probably needs only one or two exposures to an individual that achieves cognition. Subsequent exposures (even cross media) achieve their effects by way of re-cognition, and this happens in seconds or even fractions of seconds.

Take these two together: I stand in front of a shelf with gestalts being developed by the brands I see; or I think of a bank to go to; or I think of a research company to quote on a project. For all these the gestalts that develop are based on the state of the limens in my synapses. When everything else is equal, the gestalt with the lowest limens will become the dominant gestalt.

The way that a brand becomes the one with the lowest limens will be by way of being the brand I mostly use, or the one that has made me aware of it most over recent time.

This is probably how repeat purchase and advertising work. This is probably how what Millward Brown calls 'fame' works.

This is not a new model of how consumers make decisions or of how advertising works. The fact that there are some neurological works in this explanation does not make this new. It actually fits very well with what Gordon Brown, founder of Millward Brown, wrote in 1980 and what most marketers do, because most marketers have seen this work for most marketers.

For re-cognition to work, the consumer need not be exposed to the full 30 seconds of a 30-second advertisement. We have shown how fast the brain is at recognizing something. In the cats–dogs experiment this is achieved in one-tenth of a second. Inside that time frame your memory presents to your consciousness a lot of what it knows about what you are seeing (ie the developing gestalt includes much more than what you have been exposed to). The mere activation of these synapses lowers the limens. Ron Wright reports that this might be as fast as 800 milliseconds.

This is a very good explanation of what happens in neurological terms. It is a great contribution from neuroscience to understanding why people do what they do, and why marketers do what they do. By taking very diverse neuroscience findings and bringing them toward what we know in the marketing sciences we are also opening new areas for neuroscientists to explore.

Can an advertisement have an effect without it being given attention?

This brings us back to the heading of this chapter. The answer to the question affects a lot of what we argue about in marketing, and affects billions of dollars spent in the media (and the people whose families work in the media). I believe that when one frames the question as above then the answer has to be: yes.

We know from Part 1 that nearly everything in our environment enters the brain via our senses and starts a process of neural recruitment. This process of neural recruitment is simply interpretation based on memories. The end result is that we recognize what it is.

At this moment you are recognizing letters, recognizing words, recognizing sentences, recognizing it is all on a page, recognizing that the page is in a book, recognizing your hands holding the book, and so on. This process of recognition all happens along the neural pathways that were set up by previous experiences (memories, or cognitions, if you will). As this process proceeds along these pathways and synapses, the synaptic strengths are increased, ie the memories are reinforced.

Everything that enters your brain is interpreted like this and is developing gestalts. As these developing gestalts are recognized for what they are and as having limited interest to your well-being at the moment they simply fizzle out. They do not become a conscious awareness, nor do they get given attention. Yet by this time they have already reaffirmed the memories that were used to interpret them.

The key elements of this process appear, to me, to be that it is a process of re-cognition and that it happens involuntarily beyond any great level of consciousness or attention.

Let us suppose that you are in a room with friends and there is a TV in the corner. Whilst you are talking to someone and giving the person your attention the images from the TV are entering your mind and will start a process of recruitment. Generally this process of gestalt formation will mostly simply stop at: 'There is a TV showing advertising.' Sometimes this process of gestalt formation will proceed further: 'There is a TV showing that advertisement for Ford I have seen before', but this does not warrant your attention and the process will fizzle out. Despite your not giving it attention the synapses recognizing the advertisement for Ford will have received some stimulation. Sometimes the process will proceed even further because something in the advertisement makes you give it some specific attention. In this case many more synapses are stimulated and lay down stronger memories – even new memories.

To answer the question about whether an advertisement can have any effect without it receiving attention then the answer is that at the second level above it does have an effect and it is not receiving attention. At the first level there is no effect, and at the third level there is attention. For the process to reach the second level above there is a prerequisite that the advertisement has been 'cognized' before – otherwise it cannot be recognized.

The advertising effect of this

The question is: does this help to explain what we see in advertising effects?

- The S-shaped response curve of Krugman (1972) would be a direct result of this. Someone might be exposed to an advertisement and there will be no effect for several exposures. There would then be an exposure at which some attention is given – the threshold exposure. Thereafter the effect will decrease with every exposure, but still show a cumulative increase.

- In the Millward Brown Adtrack system there are many examples of advertisements launched with a 60-second execution and once this has created memories it can be cut to a 30-second execution and still has the same effect.

- John Philip Jones, in *When Ads Work: New proof that advertising triggers sales* (1995), suggests that the best media strategy for advertisements is one of continuous exposure based on the substantial database he analysed. This would be true if advertisements worked in this low attention way where subsequent exposures do not have a very different effect from the first time the advertisement was cognized. In other words, where subsequent exposures have a memory refreshing effect, that happens at a very low level of attention – if any at all.

● This is also probably how a lot of cross-media campaigns work. When a poster or print ad or radio ad or internet ad is linked to the TV campaign it often shows in research increases in the TV campaigns recall, ie when it is interpreted it brings to mind the TV campaign as part of the interpretation.

But all of this relies on the advertisement having had some attention previously so that some memory has formed. Simply: if no memory has been formed, then there is nothing to refresh.

Du Plessis's error

At the beginning of this chapter I explained that in *The Advertised Mind* I disagreed with Robert Heath's views about how emotion in advertising works. I headed that chapter 'Heath's error' as a word play on Damasio's book title.

In the January 2010 edition of *Admap*, Robert Heath published a paper entitled 'Creativity in TV ads does not increase attention', in which he argues that my views about the role of emotion being to gain attention for the advertisement are wrong. Heath is an important researcher as far as advertising research is concerned. Heath and Hyder's influential article 'Measuring the hidden power of emotive advertising' (2005) won both the David Winton Award, given to the best technical paper, and the ISBA Award, which is awarded to the paper that best indicates how research increases understanding of how advertising works.

In a private e-mail Robert told me that he wanted to title the ADMAP paper *du Plessis's Error*, referring to my chapter *Heath's Error*, but the editor changed the title. Respecting the continued debate, I decided to title this chapter *du Plessis's Error*.

Whilst I do not agree with Heath's conclusions from his experiment, I do believe that he has come up with an important piece of the neuromarketing puzzle, without doubt one that will have to be turned around several times before we know how it fits into the total picture of the brain.

The experiment

Ads for the research were rated based on a scale of 'Emotional' and the six highest and lowest rated for the experiment were used. Respondents were exposed to these ads and, by means of eye movement scanners that are able to pick up micro and very rapid eye movements (microsaccades), their microsaccades were measured as an indicator of attention.

Interesting conclusions

Heath's study yielded some interesting findings regarding attention (as measured by microsaccades). Analysing the fixations per second (FPS) during each ad against the average during the watching of the TV programme showed that high levels of emotive content were associated with an average reduction of about 20 per cent in attention levels, significant at 99.9 per cent. This is his main finding. This goes against nearly every reasonable explanation of the role of emotions. The only other variable to show any influence on attention levels was prior exposure to advertising, and this had the effect of reducing attention levels, but only for the ads that had lower emotive content. People paid no more attention to ads that featured brands or products they used than to ads that featured brands or products they didn't use and paid much the same level of attention to ads that they didn't like as to ads they did.

I am not an expert on this biometric measurement, so I went to Wikipedia to learn more:

> The role of microsaccades in visual perception has been a highly debated topic which is still largely unresolved. It has been proposed that microsaccades correct displacements in eye position produced by drifts, although non-corrective microsaccades also occur. Microsaccades were also believed to prevent the retinal image from fading, but they do not occur often enough for that purpose, considering that perfectly stabilized images can disappear from perception in a few seconds or less. The current consensus is that all fixational eye movements are important for the maintenance of visibility.
>
> (Wikipedia, 'Microsaccade')

Conclusions

Heath (2010) concludes: 'So, the conclusion I draw is that emotive creativity might facilitate communication, not – as Eric believes – by increasing attention, but by lowering attention, promoting open-mindedness and effectively encouraging the consumer to let their guard down.'

I remain unconvinced about his conclusions regarding what happens to attention. I am sure that many more experiments will be done to get to a final answer about what microsaccades actually measure about advertisements. However, Heath has certainly opened a whole new perspective on the piece of the brand advertising puzzle called 'attention', a piece that has formed a major part of the advertising debate for more than half a century.

Robert Heath has also introduced a new bio-measure to the spectrum of neuromarketing tools. Interestingly enough, given the scientists' views expressed in Wikipedia above, there appears to be a real opportunity for market researchers using their databases to contribute to the understanding of what this tool measures.

The brand soma

25

> We have considered Damasio's somatic marker theorem in Chapter 3, ie how the soma is a major input to our decisions. Brands are decisions; therefore there is a soma involved in the decision. Marketers need to manage this soma for their brands. This is not really new – marketers have been doing this to a greater or lesser extent over the years. We need to find a way to measure this soma – and this is a new thought.

What I mean by the brand soma

Antonio Damasio introduced the word 'soma' as part of his somatic marker theorem to explain how the limbic system assists the 'rational thinking' about something that it experiences (or is thinking about). What happens is that when I see, hear or think about something I do not have only the physical aspects of it 'come to mind' but also the 'how I will feel about it, or how I will feel if I use it'.

The brand soma is the 'feelings' part of the interpretation that comes to mind, and gives my rational processes a large part of the input required to 'think' about the brand as an alternative behaviour. This also allows the frontal lobes to send back impulses of alternatives to the limbic system, and receive back interpretations of these 'thoughts'. Damasio calls this the 'as if' loop.

This is not a sequential process, as it would be in a computer program, where there is clear progression via a predetermined program that 'considers' aspects of the brands. It all happens nearly instantaneously, via the states of the synapses. Thoughts are developing gestalts because of neurons recruiting other neurons. As we think about things so these thoughts trigger neurons and other thoughts. Some of these 'come to mind' (and what comes to mind is intrinsically determined by the feelings of the thought – gestalt – that is developing). Most important is that this happens very fast.

This soma comes from the limbic system, and seems to be driven by (*inter alia*) the dopamine system (when the soma is positive). Just as the neural system lays down memories of the 'what it is', so it lays down memories of 'how it makes us feel' when we experience it. When we subsequently think about it the neural system brings forth not only the 'what it is' memories, but also the 'how we feel about it' memories, or even 'This is how it should make us feel based on what we know about it.' These memories activate the dopamine system as much as the actual experience activated it (possibly even more). When we considered the reward system we saw that it is now believed that the mere thought of future consumption seems to release more dopamine than the actual process of consumption.

To marketers this is a very important thought: you cannot expect your brand to sell itself just based on what it does when people use it. The expectation of how I would feel when I use it has to be created, because the soma is especially important when the brand decision is made, ie what comes to mind when I make a decision is what matters.

What a marketer should aim for is not only managing the brand soma so that it is as positive as possible when the brand is bought, but including in the product delivery things that are surprisingly better than the consumer expected. The breakfast cereal companies used to do this very well by including toys or gifts in the package. Fast food companies often try the same tactic. Service companies are in a situation where they can do this by way of their client contacts. (There is the problem that this 'surprise' becomes part of the expectation and so if the surprise does not live up to the expectation we are back to square one.)

The brand soma is not something different from the brand. It is not something the brain interprets in a different way from anything else about the brand. When I think about the brand I know how I feel about the brand as part of what I know about the brand. My knowledge about the brand includes my feelings about the brand.

The brand soma and functionality

Nigel Hollis (in a conversation with the author) argues that we should not talk about rationality, but functionality when we talk about advertising style. Creatives often argue against 'rational' arguments, favouring the use of 'emotional' arguments. Nigel believes that what they really mean is that they are against functional arguments. This makes a lot of sense and clarifies the discussion: since emotional is part of rational, one should not be talking for or against one or the other.

But the issue is not simply what functionality I believe the brand has, but especially how this relates to me. When a brand has functionalities that I perceive as negative to me I will have a negative feeling about the brand.

My soma about a brand will be a reflection of my beliefs about its functionalities and will be an overall feeling.

Neurology

From a neurological perspective let's think about what happens. Any stimulus in the environment sets off the recruitment of neurons, as does any stimulus from inside the brain and body. I might be walking through a shop and see oranges, which sets off the process of recruitment. I might be thirsty, and this will set off the recruitment of neurons. I might recall my holiday in California, and this will set off the recruitment of neurons. I might simply be thinking of my pool party next weekend, and this will set off the recruitment of neurons.

Each of these instances sets off recruitment of different neurons. Different neuronal clouds will develop – and all will be based on my experiences. What comes to mind will be based on the status of my limens (and will come to mind very fast). All of these activations of neuronal sets will be context dependent, ie different situations will set off different activations even for an individual. All of these result in a brand soma for the individual.

It is the task of a marketer to ensure that the soma that is generated for each of these activations is positive for the brand, because each time the neuronal paths are activated the limens that form the brand soma increase.

What does the brand soma do?

The brand soma tells me how I feel about the brand. This is as simple as it is, but let us not confuse simplicity with importance.

The somatic marker theorem proposes that the memory system lays down memories of experiences in terms of the body's feelings, and that these memories, like any other memories, are used to interpret. This happens for the interpretation of everything that is around us and what we have to take decisions about. Since most of what we need to take decisions about is brands, it happens for all brands all the time.

This soma is a 'feeling' and has a positive or negative valence. The important point is that the consciousness becomes aware both of the feelings and of the functionality of what it is being presented with. By 'feelings' I mean 'How will the brand make me feel?'

Brand soma, rationality and functionality

This is where the rubber hits the road as far as the 'pieces of the puzzle' are concerned. The big debate, for decades, has been whether one should advertise emotionally or rationally.

Millward Brown, as the biggest advertising measurement company in the world, has mountains of data, and does a lot of mining of these mountains.

It also does not treat what it learns as being confidential. The learnings are regularly published as Point of View (POV) documents and are available on the website (**http://www.mb-blog.com/**) for students to use. To write up all the Millward Brown learnings would take a book much thicker than this one.

An important debate between creatives and researchers has for decades been (and will probably still be for many years) a perception by creatives that if researchers have their way then all advertisements will consist of is lots of brand mentions and a sterile list of brand performance benefits. This generalization seldom allows for the middle road: communicating a functional benefit in an emotional way. An analysis of 330 ads by Millward Brown shows that this latter route is much more effective than either of the others (Figure 25.1). The analysis was based on actual market share change – which is why the base is only 330.

FIGURE 25.1 A balanced advertising strategy is the most sales effective

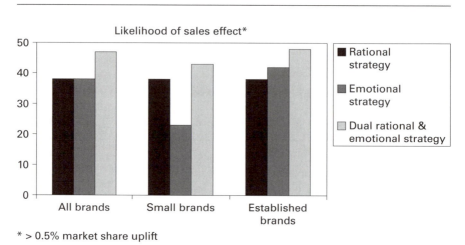

Likelihood of sales effect*

■ Rational strategy

■ Emotional strategy

□ Dual rational & emotional strategy

* > 0.5% market share uplift

It should also not be a surprise to marketers that to start a small brand mainly on an emotional platform is not a good idea – it needs to establish its 'reason for existence'. Established brands are better known and need not explain themselves. Here an emotional route works best and creates a better impact on the brand soma. However, combining the reason and the emotions is the best strategy.

Whilst Figure 25.1 depicts a rational versus an emotional execution, Figure 25.2 depicts 'feeling good'. Remember that this is what the brand soma is: feeling good. This is what Nigel Hollis suggested (in a private conversation) as the thing we should be measuring when we try to measure brand soma. The comparison in Figure 25.2 is between ads with a high 'feel-good' factor and ads with a low 'feel-good' factor, and it shows the impact that this has on the persuasion score of the advertisement and the brand appeal as a result of the advertisement.

FIGURE 25.2   Ads that evoke positive emotions have more motivational power

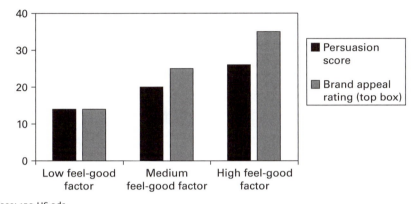

Base: 150 US ads

Whether one should use rational or emotional appeals is not an issue. People argue about whether a commercial should be emotional or rational, ie they see it as an either-or situation. The problem really is that people often are vague (or wrong) about the definition of emotional versus rational. Firstly we must recognize the new paradigm: rationality does not exist without emotions (feelings). Then we must recognize that rationality is dependent on emotions, ie not that decisions are now only emotions, but that emotions are a necessary input for rationality. Then the very important insight is Nigel Hollis's perception that in marketing we confuse functionality with rationality. The best way of viewing the debate is shown in Figure 25.3.

FIGURE 25.3   The feelings/functionality interactions

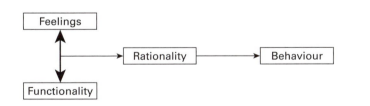

Let us, for a moment, step outside brands. There are people we all know about whom we say: 'I know these things about you are bad, but I still like you and want to be your friend.' There are also people who have positive qualities that we recognize, yet with whom we would prefer not to be friends.

None of us believe that our father, mother, brothers and sisters are all good, yet we forgive them their sins more easily than we forgive those of other people. In terms of the model in Figure 25.3, we know about their 'functionality' but we have a 'feeling' that positively predisposes us toward forgiveness and overrating their positives.

'Feelings' seems to have a multiplier effect on 'functionality', and I will spend the rest of this chapter arguing that there is a multiplier effect whereby brands that people are positively disposed to get rated more highly in all surveys by some constant. Researchers call this the halo effect.

Graham Page of Millward Brown suggested to me that the effect might be not simply a multiplier, but a contingency effect. In other words, people might first select the brands they feel positive about when they have to make a brand choice in answering research questions and then assign attributes to some of these. This would fit into the view that people use heuristics to make decisions (I discuss heuristics in Chapter 26).

I suspect that whether the brand soma is a multiplier effect, or a contingency effect, or simply some appear in our data as a constant that increases a brand's association with all positive attributes can be debated. The way that the halo effect is generally removed from our research data is to calculate the average association of the brand over all attributes and then deducting this from every association. A more sophisticated analysis would be to use a chi-square statistic, but this again simply deducts the expected association from the observed association. In other words general practice is to view the halo effect as a constant added to the brand's perception.

Whichever of these views is correct the brand soma comes into play, ie it makes one more inclined to be positive about a brand. The mathematical effect on the resultant research data will also be the same.

The multiplier effect is either positive or negative on our knowledge as far as it influences our behaviour.

Fishbein and brand utility

During the 1960s operations research became a popular science. This was especially due to computers making it possible to process large datasets.

Fishbein, borrowing from the economist Adam Smith's theories about utility, proposed an operational model whereby 'utility' can be derived from brand attribute data (Fishbein and Ajzen, 1975). He postulated that:

Utility of brand i = sum of (its perceived attributes × the importance of the attributes)

All you had to do was to ask respondents for each attribute how important it was to them, and then for each brand whether it had the attribute; then you could predict the 'utility' of the brand. You could then relate this to the price of the brand and predict sales. This is still what is conceptually being done in all brand X attribute studies, and all under Fishbein's assumption. The model sort of worked some of the time.

Several adaptations to the rule were introduced at the time: the lexicative rule, the conjunctive rule, etc. Some 'rules' were simply that the brand should be evaluated on only the top x important attributes. All of these rules did lead to improvements of the predictive nature of the model, but none stood the test of time to provide great strategic insights.

The Fishbein model has not been disproved. The problem with the model is mainly that when a brand is big it gets associated with all positive attributes more than a smaller brand. When a brand gains on one attribute it gains on all attributes. This is where the problem of 'salience' comes to the fore. The more salient a brand becomes the more it gains on all attributes.

Professor Andrew Ehrenberg discovered this Double Jeopardy phenomenon in the 1960s and found a statistical distribution that describes this (they use the brand's market share rather than its salience). This is now considered to be a fundamental law of markets. Byron Sharpe (of the Ehrenberg-Bass Institute) describes the law and its implications in his 2010 book *How Brands Grow – What Marketers Don't Know*.

How the brand soma works in practice

We see the brand soma in all our research data, whether continuous tracking data, annual usage and attitude studies or even just ad hoc studies. The measured perceptions of brands go up and down in harmony. However, we also generally see that the attributes the advertising is trying to communicate go up more than the rest when there is advertising.

Advertising (promotion) does two things:

1 It creates a general effect that increases the brand association with all positive attributes (the brand soma effect).

2 It creates a specific effect that increases the brand's association with specific attributes more than the others.

Over time the general effect increases the brand's fame while the specific effect increases the brand's position in the consumer's mind. From the perspective of research it is very important for management that both these effects are measured.

The best way to do this has to be via continuous tracking because you not only want to measure over periods that you are advertising (measuring the up phase) to see whether your positioning is reaffirmed, but you also want to know how fast the general effect dissipates. You should be especially interested in these effects for competitors' brands and in how their advertising is influencing perception of your brand.

How this shows in perceptual maps

It is interesting to consider what these two effects will do for a brand when plotted in a perceptual map (using correspondence analysis).

The stronger the general effect, the more a brand is associated with all positive attributes, which means that it will move toward the centre of the map. The stronger the specific effects, the more the brand will increase its association on specific attributes and the more it will move to the outside of the map (ie the more differentiated it will be).

Please note that you will seldom be able to have a specific effect without also having a general effect.

Marketers need to decide how far they want to be differentiated – ie be away from the centre of the market map. Too much differentiation could lead to the brand creating its own product category – which may or may not be a good thing.

Revisiting Fishbein

We left Fishbein, having looked at his model:

Utility of brand i = sum of (its perceived attributes × the importance of the attributes)

Due to the halo effect we see that for popular brands all the attributes are rated high, and for lesser popular brands all attributes are rated low. There will be some variation in the ratings based on the perceived brand differentiations. Often we will form an average rating for the brand across all the attributes we measured and then deduct this from each of the ratings – thus removing the halo effect from the data – enabling us to study the differentiation between brands.

Effectively what we have done is to rewrite the Fishbein model as:

Utility of brand i = brand soma + sum of (its perceived attributes × importance of the attributes)

This constant for brand i is simply:

- the halo effect that we estimate and remove in our data;
- the Double Jeopardy effect we see in all our data;
- the brand soma I propose.

The dopamine moment

We have moved very deep into marketing theories and the big databases like Double Jeopardy, Adtrack, the Millward Brown tracking data and halo effects, and I would like to bring the discussion back to the biology of the brain.

The somatic marker theorem suggests that the limbic system feeds the decision making with a 'feeling' component added to the physical interpretation of what the organism is faced with. This feeling component of the interpretation is based on how the body felt previously and involves the dopamine circuit. At a minimum it suggests that the dopamine memory laid down at the time the brand was experienced is involved. It suggests that memories laid down by advertising, brand experiences, promotions, packaging, word of mouth and so on (ie all the touchpoints) about expected dopamine moments matter. It suggests that the anticipation of a future dopamine moment is what is used in decision making. It therefore becomes vitally important for research to aid creative departments by identifying dopamine moments. These can be dopamine moments that consumers experienced with the brand, dopamine moments for consumers when they are experiencing the brand, or expected dopamine moments. This is rather like the ghost of Christmases past, present and future.

Without going into the evidence in this book I'd like to point creatives to the fact that it is possible to create memories. It has been shown that memories can be created in people of events that did not really occur – as long as they are reasonable. The evidence relates to even highly unreasonable events where psychologists created memories in women of being raped by their fathers when they were not – although advertising is unlikely to have as powerful an effect as repeated visits to psychologists. But suggesting that I had a great experience on the beach whilst drinking Coca-Cola is entirely reasonable – even if I actually never had such an experience. Past dopamine moments can easily be created, and often are in advertising.

Since the brand soma is strongly influenced by dopaminic memories, this should be a great focus of research – especially research aimed at helping creatives. I cannot think of a better way than focus groups to do this.

Remember that this dopamine moment is not determined by homeostatic needs, but by feelings like emotions, moods, personality and culture.

'How would using the brand make you feel?'

Nigel Hollis suggested that the question to ask if one wants to measure the brand soma is: 'How would using the brand make you feel?' This appears to me to get straight to the essence of what Damasio proposes in his somatic marker theorem. Researchers can argue about the type of scale to use, the ways that the follow-up 'Why?' question should be framed, whether this should be open-ended, or what type of prompts should be used. But this question is what matters.

It is also obvious that the issue of the brand soma has to become very important in qualitative research. Here my belief is that this question should be the major objective of any focus group. It will have to be answered before there is too much inter-respondent contamination.

I would venture as far as making this question the objective of all strategic and tactical brand decisions. The question asked for every brand decision has to be: 'If we do this, or that, to the brand, how will it make the consumers feel about using the brand?'

Using the halo effect

For a lot of research we calculate the halo effect and then ignore it. What we should be doing is to make this halo effect an integral part of our analysis and brand strategy because it might be the brand soma. Marketers should be tracking in/decreases in their brand's halo effect.

Whether the halo effect represents the brand's soma, as I believe, or is mainly a measure of salience, or just brand popularity, does not change the usefulness of my recommendation.

If an increased halo effect happens with increased popularity of a brand along the lines of the Ehrenberg Double Jeopardy Effect (see Byron Sharpe's book *How Brands Grow*, 2010) then it makes sense that growing the halo effect should be an objective of marketers.

Consumer decision making as heuristics

26

What is a heuristic?

It has become increasingly popular to view consumer decision making in terms of heuristics. 'Heuristic' is a fancy word for 'simple decision rule'.

An example often used is that of doctors, who used to have to conduct a lot of tests on patients who might be suffering from a heart attack before they could treat the patients for having a heart attack. Some of the tests involved sending blood to the laboratory. Sometimes patients had died of a heart attack before they were formally diagnosed and treatment could be started. Now doctors have a shortlist of questions, including 'How old is the patient?', 'Does the patient have a history of heart attacks?' and 'Does the patient smoke?', and some symptoms can be checked easily. Based on this, treatment for a heart attack can begin whilst the extensive tests are still being conducted. Sometimes people might now be treated for a heart attack when it subsequently transpires that they did not have one, but this simplified set of decision rules has saved many lives by making treatment available in time.

Such a simplified set of decision rules is called a heuristic. A feature of heuristics is that they save time and energy. The trade-off is that sometimes the decision might be less than optimal.

It is now increasingly accepted that people make most brand choice decisions based on mental heuristics. Think about how often you pick a brand from the shelf basically because it is your usual brand. You used it before and it did what you wanted it to do. This is a heuristic.

Neuromarketing and heuristics

We have explained how the 'as if' and 'feel-good' systems work and how dopamine is involved in decision making. I stand in front of the shelf,

I perceive many brands, what I see is interpreted via neural recruitment, including how I feel about the objects I am looking at, and I choose the one I feel best about. The one I choose will probably be the one I have used and felt good about when I did this. If that one did not make me feel good I might consider the others and will choose the one I believe will make me feel good. It might be that there is a new one on the shelf, I remember something about the advertising telling me it will make me feel good, and I might try it. I might feel that I need to save money, one brand offers a discount, the discount will make me feel better than buying my usual brand, and I might try it.

All of this goes back to how I will feel when I buy the brand. This would depend on my mood, personality and even culture. It will certainly depend on my memories, which are what I am using to interpret what I see on the shelf. It might not even be dependent on what I see on the shelf. In looking at the brands I might think about a brand that is not on the shelf and decide to go to another store to buy it because doing this will make me feel better than just buying one of the brands I see. This is a reason for the existence of speciality stores.

There will be occasions when I think really hard about what I am going to buy. When the item I am going to buy involves a lot of money, or I do not have the knowledge to evaluate the brands, I will think a lot more or use a much more extended set of heuristics.

I was once involved in doing some recording of shoppers when I watched two patently poor men standing in front of the rack for powdered soups. They were picking up brands and discussing each one. In other words, there was a lot of cognition about as simple a purchase as powdered soup. I asked them to explain what they were doing. They told me that they were sharing a chicken for dinner – their only meat for the week – and were working out which sauce they should 'risk their money on'. Another shopper might have picked up five packets and then decided later which to use.

It is not only your financial situation that determines whether you think rather than use a sweet and simple heuristic. Two years ago I taught at the Copenhagen Business School for the first time. My wife took about 30 minutes to decide on a washing powder when she first went shopping in Copenhagen. There were just too many brands and the decision became virtually impossible. I switched brands and types nearly every time I bought milk. Again this was because the numbers of varieties of milk were so much more than we had in South Africa. (In fact I just wanted full-cream milk for my morning coffee, and this seemed impossible to get.)

It is not only my wife who struggles to choose a brand of washing powder. When poor rural people in South Africa graduate to a lifestyle that includes electricity, one of the first things they will buy is a washing machine. Not having used one before they now have to choose a washing powder brand from a whole array of brands that are non-automatic, automatic and semi-automatic, with a lot of brand promises in between and different prices. The same was true when my daughter moved out of the house and had to set up in her own flat. Suddenly she was faced with a whole new scenario based on her not knowing whether she had an automatic washing machine or what.

It is well-accepted marketing wisdom in South Africa that poorer people are more brand-loyal than the wealthy. Two reasons are proposed for this: 1) price is an indicator of quality and they do not have enough money to risk a mistake; 2) a brand of even commodity goods gives them status among their peers.

What we do see in all these cases is heuristics at work (via the dopamine system). The individual differences lie in what the actual heuristic is and the individual consumer's memories.

Feelings and heuristics

There is a lot of interest among marketers in decision heuristics. It is felt that in most surveys marketers collect a lot of information from consumers about their perceptions of brands, their needs from the brands, etc. Yet the consumers are probably not complicating the purchase decision to the extent that the questionnaire implies that they do. They probably have a simple heuristic when they make decisions.

Much of what I have discussed so far in this book leads to mental heuristics based on feelings being very important for survival, ie let's not waste brain energy to solve every problem anew when we simply need to know how we felt (or expect to feel). Oatley and Jenkins recognized this:

Emotions as heuristics

Why might such simplifications be adaptive? The reason is that the world is a complex place. Even the cleverest of us, equipped with libraries, skills, technology, and all the other knowledge amassed over the last three thousand years could not know it fully or predict it entirely. Another way to put this is that only very seldom can human beings act completely rationally – seldom can we know enough to predict the best course of action. Moreover, we often have goals that are incompatible with each other, so there is no course of action that would satisfy them all. But this complexity does not remove the necessity for acting. What evolution has equipped us with, therefore, is a set of emotional states that organize ready repertoires of action. Although not perfect, emotions are better than doing nothing, or than acting randomly, or than becoming lost in thought. Emotions are heuristics.

(Oatley and Jenkins, 1996: 258)

BrandDynamics

Millward Brown (specifically Nigel Hollis and Andy Farr) has come up with a very good solution to research this. They realized that, whilst most people will be using a heuristic, the nature of the heuristic will be different for different people. For every individual there might be several important attributes that the product should have, but the importance of these to each of us will be different, and our perceptions on the extent to which the different brands have these attributes might also differ. When we look at our data on an averaged level the subtleties will be hidden. To unscramble this at an individual level is close to impossible – especially since each individual respondent might be making use of this information in a different way.

What Hollis and Farr said was that, whilst it is important to know what attributes of a brand are important and whether these are associated with the brand, it is much more important to know whether there is something about the brand that the consumer rates as important to him or her. In other words, a question like 'Which of these brands satisfy your needs?' can yield very good data without identifying what the specific need or attribute is.

The beauty of this insight was that they could derive a simple heuristic that can be applied to every consumer and every brand in every market seamlessly. From this came the Millward Brown BrandDynamics model. It is based on a series of questions that the respondent has to answer for every brand, which is then analysed at a disaggregated level. The result is interpreted as a measure of the extent to which a person is 'bonded' to the brand, and it is presented as a pyramid:

1 *Presence:* To draw a consumer into even a casual relationship, a brand needs to get on that consumer's radar screen. He or she needs to know about the brand. And this knowledge must go beyond passive name recognition; it must be an active awareness in relation to the product category. This is measured by the consumer being spontaneously aware of the brand, being aware of the brand promise or having tried it.

2 *Relevance:* If the relationship which starts with presence is to develop further, the brand must be seen as a viable choice – one that offers, and is capable of delivering, something of value at a reasonable price.

3 *Performance:* A respondent will move from relevance to performance if he or she does not mention the brand in relation to any 'performance barriers' defined for the project.

4 *Advantage:* Once the basics of presence, relevance and performance have been established, the brand can forge a deeper, more committed relationship with the consumer. But, to do this, the brand must distinguish itself from the competition in one or more ways.

5 *Bonding:* A consumer is considered to be bonded to the brand when he or she indicates that nothing else beats it.

These measures have been validated extensively by Millward Brown, showing that the higher a brand is in a person's 'pyramid' on the above measures the bigger its share of that person's wallet.

A researcher's problem with most brands that are bought based on a simple heuristic by a consumer is that, when consumers are asked why they bought the brand they did, they say something like: 'I always buy it. I like it.' This might sound like a fairly useless piece of information as far as designing brand strategies is concerned, but it reflects reality and it reflects the simple heuristic that the consumer uses. If the researcher then probes the consumer, asking why he or she does not buy another brand, the answers will be 'I don't know it', 'It does not do what I want from such a product' or 'It is too expensive.' These are really just explaining the levels of presence, relevance and performance. The respondent might say that a brand succeeds in all the above levels and has a specific advantage over other brands (getting it to level 4), but until the consumer has some feelings about the brand (that it is my brand) he or she is not considered to be bonded to the brand. Since all respondents are asked about their brand attribute associations as well, we can now look at respondents at different levels of the pyramid and see why they have moved higher than others, or what the problem is with people who did not move our brand further up the pyramid.

What makes the BrandDynamics model so interesting is that it was developed before the idea of a soma became popular. It was developed based on experience by the researchers involved with real data over a long time and many brands. Even then it was obvious to them that consumers have a heuristic and that the top end of the pyramid is really about feelings.

Different people have different heuristics in different situations

Of course they have! The way that you choose a wine over lunch when you want to order wine by the glass, or wine for your barbecue with friends, or wine when you want to impress a client, and so on will always affect your decision. The occasion matters.

The first person to recognize this in a published paper was Joel Dubow (1992), then with Coca-Cola, who explained that people choose different things to drink at different occasions. He used the term 'occasion segmentation'.

I have been involved in many questionnaire designs and some segmentation studies, and it is always very obvious that the issue becomes context related. This also often means that the questionnaire becomes ridiculously long and we need to concentrate mainly on one occasion. Often companies have different brands competing in different markets, and this then argues against simplifying the questionnaire to occasion-based segmentation, or context-dependent research.

I first encountered the term 'context-dependent' in a discussion with Nigel Hollis. We were ordering drinks on the patio in a hotel in Swaziland and

Nigel asked me: 'What non-alcoholic soft drink comes to your mind first?' I answered 'Coca-Cola.' He then asked: 'And if I asked what energizing soft drink?' I answered 'Red Bull.' He then said 'And if I asked what soft drink that is a health drink?' and I answered 'Orange juice.' He was not just changing the context of the question, but changing the context in which I would have been making a brand decision and the context in which memories come to mind. From a marketer's strategic perspective he was actually changing the market definition. With each change I changed my heuristic – not even as profound as changing my preferred brand, just changing the brand that came to mind first. He was arguing pro-salience; I was arguing pro-brand soma. What he did demonstrate was the effect of context in both salience and soma and thereby the effects of the questionnaire design.

Heuristics and questionnaire design

In many ways this is a part of the chapter that I knew I would have to write at some stage, and that I was hoping that I would never have to write. Nearly every researcher of long standing (ie old) will agree with me.

The biggest problem with nearly all questionnaires is that they are too long.

People are mostly not unhappy to answer research questions. Generally they appreciate their opinions being asked. Mostly they want to give an honest opinion.

Unfortunately, interviewers trick them into an interview by telling them it will not take too long, and then subject them to 40 minutes of ridiculously repetitive questions. No wonder there is a resistance to volunteering for market research interviews, whether this means personal interviews, focus groups or subjecting people to EEG measures or even fMRI.

The interviewers do not really have an option about misleading respondents about the length of the questionnaire – even if it is an online questionnaire – because this is what the marketers believe the respondents should be asked.

Typically the meetings with clients go fairly well until the stage where the attribute list on which the brands will be measured is being compiled.

At this point every possible perception that anyone believes anyone should (or should not) have about any of the brands is included. Somehow there seems to be a belief that if any minor view about the brand is excluded, then the whole exercise will be a waste of time. Even worse, there seems to be a belief that since the research costs a lot of money you should ask every question you can think of.

Now that I am retired from active research I honestly tell marketers and their agencies that this is what has made most research projects very difficult to execute.

Factually, people use heuristics to make a decision about brands – I do, you do, your wife or husband does, your father does, your children do. So it is likely that consumers also use heuristics.

When they are presented with a questionnaire asking them 20 or more attribute associations with 10 or more brands they think you are stupid.

Whether this questionnaire is being presented to them by someone on a face-to-face basis or on the internet via SurveyMonkey, they think you are stupid.

And when people are asked questions they perceive to be stupid they give stupid answers. For the past few years I have signed in at security entrances to buildings as James Bond. Under the section asking for the purpose of my visit I write 'to plant a bomb'. No one has yet stopped me. What is interesting about this little quirk is that the only person who gets any enjoyment from it is ... me.

When people argue that consumers do not go through a great checklist of attribute associations and their importance when they make decisions, as research methodologies imply, then they are simply criticizing the way that research treats respondents.

When we, as researchers, talk about consumers having heuristics, then we need to think about the implications that this has for our research methodologies.

Let me explain:

1 Neuroscientists like Read Montague study the brain from the perspective of it being a very efficient mechanism (almost perfect) and using minimal energy.

2 Every indication from neurosciences is that people make quick decisions.

3 All the indications post Damasio is that emotions and background feelings are a vital input to decision making – all decision making.

4 The use of emotions (against the background of background feelings) is an important input in our decision making.

5 Essentially, background feelings and specifically emotions are used by our brains as part of a heuristic in our decision making.

6 Our individual heuristics are determined by our experiences, and also our moods, personality, culture and even homeostasis at the point in time.

7 Our heuristic is always future oriented: 'What I expect from using...'.

Against this simple background a respondent would say: 'Well, you only need to ask me one or two questions.'

Factually the respondent is right. In a brand dynamics study Millward Brown gets down to the essence of the consumer's heuristic for each brand. However, to get to explain the differences in perceptions of the brand,

Millward Brown still asks respondents to complete a brand association matrix.

Where does this lead us (marketers)?

This is a piece of the brand puzzle that is going to be turned around a lot in the near future – I predict much more so than most people expect.

The past decade has seen the development of online interviewing and the establishment of online panels. Disappointingly, this has been seen as a way to do cheaper research, even if the quality is sometimes less than the alternatives.

The one beneficial aspect of interviews conducted using computers is our ability to change the direction of questions as the interview progresses. As we interview, we can simply determine what the next question should be. This is being done in many ways, but is not being done to any great extent relevant to the decision heuristics that people have.

We are all aware of the ease that this can be done with, but before we can do this dynamic changing of interview structure in a way that we can keep respondents interested, we need to understand our respondents. This is the rub.

Unfortunately, almost everything I have seen in research is simply applying normal old-fashioned questionnaires to online interviews. This is a great waste.

Of course, to ask really good questions and design really good questionnaires involve really understanding consumers, which means segmentation.

Market segmentation

27

People are all the same, except when they are different
or,
People are all different, except when they are the same.
(Matthew Angus, Millward Brown East Africa, in Hollis, *The Global Brand*, 2008)

When *The Advertised Mind* was reprinted in Chinese I was asked to write a foreword specifically for it. I explained that, when Millward Brown South Africa started to report to the Asia-Pacific region, rather than the UK, a lot changed in our lives. We were now in a region where everybody had to deal with culture and language issues on a daily basis. Our peers knew the importance of adopting practices from the United States and the UK, but also the importance of adapting these for local cultures. The term 'Think global, act local' became not just a management slogan but something that we actioned. I explained in my Chinese foreword that all humans have mainly the same brains biologically, and we all use the same parts of the brain for the same survival reason. However, different things in the environment will make the different areas in the brain respond differently between different people. Factors that will create different responses among consumers will include their cultures and their personalities (and their different experiences). Thus, although we all have similar brains that operate very similarly, we will behave differently. Among all these different behaviours there will be great similarities between what we do. Sometimes we might even be doing the same things for different reasons. Not only will the reaction to brands differ, but reactions to advertisements, packaging and so on will differ. In any market with more than one brand different people buy the different brands for different reasons.

We can restate the above in terms of heuristics: every person has his or her own heuristic to solve to decide on a brand. Everybody appears to be using similar heuristics, but while the structure of the heuristics might appear to be fairly consistent among consumers the 'data' (knowledge or memories) that drive the heuristics will be different. As a result different consumers arrive at different answers (brand decisions), or some might arrive at the same answer, for different reasons.

To the marketer the market appears to be very similar to a jigsaw puzzle. Different segments of the market (pieces of the puzzle) prefer different brands – and sometimes the same brand for different reasons. Marketers need to understand why the segments of the market act the way they do so that marketers can market their brand in such a way that the brand increases share in a specific segment, or such that more segments prefer the brand, if this can be done without losing the brand focus.

Since it is unlikely that any one brand will appeal to all people, marketers need to be focused on what they want their brand to be and not become bland. This process is called market segmentation. Often it is not done by way of formal market research, but big brands tend to use market research. Market segmentation is similar to the process where the pieces of the puzzle are sorted into groups that are obviously part of the same subsystem of the big puzzle: all the blue ones that are clearly part of the sky, all the ones that are probably part of the lake, all the ones that are probably part of the trees, and so on.

Segmentation is part of the process of target marketing. Once it has been worked out what would be a desirable segment, the whole marketing process has to be integrated to target these segments.

Segmentation has its own history. Initially segmentation was based on demographics: young people versus old people; wealthy versus the mass market; gender; and so on. Marketers soon realized that even inside the segment of (say) young, wealthy males there is still a range of brands being used and that demographic segmentation often does little to explain brand preference.

Demographics as a basis for segmentation was followed by marketers considering non-demographic variables as the basis for segmentation: psychographics, lifestyle, living standards, need states, occasion based, to name but a few. Different research companies promoted their own specialist segmentation schemes, and marketers could buy any one that they felt was appropriate.

Segmentation studies (as a marketing tool) soon experienced a set of problems. Firstly, it is expensive to conduct a tailor-made segmentation study for a brand, mainly because a segmentation study requires a fairly large sample. This often led to a situation where the marketer loaded the study with several product categories, and the study ended up doing an inadequate job for any of the categories. Secondly, segmentation studies became difficult to link to media planning information: media planning data require large samples and many questions, and often need to be input into complex media planning programs to be of any value (these programs do not accept foreign data readily). This resulted in some research agencies setting up their own general segmentation studies, which they then either syndicated across a client base or sold post facto to clients.

These generalized segmentation schemes are always interesting, because they tell us a lot about trends in society. This often results in research companies doing industry-wide presentations about their segmentation schemes – and trends in society – which often result in a 'language' where the advertising agencies and marketers at least understand which segments they are talking about (words like 'Generation X' and 'Generation Y').

These studies solve the two problems raised above: they are inexpensive and provide the link to media information. Unfortunately there is nothing that guarantees that such segmentation schemes will actually differentiate between brands in a specific product category, and as a result they seldom tell marketers anything about why some people use a specific brand. Marketers therefore end up using the segmentation as follows:

1 They decide on one of the predefined segments that they would prefer to target.
2 They brief their agencies to target this segment.
3 The agencies use the available information in the general segmentation scheme to target the required segment.

Segmentation schemes generally conclude with there being about seven segments in the market. Of these some would be unattractive to marketers and not considered as target markets. The outcome is that in many product categories and for many brands the segment that is targeted is the same! All the companies are using the same data about the segment that they target. What they know about the segment is the same, and the media they use to target the segment are the same. This happens across many product categories. As a result several banks, motor cars, foodstuffs, snacks, take-away outlet chains and so on target the same group of people!

It is little wonder that advertising styles become very similar across categories and across brands. This leads to brands becoming less differentiated and also to a decrease in brand linkage (the ability of an ad to stand out in the name of the brand).

Good segmentation should not be like this

When we consider the pieces of the brain–brand puzzle discussed earlier then it seems that products and brands operate at different levels in the systems of the brain that are described. Firstly, consumers use products to solve needs. These needs will derive from the homeostatic system especially but also from any of the other systems described. The need itself arises in a situation where the balance of the body or the balance of the brain is going to go awry. At this level the problem can be resolved by any brand – not necessarily a specific brand. Secondly, consumers use brands also to satisfy needs related to their culture, their desired social position, their personalities and so on. Here it is seldom that any brand will do, and more likely that a specific brand will be desired.

Marketers have to work with this double-layered piece of the puzzle that makes up the market:

- Marketers have the option to position their brand to a segment of the market as being the best brand to solve the problem at the first level above (homeostatic).
- Marketers have to decide whether the brand should be positioned as solving the problem at the first level, as well as solving problems at the second level (culture, personality, occasion, etc).
- Marketers very seldom (I cannot think of an example) have the option of solving a problem at the second level without also solving the problems at the first level.

Let's take maize-meal in South Africa as an example. Maize-meal is the traditional staple food in the black cultures of Africa. Traditionally the women of the kraal are tasked with grinding the maize into a meal. The king's wives have the first choice of the resultant meal, and he is allowed only the finest ground meal; then the second most important household take their pick, and so on, each taking successively less finely ground meal. The situation is made more complex in that there are two types of maize: yellow and white. The yellow variant is hardier than the white and therefore more abundant. In periods of drought the white variant becomes unobtainable. The white variant is considered to be the better-quality, and again the most senior households will take the white maize rather than the yellow. In periods of drought South Africa becomes a net importer of white maize. An important visitor to the kraal will always be offered porridge made from white, finely ground meal. There is no nutritional difference between the variants or the degree of milling. Any variant will satisfy the homeostatic need of hunger.

Marketers of branded milled maize-meal operate inside these parameters. There are many brands in the country, some selling at a premium. The positioning of these brands varies: some are yellow, some are white, some are mixed, some are more finely milled than others, some promise health (and some of these have vitamin additives), some promise strength, some of them sponsor a soccer team and have huge regional followings because of this, some brand names are in the traditional language (hoping to have a cultural bonding), some are in English (hoping to sound modern), some position themselves as being traditional (the original) and some want to appear very modern. All of the viable brands (ie those that are on the market) have found a niche of loyal supporters. The dimensions on which the brands are differentiated vary:

- Some are positioned on price (we can call this price-ographics).
- Some are positioned on demographics like regionality, culture, age or language.
- Some are positioned on benefits (we can call this benefit-ographics).
- Some are positioned on psycho-graphics (including lifestyle, VALS, etc).

It is obvious that not one type of segmentation works for all the brands in even a very basic food product category. There are many product categories in many countries, and nearly always the answer is that the brands tend to be differentiated on a different 'ographic'.

Some suggestions about segmentation studies

I have heard several people make the statement that 'market segmentation does not work'. This has to be an unconsidered statement. If there are several brands in a market, and people have a preference for one or a few brands, then the market is segmented. Even if the marketers have not consciously segmented the market, where there exists a preference for one or several brands then the market has segmented itself.

What people mean when they say that market segmentation does not work is either that they used a generalized predefined schematic that did not assist the marketer in that specific instance, or that they did a segmentation study and it was not well executed.

Three of the big names in marketing theory (Philip Kotler, John Philip Jones and Andrew Ehrenberg) have debated whether markets are really segmented or whether segmentation is just a figment of the marketers' imagination.

In 1996 RCS hosted the Great Nantucket Debate between Ehrenberg and Jones. Essentially Ehrenberg argued that since research of consumer repeat purchases shows that no one is 100 per cent brand loyal (ie everyone sometimes buys different brands) there is no such thing as market segmentation. Jones disagreed.

Recently Byron Sharpe of the Ehrenberg-Bass Institute published his book *How Brands Grow* (2010) in which he argues convincingly against the marketing doctrine of brand differentiation and specifically mentions Kotler. Brand differentiation is the execution of market segmentation. Sharpe argues that the 'past world model' is brand *differentiation* and the 'new world model' is brand *distinctiveness*. His book is due to become one of the important marketing books that everybody should read.

The ongoing nature of this debate and its very important implications for new brands and whether one should have range extensions indicate that this part of the brand puzzle is still very actively under scrutiny. I hope some of the insights about the working of the brain will contribute to this.

The first step for a successful useful segmentation is to recognize that it is unlikely that any one of the 'ographics' is going to 'explain the market' satisfactorily. In fact, it is likely that several will be involved.

The best practice we use is to identify from the start that we are looking for market-ographics (which can be a combination of any of the 'ographics'). Thus for the cigarette market we are looking for smoke-ographics, for the sugar market we are looking for sweet-ographics, and so on. Not surprisingly in these two specific studies there were 'ographics' that appeared in both studies. Age was a determinant for certain cigarette brands not being used (these brands were seen as not fashionable anymore because older people use the brand) and for sugar consumption (mothers in the age bracket that have young children had certain concerns about sugar, and younger girls had a different set of concerns about sugar consumption). Similarly health consciousness was a determinant in both markets. Thus a demographic and a lifestyle measure had influences in explaining both markets.

The best way to start a segmentation study is not to start off with consumer research, but to start off with the company staff. Ask them to describe the consumers of the different brands in the market. If you can get them not just to feed back the target markets described in the brand plan but to talk about experiences you get a great wealth of the type of 'ographics' that might be important in the market.

When doing segmentation studies we really have to follow the disciplined ways of academics. In working towards a PhD, candidates have to do a literature review so that they can use what has been done by others and build on this. There exist a number of 'marketing scales' books. These are really thick books! In these are all the scales used in studies that have been published in academic journals. The benefit of this is that the questions used have been validated by statistical analyses, and serve as a great source for inspirations. However, this involves a lot of work for the researcher and is therefore seldom done.

Only when these two sources have been exploited should one start with consumer research, focus groups and then a large-scale quantitative study with all the potential 'ographics' measures elicited. Often a data reduction study might be required before this.

A common mistake is for researchers to include a lot of media questions in the belief that it is necessary to identify the media strategy for the resultant market segments. This is mostly because researchers have not been media planners. Media optimization programs require very detailed media information, and it is nearly impossible to input data into these specialist programs from a different source from that which they were written for.

When media information is collected inside a segmentation study it is too bland owing to the available space in the questionnaire for it to be used by media planners. It is much better to concentrate on doing a very good segmentation using all available space to collect segmentation data.

Once the segments have been derived for the specific market they are intended for there will be an abundance of information to describe each segment and explain what the determinants of the decision making are (the common heuristic). This is what should be used as input to the marketer's strategic decision-making process.

The final step should then be a data reduction stage (a statistical program like CH-AID). This should determine a few questions that can be asked in any survey to classify the respondent into one of the segments. These statements can then be used as a passenger question in a large-scale media survey like TGI that collects media planning data in such a way that they are readily input for media optimization programs. The statements can also be used when focus groups are recruited, which is a very useful step after the quantitative research process is done. They can then also be used for any pre-testing of proposed marketing activities or even for tracking.

Neuromarketing and segmentation

One of the first steps in any marketing strategy is to identify as clearly as possible which segment of the market one is targeting with the brand. This becomes the focus that keeps everything else aligned: the creativity, the media strategy, the distribution strategy, the promotions strategy, the pricing strategy, the packaging and all the research.

The neurological insights that this book discusses lead us to understand that there are many drivers of such segmentation. Issues like the physical product performance benefits often determine which segment it can aim for, but we also need to include feelings about the brand and the consumption of the brand. At the same time marketing can teach neurologists an important lesson: people will feel differently about a brand, and sometimes for the same reasons and sometimes for different reasons. In other words, when brain scans are conducted the readings will be different for different brands, or even different for the same brand among different people, or appear exactly the same for fundamentally different reasons.

Simply scanning the brains of people whilst exposing them to a brand or an advertisement could be an exercise in futility (or be very misleading) unless we first understand the segments and the motivations in the market. Simply dividing the consumers to be scanned into users versus non-users is not a good experimental design. (Thomas Ramsoy made me aware that brain scanning is very dependent on the experimental design. Simply placing people in scanners and measuring what lights up is not an experimental design.)

What we need to understand – from segmentation – is what the different heuristics are for the different consumer segments. This really boils down to trying to understand what the 'dopamine moment' is for the product category for specific consumer types, because marketers want their brands to evoke more dopamine at the point of decision making than the competitor brands.

Segmentation and neural studies – a chocolate example

Two of my students wanted to do their theses basically on the stuff of this book. They are doing them in the Copenhagen Business School's

Neuro-Decision Making Unit, which has access to all types of neuro-measurement methodologies, including fMRI. They had to look for a business issue, and they chose Mars, believing that sweets are a natural product for such an investigation into emotions and the measurement of emotions. Their sample would be people who buy snacks.

The result of their study is still outstanding at the time of publication of this book, but I gave them some advice that has nothing to do with understanding the neuropsychology of the brain, but everything to do with marketing experience. The target market for nearly every chocolate is females. Is there a neurological difference between female brains and male brains? If you can explain this neurologically you are on to something; if not, then why can't you explain this? There are very distinctly different chocolate consumers, who are easily identifiable by segmentation analysis and can therefore be identified by a battery of questions. These include:

- people who simply cannot resist chocolate, have a sweet tooth and can be termed addicts;
- people who reward themselves with chocolate when they have done something, eg shopped or stood in the queue at the till;
- people who go to the gym and eat diet food, so they then have chocolate for energy;
- people who buy chocolate for their children, buying approval, and then feel good about not eating it themselves;
- people who do not really like chocolate, including many males; and
- people who do not care and eat chocolate, smoke and so on.

All of the above segmentations will have very different reactions in terms of whether a person's dopamine system responds to exposure to a brand. As I am not a chocoholic, my dopamine system will probably not respond to any brand used as a stimulus. The brain response of an anorexic would be very interesting because of the conflicting areas that might respond. It might even be that the same areas in the brain light up for very different reasons. Somebody who likes sport for exercise and sees chocolate as a source of energy will be very different from someone who sees chocolate as a snack on the way to work in place of breakfast, who will be different again from someone who wants to have a Kit Kat break.

The point I am making is that I have this marketing knowledge from having done a segmentation study for the Sugar Association, and this knowledge already has an impact on the way one should be interpreting the result of fMRI studies, based on pre-screening the respondents.

Advertising budget, brand life cycle, synapses and brand soma

28

Marketing can be described as 'making big decisions that affect small things'. Advertising budgets run into millions of dollars, and the aim of these dollars is to influence a few million very small synapses in people's brains.

Neuromarketing is becoming involved because it measures neuronal activation, ie predicts whether advertising has the potential to lower the limens in synapses.

Budget setting is a combination of science, gut feel and accounting. There exists a substantial contribution from large empirical databases that gives marketers insight into what would be good guidelines – but these are mostly ignored (or marketers and accountants are not aware of them).

Ideally the budgeting process should include:

1 reviewing current activities and determining their success:
   – whether they are successful or not;
   – whether this is due to/despite of underspending or overspending;
2 if the current activities are deemed to be not successful, reviewing potential alternatives – especially as to whether they would be more successful than the current campaigns;
3 determining a budget level at which these new activities will actually be effective.

Biometrics is already being used to assist in step 2 above. I am not aware of it being used as input to steps 1or 3 above, but that certainly has to come.

However, the piece of the brand puzzle relating to the setting of a budget level is itself also changing these days, and it is worth discussing these changes, because to some extent if neuromarketing is going to be applied to these big decisions then one needs to know that the piece of the puzzle we are using the techniques for is shifting.

Setting the budget

The textbook recommended way to set marketing budgets is to start with a task orientation: what is the advertising supposed to achieve and what needs to be done to achieve this? The cost of these tasks is calculated and then this is reviewed against what funds are available and also the risk propensity of the company.

Most of the work involved lies in obtaining costs for the various alternatives. However, the real determinant of the ultimate decision is 'available funds'. In many cases a lot of the work wastage would be reduced if we started off with the marketing budget and then determined the best way that this should be invested.

The reality of business is that mostly the budgeting rule for all the items to be budgeted for is to spend the same proportion of income per item as was spent last year. Every business knows that most of the costs will increase at inflation rate, and some costs will increase much more or much less, and these need to be taken into account. For established brands this means that, if a brand spent about 10 per cent of its revenue on advertising last year, then it will be spending 10 per cent of its projected revenue this year. It is seldom that a marketing department will argue for a reduction, and it is seldom that the financial department is in a situation where an increase can be allowed.

This reality of how budgets are set ignores the actual leverage of advertising, can lead to over- or underinvesting, and causes the brand life cycle phenomenon.

Peter Field and AC Nielsen

The marketing consultant Peter Field explains that the problem is, in reality, much worse than I suggest above, and also that AC Nielsen has shown the relationship I will be discussing to hold currently in the UK market:

> In many ways, these are delusional times. The more we are all asked to do more with less, the more we think that it is always possible.

So the focus these days is on challenging communications to achieve more, rather than challenging clients to invest more in their brands.

But account planners should know better than this – it was established some years ago by Professor John Philip Jones and Millward Brown, among others, that even the most effective campaigns will fail to generate growth for the brand if it is not backed with sufficient share of voice (SOV). More recently, Malik PIMS has shown the effects on market share of cutting marketing expenditure in a recession. Thus, all brands have an equilibrium SOV at which their market share is stable: if SOV rises or falls from this level, then so too will market share.

(Field, 2009)

He describes the Nielsen analysis and their conclusions:

The IPA asked Nielsen to explore whether, by combining its media and FMCG sales data, it could extend the IPA data-BANK findings on how SOV drives market share. Extend in two senses: from the limited IPA world of super-effective campaigns to average ones and from an IPA base of campaigns going back 30 years to one that is entirely up-to-date. The results were presented in June at the IPA.

Nielsen's analysis included two years of media and sales data over the period ending August 2008, for 123 brands in 30 FMCG categories.

The brands and categories were chosen to reflect the diversity of the FMCG landscape. They included new and established brands, brand leaders, challengers and smaller niche players. They included a few brands that had entered campaigns into the IPA Effectiveness Awards and a great number that had not: a typical cross-section. They included brands with celebrated online campaigns and those that made little or no use of online beyond a website.

Nielsen looked at the impact of brands' SOV in the first year on sales over the two-year period and used 'base sales' to exclude the sales effects of distribution changes, price promotions and other in-store activity. The scale and rigour of the analysis undertaken is hugely impressive and the results invaluable.

Perhaps the most important result is that the relationship between SOV and share of market (SOM) growth is confirmed, and is still strong.

Eye-catching online initiatives, such as the Cadbury 'Gorilla' viral, may produce occasional uplifts, but brands like Cadbury still depend on SOV to maintain or build market share over the longer term.

The lesson for account planners is clear: brand targets as well as campaign and agency assessments cannot be divorced from the communications budget. A target that is realistic with one budget level can become unrealistic when this is lowered. And a campaign that might have generated strong growth with sufficient budget can fail without it. Fortunately, the Nielsen study now provides us with a powerful framework.

(Field, 2009)

FIGURE 28.1 Typical annual market share and advertising share data

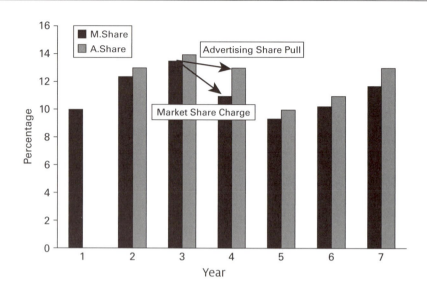

The dynamic difference model

I can only give an introduction to this model and its implications for the brand budget here; a much more complete exposition is given at **http://www.budgetforadv.com/**.

The model was popularized by James O. Peckham, retired Chairman of AC Nielsen, in 1967, when he analysed Nielsen's massive database of advertising share (AS) and market share (MS) data in several countries for many FMCG products. Most companies show AS/MS data in their annual plans but mostly as a static analysis, ie they compare the AS to MS ratio for every year. (See Figure 28.1.) Peckham did a dynamic difference analysis, which compares the difference between years, ie the extent that AS in year 4 is above or below the MS of year 3, and the resultant shift in MS between years 3 and 4. For a very good discussion of the dynamic difference analysis see Jones and Slater's *What's in a Name?* (2003).

Peckham used simple linear regression to look for a relationship between these variables. The two parameters that are estimated he called: 1) advertising leverage (the slope of the line): the increase in market share that can be expected from an increase in advertising share; 2) brand leverage (where the line intersects the vertical axis): the increase or decrease in market share that can be expected if advertising share is held at the same level as the current market share. (See Figure 28.2.) He found a statistically significant fit to the data for about 70 per cent of the brands that he analysed, and these were mainly established brands (or, to put it differently, if he analysed only

FIGURE 28.2 The dynamic difference analysis – Peckham's terminology

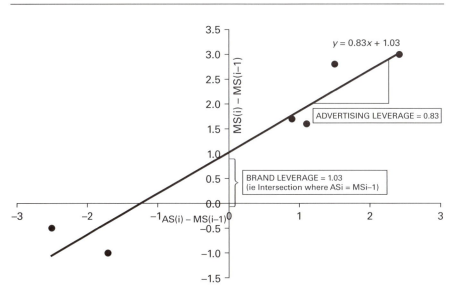

established brands, he would have found much more than 70 per cent had a good fit to the data).

Peckham's findings have been replicated in several published studies over the years for different product categories and different countries. Nearly all of these studies used a static analysis, but if a static analysis fits the data then so will a dynamic analysis. The dynamic analysis is just a lot more useful for setting budgets.

Implications for 'percentage of revenue' budget

Unfortunately most marketers forget that it is simple mathematics that, if the competitors spend a fixed amount, you get incrementally less advertising share for your dollar as you spend more. Let's assume that the competitors' combined spend is $10 million. Then you will get 9 per cent advertising share for your first $1 million. However, if you increase your advertising budget tenfold to $10 million you do not get 90 per cent advertising share, but only 50 per cent. (See Figure 28.3.)

The dynamic difference line shows the increased AS you will need if you want to increase your MS by (say) one point. It does not highlight the fact that the extra AS you need to buy will cost you increasingly more as your

FIGURE 28.3   Your advertising share per dollar spent, if all competitors spend $10 million

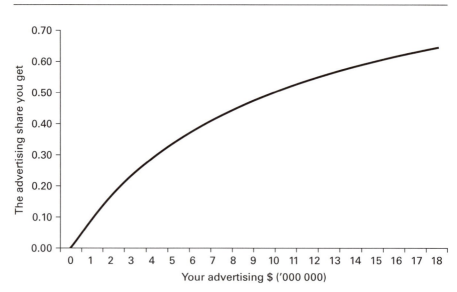

own market share increases, or that your income from an extra market share point grows linearly.

If there is a fixed relationship between your advertising share and market share, as there is for most brands, if your competitors are not likely to reduce their advertising investment and if you want to gain one point market share next year, then you need change to the percentage of revenue that you invest in advertising. Figure 28.4 shows an example. In this example beta refers to the advertising leverage of the brand:

1 With beta at 0.5 the brand will gain 0.5 market share point for one point increase in advertising share.

2 With beta at 1 the brand will gain 1 market share point for one point increase in advertising share.

3 With beta at 1.5 the brand will gain 1.5 market share points for one point increase in advertising share.

The mathematics and a more complete explanation are set out at **http://www.budgetforadv.com/**.

What it is important for marketers to note is that for this hypothetical example the percentage of revenue that needs to be budgeted for another point market share growth increases as the brand grows from a 6 per cent market share to a 12 per cent market share!

FIGURE 28.4 Percentage of income required for 1 per cent growth for different advertising leverages (total market $200 million)

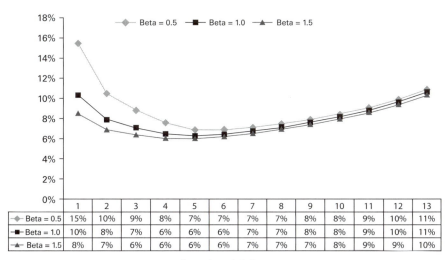

	1	2	3	4	5	6	7	8	9	10	11	12	13
Beta = 0.5	15%	10%	9%	8%	7%	7%	7%	7%	8%	8%	9%	10%	11%
Beta = 1.0	10%	8%	7%	6%	6%	6%	7%	7%	8%	8%	9%	10%	11%
Beta = 1.5	8%	7%	6%	6%	6%	6%	7%	7%	7%	8%	9%	9%	10%

Current market share

This is a big ask of the brand

Let us assume that:

1 the total market revenue is $100 million;

2 the competitors combined invest $10 million in advertising;

3 your brand's dynamic difference line suggests that if you invest in buying one AS point more than your current MS you will gain 1 MS point (ie advertising leverage = 1).

If we start with your market share in year 0 being 6 per cent then the outcome shown in Table 28.1 will result if your objective each year is to gain 1 MS point.

In this example the marketing director will – each year – have to get a bigger percentage of the brand's revenue for advertising and therefore a bigger percentage increase in the advertising budget than the percentage by which the revenue will increase.

This is all just straightforward mathematics based on the assumption that the competitors will not decrease their advertising budgets.

Brand life cycles

It is common marketing wisdom that brands have life cycles, ie go through a period of growth and then go into decline.

TABLE 28.1   As market share grows, the required advertising investment needed for more growth is bigger than the growth in income

Year	Desired MS	Revenue	Required AS	Cost of required AS	Percentage of revenue	Percentage revenue increase	Percentage advertising increase
1	6%	6	6%	0.64	0.106		
2	7%	7	7%	0.75	0.108	1.17	1.18
3	8%	8	8%	0.87	0.109	1.14	1.16
4	9%	9	9%	0.99	0.110	1.13	1.14
5	10%	10	10%	1.11	0.111	1.11	1.12
6	11%	11	11%	1.24	0.112	1.10	1.11
7	12%	12	12%	1.36	0.114	1.09	1.10
8	13%	13	13%	1.49	0.115	1.08	1.10
9	14%	14	14%	1.63	0.116	1.08	1.09
10	15%	15	15%	1.76	0.118	1.07	1.08
11	16%	16	16%	1.90	0.119	1.07	1.08
12	17%	17	17%	2.05	0.120	1.06	1.08
13	18%	18	18%	2.20	0.122	1.06	1.07
14	19%	19	19%	2.35	0.123	1.06	1.07
15	20%	20	20%	2.50	0.125	1.05	1.07
16	21%	21	21%	2.66	0.127	1.05	1.06
17	22%	22	22%	2.82	0.128	1.05	1.06
18	23%	23	23%	2.99	0.130	1.05	1.06
19	24%	24	24%	3.16	0.132	1.04	1.06
20	25%	25	25%	3.33	0.133	1.04	1.06
21	26%	26	26%	3.51	0.135	1.04	1.05

Consider what would happen if the brand grows from 6 per cent market share to 18 per cent over a 13-year period of steady gains, resulting in revenue trebling, and the company decides to keep the advertising budget as a percentage of revenue static in the following years (ie at 12.2 per cent). This happens in many companies: 'The brand grew when we invested less in advertising, so it should grow with less.' The brand's growth will slow down and eventually decline, thus producing a near perfect brand life cycle. At **http://www.budgetforadv.com/Case_Study__Bols_Brandy.html** I tell the story of a brand I worked on where exactly this happened. We did accelerate the process when the market share started not to grow as fast as in the past, because we believed in the brand life cycle and we relaunched, repositioned, rebranded and so on.

Jones's advertising intensity curve

John Philip Jones analysed the AS/MS relationship for 666 brands from 23 countries, three-quarters from the various types of repeat-purchase packaged goods and the rest from other types of advertising. He calls the resultant curve (which he reproduced per market analysed) the advertising intensity curve. (See Figure 28.5.)

This analysis shows that, in the real world, brands with smaller market share tend to buy more advertising share than their market share, and also that brands with larger market shares tend to buy less advertising share. This is such a general phenomenon for all brands and all countries that we should view this as a law of marketing.

From Figure 28.5 it would appear that for larger brands a 'relatively' smaller advertising share is required to support their market share than for smaller brands. In other words there appears to be an economy of scale. According to Jones and Slater (2003), 'What this arithmetic shows is that the advertising investment behind large brands is more productive, dollar for dollar, than the investment behind small brands. This difference is robustly quantifiable, and if we are able to understand the reason for this phenomenon, we

FIGURE 28.5   The AS/MS relationship

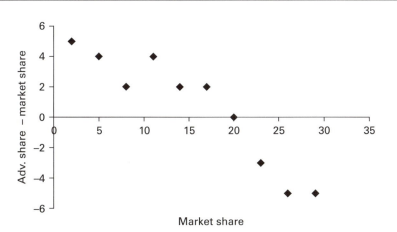

shall receive valuable clues to measuring the long-term effects of advertising.' Jones and Slater suggest that there are at least five reasons for this phenomenon, mostly to do with benefits of scale.

What I am suggesting here is that the main reason for this phenomenon is that the brands in a category try to invest the same percentage of revenue as each other! If they all invest the same percentage then the bigger brands will get a lower advertising share and the smaller brands a higher advertising share proportionate to their market shares.

Brand life cycle: a self-fulfilling belief?

Jones and Slater (2003) make the point that the brand life cycle is a self-fulfilling prophecy. 'It is, however, rather more common to find examples of the opposite: of once substantial brands whose popularity has dwindled. This should immediately prompt us to ask how many reductions in market share of existing brands following the launch of new brands are *caused by a conscious transfer of resources* from the old to the new.'

In fact, I would add that it might not even be a conscious decision, but an unwitting underinvestment in the brand because of a belief that if it grew at the previous percentage of income invested in advertising that is enough (and a false hope that one can even reduce this).

Jones and Slater (2003) continue:

> This often represents tragic misjudgment, because the growth of added values in an old brand represents a genuine investment that is all too often sacrificed through a misplaced belief in the inevitability of the brand's decline. To make matters worse, the new investment for which so much is sacrificed produces in many cases an unsuccessful or mediocre new brand. Remember that most new brands *are* unsuccessful.
>
> One of the temptations to milk a brand (to turn it into a cash cow) is the fact that the withdrawal of support means an immediate increase in profit. But this is temporary, because sales invariably decline, so that the brand after a time yields not only a much reduced profit, but also often a drastically reduced contribution to overhead.

Optimizing advertising budgets

For a company with several brands, and especially when these are in different markets, the dynamic difference makes a very useful tool with which to allocate the company advertising budgets between the brands.

The size of the total market determines the income that will be generated by each market share point increase. The existing market share, the expected competitive investment in advertising and the advertising effectiveness (dynamic difference) determines the cost of the additional market share point. From here it is a simple exercise to calculate where the funds would be best invested.

The algorithm, needs to be run stepwise because the relative cost of an advertising share point changes with each increase in market share. This result in the investment decision changing over each iteration of the model.

The data needed for such a programme is the stuff that is included in all brand plans. Where they are not explicitly included, the brand manager can be told that his proposed budget for next year suggests that he expects x per cent market share for a y per cent advertising budget, which implies a specific dynamic difference curve. This leads to a discussion about what reasons he has to expect such a reaction for his advertising.

This programme leads to a very sound basis for discussions between brand teams and especially for budget meetings between the finance department and the marketing department.

The changing pieces of the puzzle

This book is about the changing pieces of the brain–brand puzzle, and this is where the intersection between neuroscience and marketing knowledge becomes really interesting.

Since the 1980s the debate about 'advertising as publicity' has carried on apace. We can recognize this in the popular marketing media (and even journals) under the guise of arguments that, as long as you advertise, it does not matter what you say. In fact, these arguments have changed some of their tenor since the importance of emotions in advertising has become recognized, and now suggest that, as long as your advertisement is noticed, it does not matter what you say.

Sharpe (2010) describes this as the shift from concentrating on the advertising message content to concentrating on the emotional content (ability to attract attention) as one of the changes in the pieces of the marketing puzzle differentiating between the 'old approach' and the 'modern approach'.

The Peckham type of analyses, in the 60–70 per cent of cases where it leads to a statistical fit of the data, shows clearly that some brands have higher advertising sensitivities than others. This might be because the brand is reliant on advertising or because the brand has a good advertising campaign (or both). Thus, even if the 'advertising needs to be mere publicity' arguments are right, there is still a difference in the effectiveness of different campaigns.

Moreover, I have shown empirical data from the Millward Brown database that for smaller brands an informative style of advertising is required, whereas large, well-known brands get better results from an 'emotional' campaign, ie mere publicity works better for brands where the functionality of the brand has been established.

If we now want to think about how this relates to John Philip Jones's advertising intensity curve, things become much more interesting. Jones considers the advertising intensity curve as a category phenomenon, ie the result of what the individual brands do. In this there is little recognition for individual campaigns' effectiveness relative to the others, nor for the fact that bigger brands might have to spend more money, proportionately to their income, on advertising to maintain market share growth. Jones does, however, correctly point out that this leads to the life cycle of brands being a self-fulfilling prophecy.

However, and this is where the pieces of the puzzle really meet, I proposed an argument that suggests the halo effect is a major piece of information of the brand and that it is generally ignored in research presentations (especially in tracking studies). Yet the halo effect is largely a result of advertising pressure. In other words it is more inclined to appear to be supporting the argument about advertising being publicity!

This gets us directly into the area of neuroscience. I explained Damasio's concept of the soma, and tried to relate this to a brand soma (a 'general feeling' about the brand, which underlies the background to how we think about the brand). This brand soma is influenced by all our experiences (touchpoints) with the brands, especially the feeling of a presence of the brand, ie memories.

PART SIX
My conclusions

What this was all about

29

At the turn of the century things changed not only for marketers, but for other disciplines as well. Damasio, a neuroscientist, changed the way that we thought about why we have emotions. fMRI gave us the technology to look inside living people's skulls. Neuromarketers started to use bio-measures of the brain.

These three major changes happened largely independently, but happened at the same time and had an influence on each other. Books about these things became very popular and often did not differentiate between these changes in our knowledge. A lot of conference speakers, popular press reporters, took some things out of context creating confusion and unrealistic expectations (or interpretations of what is happening).

It is obvious that if we now think differently about how people make decisions then this impacts on marketers, advertisers and market researchers. In this book I attempted to bring together the changed views about decision making and marketing.

Damasio, who has changed the paradigm about the role of emotions, explains that emotions happen against the background of background feelings. He does not go into any depth about what these feelings are, how they work, etc. There are others that do talk about what these background feelings are and describe their functions. None of these authors wrote marketing books. However, what they say is important to marketers to understand what is changing. As a result this book has to explore areas that are more biological than the readers might have expected. Only once these have been introduced could we start to look at the marketing implications.

All the books, academic papers and conference talks that go under the title neuromarketing mainly discuss the output of bio-measurement systems (EEG and fMRI). This is very important, but it ignores largely the bigger picture of what neuroscience has contributed to our understanding of the decision making process (or brand choice).

From very small things to very big things

This book started with very small things, neurons and synapses, and ended with very big things: brand budgets.

In this chapter we review how these things relate to each other, and the best way to do this is to walk the opposite route – from very big to very small.

Brand budget

Marketing budgets are big ticket items for any company irrespective of how small the company is. Mathematically, underspending can be just as damaging as overspending and this can lead to self-fulfilling brand life cycle prophesies.

For, at least, 70 per cent of brands, the dynamic difference analysis, relating market share to advertising share provides a very good way to start the budgeting process. This helps in decisions not only about how much should be invested in advertising, but also whether new campaigns should be considered, or even whether a total brand repositioning should be done.

The driving statistic for this decision is the advertising leverage, which will be partly comprised of measures like Millward Brown's Awareness Index obtained from tracking studies. This will also relate to mere ad-liking, as explained in *The Advertised Mind*.

Heuristics

The dynamic difference analysis not only provides an advertising leverage, but also a variable called brand leverage – a single number indicative of brand strength. This is not unlike the Brand Voltage measure that Millward Brown derives from its brand dynamics research.

To a large extent these brand strength measures are dependent on the heuristics that consumers use – especially the top levels of the heuristics: 'It's the brand I usually buy', etc.

Different people might have different heuristics. It is important that marketers understand these people as segments with similar heuristics, else the analysis of what consumers want becomes too averaged to yield good insights.

Halo effect and brand soma

These heuristics that consumers use is very dependent on their feelings about the brand, very similar to the soma concept of Damasio. For marketing purposes I coined the term brand soma to differentiate this from the soma people use for all decision making.

This brand soma is probably best measured by the halo effect we see in image data. This halo effect will also be a reflection of how the brand is faring on the heuristics of consumers. It should be the foundation of every marketing strategy to grow this halo effect.

Advertising has two effects: the brand soma as measured by the halo effect, and the specific communications effect it is trying to achieve, and these might mostly be the same thing. This is really central to the modern debate of how advertising is supposed to work – the mere advertising effect.

Segmentation

When more than one brand exists in a market and one is bought more often by some people then the market is segmented. This is true whether the marketers intentionally segment the market by brand differentiation or not.

In terms of the path that we are now walking backwards: some people have a more positive brand soma for one brand than the other. Or, the brand is at a higher level of the decision tree in their heuristic.

The market may be segmented by demographics, or some pre-packaged segmentation scheme.

From a neuroscience point of view there are some background feelings that exist and these have an effect on what brand some people prefer versus the brand others prefer. We identified moods, personality and culture because these do have a neuroscience base.

These three factors have a strong influence on why people use brands – ie their personal heuristic and the brand soma to them.

Good marketing will try to grow the brand inside these segments, or might decide to grow the brand in other segments.

Emotions

Emotion is a very important determinant of what, and how, people will react to things in their environment. This happens firstly by people giving attention because they experienced an emotion. This might be giving attention to an advertisement, or it might be giving attention to a brand.

In the case of an advertisement we are looking at the effects on the advertising leverage and the awareness index. In the case of the brand we are really looking for an effect on the brand soma.

Emotions play off against the background of feelings: mood, personality and culture (at least).

Understanding feelings

Current neuromarketing techniques mainly measure emotions using EEG. However, emotions play off against the background of background feelings.

There is a lot of potential confusion in the way that different people use the term emotion and feeling. Therefore it is necessary to set up working definitions for these.

Little is written about background feelings, even by Damasio, so it is necessary to explain them in greater depth if the concept is to be used sensibly in marketing, advertising and market research.

Interpretation and memories

Nothing happens if the brain does not interpret its environment and its thoughts. If people cannot interpret an advertisement it did not happen. If people cannot interpret that the thing they see on the shelf is a brand, nothing can happen.

Interpretation is based on one's memories. A one-month-old baby cannot interpret that it is in front of a television set and seeing a BEN10 story, it cannot interpret a brand. It can basically only interpret its mother's face. As it forms memories (learns) it soon learns to interpret its environment.

All our behaviours are based on our memories. (Even if you argue that our behaviour is based on our subconscious, then all theories about the subconscious still recognize that it is driven by memories.)

Neurons and neural networks

To understand how memory works and that it is the flipside of the interpretation coin, one needs to understand how neurons and synapses work (biologically) and that as networks they produce gestalts.

Is the future what it was?

30

Everybody loves an author to speculate about the future. They know that he will be wrong.

Is there a future for neuromarketing?

I foresee that neuroscience's bio-measures and theories about the brain will have a big impact in marketing practice and theories.

The scepticism I have occasionally expressed merely suggests that when people recklessly make exaggerated claims for what neuromarketing can achieve now, they will impede the growth of neuromarketing to the detriment of marketing and market research.

Our industry is quick to say 'It has been proven that research does not work,' or 'It has been proven that segmentation does not work.' With these types of generalized, and unsupported, statements we are prone to throw out the baby with the bath water.

The contribution to marketing from the neurosciences will be at two levels. At a lower level there will be bio-measurement techniques like EEG, used to identify whether there is electronic activity when respondents are exposed to adverts, pack designs, brand logos, etc. At a higher, more general, level there will be greater insights about how decisions are made, how people differ culturally, how their personalities differ, etc.

Obviously these two levels are not independent. The more experience we have at the lower level, the better we will do at the higher level (theories); and when we start to raise good theories that are empirically supported we will design better experiments at the lower level.

What the future will bring

More insight into background feelings

When we read the literature on the subject from other disciplines, it is clear that what Damasio calls background feelings have a strong influence on emotions, and that what we measure at this stage in the development of neuromarketing is mostly emotions.

It is clear that homeostasis, moods, personality and culture are neuroscience issues, and have a big impact on brand marketing and decision making in general. However, current technology does not allow us to learn much in isolation. Real progress will come when we start to combine introspective questions with these measures via well-designed experimental designs – much like Read Montague has done.

I would hope that as we are taking bio-measures we will be developing databases relating the measures of research to these things and find ways that we can identify background feelings via EEG (or some technology) – or, at least, their effects on the measures of emotions. Without a more rigorous meta-analysis of results, practitioners will be left applying only judgment as to what the results really mean.

Technological improvements

Already the bio-measuring equipment is portable (Bluetooth) and dry technology. Obviously there will be great advances in the miniaturization of the equipment as well as the range at which it can be used.

Presumably fMRI or similar technology will give us headsets that are small and whose readings will be faster.

However, the biggest advance we can expect is that the spatiality of EEG equipment will improve – ie that smaller brain areas can be read and that better identification of specific electronic activity will give us new things to measure. Or even that the equipment will increasingly be able to read the deeper brain areas like the limbic system.

Brain activation

Transcranial magnetic stimulation (TMS) already gives us the technology to activate, or deactivate, brain areas, as explained in Chapter 17.

When the media talk about a 'buy button', the image that comes to mind is very much that there will be technology whereby we can activate an area in the brain that causes people to desire a specific brand. In some science-fiction way we can imagine that with this technology we activate the dopamine pathways when a consumer uses our brand, or is near it at the shelf, which would lead to them purchasing our brand. Whatever the secret desires of marketers this is simply not going to happen.

However, with TMS we will be able to knock out certain parts of the brain and inspect the influence this has on decision making, or we can stimulate areas of the brain and inspect what happens. Let's say that we are interested in testing the hypothesis that the background feeling of hunger has an effect on what we give attention to. We might, some day, be able to knock out or stimulate the parts of the hypothalamus that signal hunger and then do research on what is given attention to.

Let me hasten to add that I am unlikely to volunteer for such an experiment.

Before we rush to make laws prohibiting research in this area, let us look at the big medical advantages this will have. People with epilepsy will be wearing sensors and when these detect the onset of a fit the deactivator TMS will knock out the area in the brain where the fit starts. Recovering alcoholics and smokers can wear these bands and each time they feel the desire to drink or smoke the deactivator TMS will knock out the areas responsible. Air traffic controllers will wear these headbands and when their arousal levels drop (or increase) the headband will activate parts of the brain that make them more alert. The applications of TMS are potentially far-reaching. The application to marketing is one of the least important of the potential applications.

Trained respondents

There are companies that are trying to make the EEG equipment so cheap that they can be distributed to members of a large panel so that these people can become respondents in surveys. Part of the problem is that these people need to be trained to use the equipment. But that problem will disappear as the equipment becomes familiar in other contexts.

Already there is a meditation self-help product that uses galvanic skin response (GSR) to teach you how to relax. There are a few computer games that use GSR to activate actions on the screen. The next step will be to include EEG and eye scanning into games, thereby creating a whole segment of the population that own, and use, bio-measuring equipment. Other markets will open when teaching applications and so on are found. I believe NeuroFocus has recently launched such a game.

Take the example of using TMS to prevent an epileptic fit. This can be taken several steps further. Imagine one of these things being able to detect the onset of a stroke or heart attack. In both these cases there exist heuristics that can identify the situation and in both cases an early warning is vital. We might all be wearing these things for our health.

Once enough people are wearing these things (for health reasons) we might be able to persuade them to become part of media research. It will even be possible for the equipment to be activated by internet ads. In fact, the equipment will also tell us how much attention consumers give to the advertising/brand and even the dopamine levels caused.

Academic training

At the moment there are not enough universities that are teaching a course related to neuromarketing or neuro-economics or neuro-decision making.

The problem is really a chicken and egg situation: where will the teachers come from if the discipline is only a few years old? And where are the practitioners going to come from?

The main question that an academic institute will have to ask is whether the course is going to be predominantly neuroscience or marketing. With the students being students of commerce, I believe that they need to be taught enough about the functions of the brain to allow them to understand why some approaches to marketing are good practice. I would see them being taught which marketing empirical databases exist so that they can look for areas where their future experience might assist neurologists.

In other words, courses should concentrate on the area where neuroscience touches on marketing, and students should approach this from the perspective of marketing.

They should, most certainly, at the end of the course know what questions they should ask purveyors of neuromarketing measures.

Summary implications for neuromarketing

1. The technology is going to get smaller, cheaper, easier, faster, better.

2. It will become more pervasive and more used – across a vast range of needs and uses.

3. As marketers we will inevitably want to harness it, and this will be easier to do – so it will happen.

4. We need to beware simplistic conclusions – we are going to be learning much and will need to amend our views as new evidence emerges.

5. Too many commercial operators draw inferences form neuroscientific measures alone, which they present as definitive conclusions.

6. Neuroscientific measures need to be linked with real-world observation of attitudes and behaviour. And because many of these techniques are expensive, we must identify how and when they add value to existing techniques. And we need to create databases so that we can cross-reference results and provide general learning.

7. We will understand more about people's (buying) decision making in future but we already know that there is no 'buy button' – there are no simple triggers that are going to allow the marketer to ensure that a decision goes in their favour. Where research should focus is in understanding the interplay of processes when people make real choices.

8. More understanding of decision making will require more sophisticated and informed marketing. And it will require better experimental designs than simply taking bio-measurements of a few people in isolation from normal research methodologies. Neuroscience is just one more way to provide that information.

So there is a need to get to grips with the practice and theory of neuromarketing – it's not a fad and it's not going away. I hope that this book has helped start you down that path.

REFERENCES

Angus, M (2008) Light on a dark continent, in *The Global Brand: How to create and develop lasting brand value in the world market*, ed N Hollis, Palgrave Macmillan, New York

Baars, BJ and Gage, NM (eds) (2007) *Cognition, Brain, and Consciousness: Introduction to cognitive neuroscience*, Elsevier, Amsterdam

Baars, BJ and Ramsoy, T (2007) The tools: Imaging the living brain, in BJ Baars and NM Gage, *Cognition, Brain, and Consciousness: Introduction to cognitive neuroscience*, Elsevier, Amsterdam

Brizendine, Louann (2007) *The Female Brain*, Broadway Books, New York

Brizendine, Louann (2010) *The Male Brain: A breakthrough understanding of how men and boys think*, Broadway Books, New York

Cohen, G, Kiss, G and Le Voi, M (1993) *Memory: Current issues*, 2nd edn, Open University Press, Buckingham

Damasio, A (1995) *Descartes' Error: Emotion, reason, and the human brain*, Avon, New York

Damasio, A (1999) *The Feeling of What Happens: Body and emotion in the making of consciousness*, Harcourt Brace, Orlando, FL

Darwin, C (2006 [1872]) *The Expression of the Emotions in Man and Animals*, in C Darwin, *From So Simple a Beginning: The four great books by Charles Darwin*, WW Norton, New York

de Bono, E (1969) *The Mechanism of Mind*, Simon & Schuster, New York

de Sousa, R (1990) *The Rationality of Emotion*, MIT Press, Cambridge, MA

Dubow, JS (1992) Recall first – but not recall alone, in *Proceedings of the Ninth Annual ARF Copy Research Workshop*, Advertising Research Foundation, New York

du Plessis, E (2005) *The Advertised Mind*, Kogan Page, London

du Plessis, E (2007) DVRs, fast-forwarding and advertising attention, *Admap*, September

du Plessis, E (2009) Digital video recorders and inadvertent advertising exposure, Special issue, *Journal of Advertising Research*, **49** (2), June, pp 236–39

Ehrenberg, A (1958) The pattern of consumer purchases, *Applied Statistics*, **8** (1)

Ephron, E (1997) Recency planning, *Journal of Advertising Research*, **37** (4), July–August

Field, P (2009) Account planners need to care more about share of voice, *Admap*, September

Fishbein, M and Ajzen, I (1975) *Belief, Attitude, Intention and Behavior: An introduction to theory and research*, Addison-Wesley, Reading, MA

Franklin, S (1997) *Artificial Minds*, MIT Press, Cambridge, MA

Frith, CD (2007) *Making Up the Mind: How the brain creates our mental world*, Blackwell, Blackwood, NJ

Gladwell, M (2005) *Blink: The power of thinking without thinking*, Little, Brown, New York

Greenfield, S (1995) *Journey to the Centers of the Mind: Toward a science of consciousness*, WH Freeman, New York

Griffiths, PE (1997) *What Emotions Really Are*, University of Chicago Press, Chicago

Hansen, F and Christensen, SR (2007) *Emotions, Advertising and Consumer Choice*, Copenhagen Business School Press, Copenhagen

Heath, R (2010) Creativity in TV ads does not increase attention, *Admap*, January

Heath, R and Hyder, P (2005) Measuring the hidden power of emotive advertising, *International Journal of Market Research*, **47** (5)

Hollis, N (2008) *The Global Brand: How to create and develop lasting brand value in the world market*, Palgrave Macmillan, New York

Jaffe, J (2005) *Life after the 30-Second Spot*, Wiley, New York

Jones, JP (1995) *When Ads Work: New proof that advertising triggers sales*, Lexington Books, New York

Jones, JP and Slater, JS (2003) *What's in a Name? Advertising and the concept of brands*, ME Sharpe, New York

Krugman, HE (1972) Why three exposures may be enough, *Journal of Advertising Research*, December

LeDoux, J (1996) *The Emotional Brain: The mysterious underpinnings of emotional life*, Simon & Schuster, New York

Levitt, T (1983) The globalization of markets, *Harvard Business Review*, May–June

Lindstrom, M (2005) *Brand Sense: Sensory secrets behind the stuff we buy*, Free Press, New York

Lindstrom, M (2008) *Buy-ology: How everything we believe about why we buy is wrong*, Random House, New York

Montague, R (2007) *Your Brain Is (Almost) Perfect: How we make decisions*, Plume, New York

Oatley, K and Jenkins, JM (1996) *Understanding Emotions*, Blackwell, Blackwood, NJ

O'Connell, A (2010) Advertisers: Learn to love the DVR, *Harvard Business Review*, April

Packard, V (1957) *The Hidden Persuaders*, Pocket Books, New York

Page, G and Raymond, J (2006) Cognitive neuroscience, marketing and research: Separating fact from fiction, ESOMAR Annual Congress, London, September

Pradeep, AK (2010) *The Buying Brain: Secrets for selling to the subconscious mind*, Wiley, New York

Sharpe, B (2010) *How Brands Grow: What marketers don't know*, Oxford University Press, Melbourne

Weisberg, DS *et al* (2008) The seductive allure of neuroscience explanations, *Journal of Cognitive Neuroscience*, **20** (3), March, pp 470–77

INDEX

Also available from **Kogan Page**

Find out more; visit **www.koganpage.com** and
sign up for offers and regular e-newsletters.